BIRDS
OF THE
HULL AREA

Richard K Broughton

Kingston **Press**

British Library Cataloguing in Publication Data.
A catalogue record for this book is available from the British Library.

First published 2002

Published by Kingston Press

ISBN 1 902039 13 1

Kingston Press is the publishing imprint of Kingston upon Hull City Libraries, Central Library, Albion Street, Kingston upon Hull, England HU1 3TF.
Email: kingstonpress@hullcc.demon.co.uk
Internet: www.hullcc.gov.uk/kingstonpress

Printed by Kingston upon Hull City Council Printing,
35 Witham, Kingston upon Hull, England HU9 1DA

ACKNOWLEDGEMENTS

The author wishes to thank: Peter Bonavia; the monthly journal British Birds; Joyce Broughton; Matthew Broughton; the Centre for Ecology and Hydrology; Joe Curl; Geoff Dobbs and the Hull Valley Wildlife Group; Ray Eades; Brian Fendley; Michael Flowers; Laura Gundy; Steve Howard and Kingston Press, Samantha Jackson; Rick Lyon and the Hull Daily Mail; Richard Middleton and the Hull Natural History Society; Paul Milsom; Brett Richards; the Yorkshire Naturalists' Union and especially Claire Walker.

CONTENTS

FOREWORD

by Geoff Dobbs, Chairman of the Hull Valley Wildlife Group

The start of a new millennium is a timely occasion for the publication of a summary of all the birds seen in the Hull area. Pressure on habitat for wildlife has never been so great, with urban sprawl and industrialisation continuing apace. At the same time, however, the number of people who show an interest in wildlife, and birds in particular, is constantly increasing. Watching birds is a popular recreational activity for many members of our community. This interest is accompanied by increased awareness of our responsibilities to protect and preserve both wildlife and its habitat. The quality of life in the Hull area relies on improved housing standards and employment opportunities, but at the same time, the maintenance of our attractive "green" environment. There is a need to ensure that we conserve and enhance those natural resources that contribute so much to our quality of life. This book will provide an important source of information to help us judge our efforts in the future.

Local Biodiversity Action Plans (LBAPs) are currently being developed for both the City of Hull and its immediate environs. It is to be hoped that we can maintain the variety of wildlife in our community by carefully identifying key habitats and species, and developing plans to protect them. The Victorian parks are our jewels, the green corridors of the River Hull, Holderness and Barmston drains and disused railway lines are our lungs, but house gardens provide much of the bread and butter habitat for our birds. It is in your own back yard that you can start to help conserve the local avifauna!

Eight birds have been selected as target species for the Hull LBAP: Mute Swan, Skylark, House Martin, Song Thrush, Spotted Flycatcher, Tree Sparrow, Linnet, and Reed Bunting. Some of these species are well known to the public, but others have become increasingly rare in recent years. Mute Swans have suffered in the past through lead poisoning, but are now recovering and present a splendid sight on some of our open waters. House Martins, increasingly rare Spotted Flycatchers and the almost locally extinct Tree Sparrows can all be helped with careful nest-box schemes. Sensitive gardening, avoiding the use of chemical slug pellets, will help Song Thrushes to survive. The loss of scrub and old dock and scrubby wastelands is affecting our Linnet population. Reed Buntings will thrive as long as we protect the reed beds along our rivers and drains, and the sweet song of the Skylark will still be heard on the outskirts of the city if we keep some rough pasture land for nesting.

Since the publication of Patrick Boylan's Hull Museum booklet *Birds in Hull* in 1967, some obvious changes have taken place to our avifauna. Skeins of Pink-footed Geese are no longer a common sight over the city and farmland birds such as Lapwing, Skylark, Tree Sparrow, Linnet and Yellowhammer have all declined in the surrounding countryside, following national trends. Concerns are now being expressed over a recent decline in Starling and House Sparrow numbers in many of our cities. It is not all doom and gloom however: Great Crested Grebes now breed in Hull, and the numbers of Canada and Greylag Geese in our parks have mushroomed. Sparrowhawks were virtually unknown in Boylan's day, but are now resident and can seen daily by the keen-eyed observer. Collared Doves are now ubiquitous and Magpies much more numerous. Also more regularly observed are Lesser Whitethroats, Blackcaps, and Long-tailed Tits, the latter perhaps benefiting from recent mild winter weather.

Monitoring changes in the populations of our birds is something everyone can help with. Every record is significant. My own observations started as a young lad in 1966 when I counted 575 Mallard and saw 10 Bullfinches in East Park. Both these species have since declined, with Bullfinches now a rare sight in most parts of Hull. Also that year I saw my first Waxwing in my garden in East Hull, a species that still brings excitement during its periodic winter invasions from sub-arctic Scandinavia and beyond.

If you would like to contribute to the recording and conservation of our local birds, sightings and counts for Hull and East Yorkshire should be sent to the Recorder of the Hull Valley Wildlife Group, Paul Ashton, 4 St. Aiden's Close, Market Weighton, YO43 3HE or email hvwg@care4free.net

There are several groups active in Hull and East Yorkshire that you can join if you wish to learn more about the birds and wildlife in the region:

Hull Valley Wildlife Group
670 Hotham Road, Hull HU5 5LE.
www.hvwg.co.uk

East Yorkshire Birdwatchers
5 Antholme Close, Tween Dykes Road, Sutton-on-Hull HU7 4XX

Hull Natural History Society
12 Meaux Road, Wawne, East Yorkshire, HU7 5XD

Royal Society for the Protection of Birds (RSPB)
East Yorkshire Members Group, 17 St Aidan's Road, Bridlington, East Yorkshire, YO16 5SP.
www.eymg.freeserve.co.uk

South Holderness Countryside Society
The Old Station, Station Road, Patrington, East Yorkshire, HU12 0NE.
members.aol.com/coteds1/shcc.html

INTRODUCTION

Hull has many amateur naturalists and birdwatchers that do not, or maybe cannot, visit the top Yorkshire birdwatching sites on a regular basis. For them the interest is a local affair and something to be indulged on a Sunday morning or after work. Others are content just to watch the bird table from their kitchen window. Luckily, however, it is very easy for residents of even the most built up areas of the city to get out into the surrounding countryside or to a green oasis within the city itself. The Hull area is quite a green conurbation, with its large municipal parks and cemeteries, old rail trails, wide drains and boundary hedges, the Humber shore, pockets of undeveloped land and the fringing farmland. This provides many opportunities for people to connect with the wildlife around them, especially birds. The diversity of local habitats, from tidal mudflats to suburban avenues, and Hull's geographical location within Britain and Europe, means that a wide range of species pass by, through or over the area. From oceanic seabirds on the Humber to migrants from Scandinavia, eastern Europe and Africa to vagrants from the Mediterranean, Asia and the Americas, all have visited the Hull area and they continue to do so.

These things were the inspiration for this book. I have tried to write a definitive local avifauna for those folk who have noticed that we are not alone in this world and want to know more about the birds they share their city and villages with. This book covers what species there are, where they are, why they are there and how they have coped alongside us. The scope is purposefully broad in order to accommodate everyone with an interest in Hull's birdlife, from the garden birdwatchers to the dedicated birders and twitchers. The species accounts for common birds are therefore just as detailed as those for the scarcer ones, often more so.

The number of bird species reported in the Hull area up to March 2002 stands at 276. Deciding how many of these are genuinely wild birds is not easy, however. There is a confusing gradation between clearly inadmissible birds that have very recently escaped from captivity (such as the Zebra Finch), through escapees that can live happily in the wild and even breed (e.g. Muscovy Duck), to those that have established naturalised populations (like the Canada Goose). Then, of course, there are the others that are here totally under their own steam, such as the Blackbirds in your garden or a Black Kite overhead. Furthermore, there are those birds that may occur as escapees as well as being potential vagrants (such as White Stork), and others that are wild but may have endured part of their journey to the Hull area in captivity (e.g. Red-headed Bunting). Adding to this confusion is the question of rare birds that were not accepted by certain reports committees, such as Red-footed Falcon. Excluding all of those species that have even the suggestion of doubt over their identification or status as a genuine wild bird whittles the list down to something like 245, this including truly naturalised species like the Ruddy Duck. The true figure is likely to be somewhere between the two, however, and I would tentatively put it around the 250 mark. Of this number, at least 84 are known to have bred within the Hull area in the last 50 years. A further dozen or so either possibly bred within that period or were certainly breeding beyond it. The number of regularly breeding birds, those that nest in the Hull area in all or most years, is around 69. Several species included in the latter are just hanging on by a toehold after long term declines and are likely to be lost in the near future. Some, such as the Lesser Redpoll, may have already been lost as regular breeding birds along with the Turtle Dove, Redshank and Snipe.

There are some notable omissions from the systematic list. Regular east coast migrants such as Bluethroat, Common Rosefinch, Barred Warbler and Sooty Shearwater have never been recorded in the Hull area. Vagrants such as Ring-necked Duck, Pectoral Sandpiper, Glossy Ibis, Alpine Swift, Serin and Woodchat Shrike might also have been expected to have turned up at some point during the last century or so. Other birds, such as Raven, Stone Curlew and Great Bustard probably occurred in the dim and distant past but are highly unlikely to do so now. Having said that, I would have listed Red Kite there a few years ago and look at them now (see the entry for that species). That is one of the joys of birdwatching – you never know what will turn up next. Who, though, could have predicted that the Hull area would be able to claim such exotic species as White-tailed Eagle, Pallas's Sandgrouse, Laughing Gull, White-billed Diver, Little Bustard and, perhaps, Long-billed Dowitcher and White-throated Sparrow? As one Hull birder said to me many years ago, "any bird can turn up anywhere".

Richard K Broughton
May 2002

THE HULL AREA

The area covered by this book is depicted in the map below. The 'Hull area' as dealt with here broadly falls within an arc drawn from the Humber Bridge in the west, up around Skidby and Dunswell over to Wawne and Swine, then down past Bilton and Hedon and ending at Paull. This area consists of the city of Hull and the nearby villages in adjoining parts of the East Riding, as well as the middle stretch of the Humber estuary. The map shows that much of the open space between Hull and the villages is farmland, mainly arable, but there are also many patches of mown and rough grassland, pasture and other unploughed land. Several significant pockets of open land can be found within Hull itself, particularly the parks. Besides the mighty Humber, the main waterways are the River Hull and the Holderness and Barmston Drains that run north to south through the area. There is little in the way of stillwaters, the main bodies being East Park lake, the Bransholme Sewage Works reservoir and the eastern docks. Woodland is also at a premium, with most of the mature trees being found to the west of the area. Being a floodplain and former saltmarsh, virtually all of the Hull area is low lying and flat. Only in the extreme west, where the silts and clays give way to to the chalk foothills of the Wolds, does the ground begin to rise and undulate.

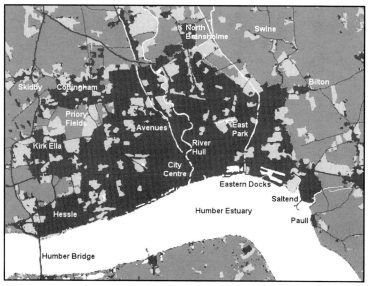

Map derived from the The Land Cover Map of Great Britain, 1990. Copyright NERC, acknowledgements CEH Monks Wood.
black = built-up areas, white = water, dark grey = tilled arable land,
light grey = pasture/rough grassland/parkland/mown grass/scrub.

WHERE TO WATCH

Birds can be seen anywhere in the Hull area but, like all areas, some places are better than others. Several areas are particularly worth visiting, either because they have a notable complement of species, are easy to work, or both. Most of these have a strong watery element and all encompass a good mix of habitat. Both of these factors are important in attracting a good range of species. The following are a few locations, but this is by no means an exhaustive list.

- Priory Fields
- East Park
- Bransholme Sewage Works
- Saltend
- North Bransholme
- Humber Bridge Country Park

Key: ** breeding in most years*
              ** rare/occasional breeding
              [ ] denote dubious origin or unconfirmed records

Priory Fields

The Priory Fields sit between Cottingham and Hull and are dissected by Priory Road and the Hull to Cottingham railway line. The area is comprised of 160 ha of pasture, rough grassland, farms and arable fields, with around 10 miles of hedgerow and a few small copses and thickets. The fields are subject to flooding in winter and there are several wet ditches and dykes. Besides having an important flora, the area is also very good for birds. Several species that have drastically declined elsewhere, such as the Tree Sparrow, Willow Tit and Yellowhammer, still cling on here.

All year: Mallard*, Sparrowhawk, Kestrel, Red-legged Partridge*, Grey Partridge*, Pheasant*, Moorhen*, Woodpigeon*, Collared Dove*, Skylark*, Pied Wagtail*, Wren*, Dunnock*, Robin*, Blackbird*, Song Thrush*, Mistle Thrush*, Long-tailed Tit*, Willow Tit*, Blue Tit*, Great Tit*, Magpie*, Jackdaw, Rook, Carrion Crow*, Starling*, House Sparrow*, Tree Sparrow*, Chaffinch*, Greenfinch*, Goldfinch*, Linnet*, Bullfinch*, Yellowhammer*.

Summer: Cuckoo*, Swift, Swallow*, House Martin*, Meadow Pipit*, Sedge Warbler*, Whitethroat*, Blackcap*, Willow Warbler*, Spotted Flycatcher, Reed Bunting*.

Winter: Golden Plover, Lapwing, Snipe, Great Black-backed Gull, Herring Gull, Common Gull, Black-headed Gull, Redwing, Fieldfare.

Passage/occasional: Greylag Goose, Canada Goose, Shelduck, Teal, Merlin, Woodcock, Curlew, Redshank, Lesser Black-backed Gull, Stock Dove, Tawny Owl, Barn Owl, Little Owl, Short-eared Owl, Great Spotted Woodpecker, Yellow Wagtail, Whinchat, Wheatear, Lesser Whitethroat, Chiffchaff, Spotted Flycatcher, Coal Tit.

Scarce/rare bird records: Wigeon, Goosander, Oystercatcher, Dunlin, Ruff, Jack Snipe, Black-tailed Godwit, Common Sandpiper, Laughing Gull, Turtle Dove, Kingfisher, Wryneck, Waxwing, Redstart, Garden Warbler, Pied Flycatcher, Treecreeper, Jay, Hooded Crow, Brambling, Lesser Redpoll, Corn Bunting.

East Park

Most people in the Hull area have visited East Park at some point. The lake is the dominant feature in the park but the wooded islands, animal enclosure, shrubberies and plantings give an open woodland feel to several parts. Playing fields provide yet more variety. East Park has a respectable bird list and has hosted several rarities, with passage migrants and winter wildfowl adding an interesting dimension to the birding. There is a very large winter roost of Carrion Crows and Collared Doves around the islands and animal enclosure. Early mornings are always best for birding in East Park, when there is much less disturbance from visitors, and it can be a rewarding local patch if watched regularly.

All year: Great Crested Grebe★, Mute Swan★, Greylag Goose★, Canada Goose★, Mallard★, Sparrowhawk★, Kestrel, Moorhen★, Coot★, Tawny Owl★, Feral Pigeon, Woodpigeon★, Collared Dove★, Great Spotted Woodpecker★★, Pied Wagtail★, Wren★, Dunnock★, Robin★, Blackbird★, Song Thrush★, Mistle Thrush★★, Blue Tit★, Great Tit★, Treecreeper★★, Magpie, Carrion Crow★, Starling★, House Sparrow★, Greenfinch★.

Summer: Swift, House Martin, Swallow, Blackcap★, Spotted Flycatcher★.

Winter: Little Grebe, Barnacle Goose, Pochard (has bred), Tufted Duck, Goosander, Black-headed Gull, Common Gull, Herring Gull, Grey Wagtail, Redwing, Long-tailed Tit.

Passage/occasional: Cormorant, Grey Heron, Wigeon, Teal, Goldeneye, Woodcock, Common Sandpiper, Lesser Black-backed Gull, Great Black-backed Gull, Stock Dove, Kingfisher, Skylark, Sand Martin, Meadow Pipit, Fieldfare, Lesser Whitethroat, Chiffchaff, Willow Warbler, Goldcrest, Coal Tit, Rook, Jackdaw, Chaffinch, Bullfinch.

Scarce/rare bird records: Red-necked Grebe, Slavonian Grebe, Night Heron, American Wigeon, Pintail, Garganey, [Ferruginous Duck], Scaup, [Bufflehead], Smew, Ruddy Duck, Temminck's Stint, Mediterranean Gull, Laughing Gull, Iceland Gull, Hoopoe, Waxwing, Black Redstart, Ring Ouzel, Yellow-browed Warbler, Wood Warbler, Pied Flycatcher, Marsh Tit, Crossbill.

Bransholme Sewage Works

The Bransholme Sewage Works, sandwiched between Thomas Clarkson Way and the River Hull half way between Sutton Park and Kingswood, comprises a deep reservoir, a narrow wooded plantation and the old water treatment works and sludge pits. The reservoir, while attractive to passage and wintering wildfowl, has limited appeal to breeding waterbirds due to the concrete banks. There is no access to the reservoir itself, although it is easily seen from the banks of the River Hull, while the plantation has free access and a muddy track running through it. The reed beds fringing the River Hull hold good numbers of Reed Warblers.

All year: Mute Swan**, Mallard*, Kestrel*, Sparrowhawk*, Pheasant*, Moorhen*, Coot*, Stock Dove*, Woodpigeon*, Collared Dove*, Tawny Owl*, Pied Wagtail*, Wren*, Dunnock*, Robin*, Blackbird*, Song Thrush*, Blue Tit*, Great Tit*, Magpie*, Carrion Crow*, Starling*, House Sparrow*, Chaffinch*, Greenfinch*, Goldfinch*, Linnet*, Reed Bunting*.

Summer: Little Grebe**, Cuckoo, Swift, House Martin, Swallow*, Sedge Warbler*, Reed Warbler*, Lesser Whitethroat*, Whitethroat*, Blackcap*, Chiffchaff*, Willow Warbler*.

Winter: Gadwall, Pochard, Tufted Duck, Woodcock, Redshank, Black-headed Gull, Common Gull, Meadow Pipit, Grey Wagtail, Fieldfare, Redwing.

Passage/occasional: Little Grebe, Great Crested Grebe, Cormorant, Canada Goose, Greylag Goose, Shelduck, Wigeon, Teal, Shoveler, Goldeneye, Common Sandpiper, Redshank, Lesser Black-backed Gull, Herring Gull, Great Black-backed Gull, Turtle Dove, Barn Owl, Kingfisher, Skylark, Sand Martin, Whinchat, Wheatear, Mistle Thrush, Grasshopper Warbler, Goldcrest, Jackdaw, Rook, Siskin, Yellowhammer.

Scarce/rare bird records: Red-necked Grebe, Whooper Swan, Garganey, Ferruginous Duck, Scaup, Long-tailed Duck, [Bufflehead], Goosander, Ruddy Duck, Hobby, Little Ringed Plover, Mediterranean Gull, Yellow-legged Gull, [Caspian Gull], Kittiwake, Rock Pipit, Stonechat.

Saltend

Access is restricted at Saltend so the only way to view the mudflats is to park either at Paull or the North Sea Ferry terminal, west of King George Dock, and then walk along the Humber embankment to overlook the estuary. Paull is by far the quickest option, with the ferry terminal route involving a two-mile walk past the docks. Only one end of the mudflats can be seen from each vantage point. The Saltend mudflats are the very best site for waders and wildfowl in the Hull area. Looking out over the estuary is also likely to produce seabirds and passing migrants. The fields and industrial areas behind the embankments are also worth a look for passage migrants and farmland birds. The once productive Growths/Saltend Marsh area, between King George Dock and Saltend itself, has now largely gone due to development.

All year: Cormorant, Grey Heron, Shelduck, Mallard*, Sparrowhawk, Kestrel*, Pheasant*, Grey Partridge*, Moorhen*, Lapwing, Ringed Plover, Bar-tailed Godwit, Curlew, Redshank, Black-headed Gull, Common Gull, Lesser Black-backed Gull, Herring Gull, Great Black-backed Gull, Feral Pigeon*, Stock Dove, Woodpigeon*, Collared Dove*, Skylark*, Meadow Pipit*, Pied Wagtail*, Wren*, Dunnock*, Robin*, Song Thrush*, Blackbird*, Long-tailed Tit*, Blue Tit*, Great Tit*, Magpie*, Carrion Crow*, Starling*, House Sparrow*, Greenfinch*, Goldfinch*, Linnet, Bullfinch, Reed Bunting*.

Summer: Cuckoo*, Swift, Swallow, House Martin*, Sedge Warbler*, Whitethroat*, Willow Warbler*.

Winter: Little Grebe, Great Crested Grebe, Shag, Teal, Pochard, Tufted Duck, Goldeneye, Red-breasted Merganser, Goosander, Merlin, Coot, Golden Plover, Dunlin, Woodcock, Short-eared Owl, Rock Pipit, Grey Wagtail, Fieldfare, Redwing, Bearded Tit.

Passage/occasional: Red-throated Diver, Fulmar, Gannet, Mute Swan, Pink-footed Goose, Greylag Goose, Canada Goose, Wigeon, Gadwall, Pintail, Scaup, Common Scoter, Eider, Hobby, Peregrine, Red-legged Partridge, Oystercatcher, Grey Plover, Knot, Sanderling, Little Stint, Curlew Sandpiper, Purple Sandpiper, Ruff, Black-tailed Godwit, Whimbrel, Greenshank, Common Sandpiper, Turnstone, Arctic Skua, Mediterranean Gull, Little Gull, Kittiwake, Sandwich Tern, Arctic Tern, Common Tern, Black Tern, Guillemot, Turtle Dove, Long-eared Owl, Kingfisher, Sand Martin, Yellow Wagtail, Black Redstart, Redstart, Whinchat, Wheatear, Ring Ouzel, Lesser Whitethroat, Blackcap, Chiffchaff, Goldcrest, Spotted Flycatcher, Pied Flycatcher, Yellowhammer.

Scarce/rare bird records: Black-throated Diver, White-billed Diver, Great Northern Diver, Red-necked Grebe, Leach's Petrel, Manx Shearwater, Bittern, [Purple Heron], Whooper Swan, Bewick's Swan, Bean Goose, White-fronted Goose, Barnacle Goose, Brent Goose, Long-tailed Duck, Velvet Scoter, Smew, Black Kite, Marsh Harrier, Hen Harrier, Common Buzzard, Osprey, Common Crane, Avocet, Little Ringed Plover, American Golden Plover, Pacific Golden Plover, Temminck's Stint, Broad-billed Sandpiper, Spotted Redshank, Wood Sandpiper, Grey Phalarope, Pomarine Skua, Great Skua, Ring-billed Gull, Iceland Gull, Glaucous Gull, Little Tern, Razorbill, Little Auk, Puffin, Water Pipit, Waxwing, Yellow-browed Warbler, Firecrest, Red-backed Shrike, Lesser Grey Shrike, Great Grey Shrike, Twite, Mealy Redpoll, Arctic Redpoll, Crossbill, Lapland Bunting, Snow Bunting.

North Bransholme

The land to the east and southeast of North Bransholme is a mixture of low-lying farmland with hedgerows, copses and dykes, and abandoned farmland that has reverted back to marshy grassland and carr. There are numerous ponds and flashes, including the more substantial Bransholme Fishing Pond, and flooding is likely on the arable fields in wet winters. The wide Holderness Drain that bounds the area to the east is a major waterway that has lush marginal vegetation. The mix of arable, rough grassland, hedgerow and water supports many traditional farmland birds, several of which may have their last breeding grounds within the Hull boundary here. Many marsh-loving species can also be found in the wetter areas.

All year: Mute Swan, Mallard*, Sparrowhawk, Kestrel*, Grey Partridge*, Red-legged Partridge*, Pheasant*, Moorhen*, Coot*, Lapwing*, Feral Pigeon, Stock Dove*, Woodpigeon*, Collared Dove*, Barn Owl*, Tawny Owl*, Skylark*, Meadow Pipit*, Pied Wagtail*, Wren*, Dunnock*, Robin*, Song Thrush*, Blackbird*, Long-tailed Tit*, Blue Tit*, Great Tit*, Magpie*, Carrion Crow*, Rook, Jackdaw, Starling*, House Sparrow*, Tree Sparrow**, Chaffinch*, Greenfinch*, Goldfinch*, Linnet*, Yellowhammer*, Reed Bunting*, Corn Bunting**.

Summer: Cuckoo*, Swift, Kingfisher*, Swallow*, House Martin, Grasshopper Warbler*, Sedge Warbler*, Reed Warbler*, Lesser Whitethroat*, Whitethroat*, Blackcap*, Willow Warbler*, Chiffchaff*.

Winter: Cormorant, Teal, Golden Plover, Snipe, Woodcock, Black-headed Gull, Common Gull, Short-eared Owl, Fieldfare, Redwing.

Passage/occasional: Little Grebe, Grey Heron, Greylag Goose, Canada Goose, Shelduck, Goldeneye, Merlin, Water Rail, Oystercatcher, Dunlin, Curlew, Whimbrel, Jack Snipe, Redshank, Common Sandpiper, Green Sandpiper, Lesser Black-backed Gull, Herring Gull, Great Black-backed Gull, Turtle Dove, Long-eared Owl, Great-spotted Woodpecker, Sand Martin, Yellow Wagtail, Grey Wagtail, Whinchat, Wheatear, Ring Ouzel, Mistle Thrush, Goldcrest, Spotted Flycatcher (has bred), Willow Tit (perhaps bred), Lesser Redpoll, Bullfinch.

Scarce/rare bird records: Great-crested Grebe, Fulmar, [Whooper Swan], Barnacle Goose, Smew, Goosander, Marsh Harrier, Hen Harrier, Osprey, Hobby, Peregrine, Quail, Little Ringed Plover (has bred), Temminck's Stint, Spotted Redshank, Kittiwake, Iceland Gull, Glaucous Gull, Little Owl, Green Woodpecker, Waxwing, Redstart, Stonechat, Red-breasted Flycatcher, Great Grey Shrike, Jay, Brambling, Mealy Redpoll, Lapland Bunting, Snow Bunting.

Humber Bridge Country Park

The Humber Bridge Country Park is an old chalk quarry that has been colonised by scrubby woodland. Ponds, areas of meadow and the Humber shore provide further variety and interest for the birder. There are trails throughout the park and access is easy on foot or by car. The park holds a good variety of woodland birds, including local rarities such as the Hawfinch and Garden Warbler, and the Humber is always worth a look for waders and wildfowl at low tide, particularly on the sand banks. There is also the chance of seabirds offshore.

All year: Cormorant, Mallard*, Sparrowhawk*, Kestrel*, Pheasant*, Moorhen*, Black-headed Gull, Common Gull, Herring Gull, Feral Pigeon, Stock Dove*, Woodpigeon*, Collared Dove*, Tawny Owl*, Great Spotted Woodpecker*, Skylark*, Meadow Pipit*, Pied Wagtail*, Wren*, Dunnock*, Robin*, Song Thrush*, Blackbird*, Mistle Thrush*, Long-tailed Tit*, Coal Tit*, Blue Tit*, Great Tit*, Treecreeper*, Magpie*, Carrion Crow*, Rook, Jackdaw, Starling*, House Sparrow*, Chaffinch*, Greenfinch*, Goldfinch*, Linnet, Bullfinch*, Hawfinch*.

Summer: Cuckoo*, Swift, Sand Martin, Swallow, House Martin, Sedge Warbler*, Lesser Whitethroat*, Whitethroat*, Blackcap*, Garden Warbler*, Willow Warbler*, Chiffchaff*, Spotted Flycatcher*.

Winter: Golden Plover, Lapwing, Ringed Plover, Dunlin, Woodcock, Curlew, Redshank, Turnstone, Great Black-backed Gull, Fieldfare, Redwing, possibly Brambling, possibly Siskin.

Passage/occasional: Little Grebe, Great Crested Grebe, Fulmar, Gannet, Grey Heron, Mute Swan, Shelduck, Wigeon, Teal, Scaup, Common Scoter, Goldeneye, Oystercatcher, Ringed Plover, Kittiwake, Sandwich Tern, Common Tern Arctic Tern, Black Tern, Turtle Dove, Little Owl, possibly Redstart, Wheatear, Whinchat, Reed Warbler, Goldcrest, Willow Tit, possibly Pied Flycatcher.

Scarce/rare bird records: Leach's Petrel, [White Stork], Whooper Swan, Barnacle Goose, Brent Goose, Honey Buzzard, Osprey, Marsh Harrier, Hen Harrier, [Red-footed Falcon], Hobby, Peregrine, Pomarine Skua, Artic Skua, Long-tailed Skua, Great Skua, Mediterranean Gull, Sabine's Gull, Little Gull, Puffin, Red-breasted Flycatcher.

LOOKING OVER THE SALTEND MUDFLATS AT PAULL. Thousands of wading birds congregate here between autumn and spring, while seabirds can be seen on the estuary and migrants may be found in the fields and bushes. This is one of the most important sites for birds in the Hull area.

THE CHURCHYARD OF ST. JAMES' AT SUTTON. The mature trees, shrubberies and lawns are typical of many of the churchyards and cemeteries throughout Hull and the villages, and are a haven for Robins, Wrens, Blackbirds, Song Thrushes and Tawny Owls in otherwise built-up areas.

THE BOATING LAKE AT EAST PARK, home to large flocks of Greylag and Canada Geese and a wide variety of passage and wintering waterfowl. This is the only regular breeding site for the Great Crested Grebe in Hull, while the islands hold important roosting flocks of Carrion Crows and Collared Doves.

HESSLE FORESHORE, looking towards the woodland of the Humber Bridge Country Park and North Ferriby in the distance. Turnstones, Redshanks and Oystercatchers may be seen on the shoreline here and seabirds often pass offshore. The maturing woodland holds Hawfinches, Sparrowhawks and Garden Warblers.

THE HOLDERNESS DRAIN AT NORTH BRANSHOLME. Kingfishers may be found here in summer while Sedge Warblers, Reed Buntings and Yellowhammers breed along the banks.

THE RIVER HULL AT WAWNE, looking south towards Hull, where Skylarks nest in the adjoining fields and Yellow Wagtails may stop off on passage. Although Moorhens creep among the marginal vegetation, the strong tidal flow of the sediment-laden river prevents other waterbirds, such as Kingfishers and Mute Swans, from taking full advantage.

A ROOSTING TAWNY OWL at the Hedon Road Maternity Hospital. Tawny Owls occur throughout the Hull area, wherever there are mature trees to nest in and plenty of small birds or rodents to eat.
(Photograph courtesy of Michael Flowers).

A MALE BRAMBLING rescued after colliding with a window in Hedon Road Cemetery in April 1987. A scarce winter visitor to the Hull area from Scandinavia, this bird was later released to continue on its journey. (Photograph courtesy of Michael Flowers).

GAZETTEER OF BIRDS

Red-throated Diver
Gavia stellata

A handful of Red-throated Divers enter the mid and upper Humber each year, usually in late autumn and winter, and there is a scattering of records from the waterfronts of Hull and Saltend. The Hull Scientific and Field Naturalists' Club found an oiled bird on the Humber shoreline at Hull on 21st January 1963, with two others between 1960 and 1966. Intensive coverage at Saltend and the eastern docks in 1985 gave a better indication of the status of Red-throated Divers in the Hull area; birds were scarce in the first part of the year with singles in January and April while November had one on 10th, two on 15th, five on 16th and two again on 19th. All of these birds were fly-bys along the Humber, though the 10th November bird headed off north over Hull. In 1986 singles were seen off the eastern waterfront on single dates in January and February and twice in November, with three at Saltend on 20th September 1990. Autumn then, anytime between September and November, is the primary season for Red-throated Divers on our stretch of the Humber, with occasional birds being possible throughout the winter until April.

Black-throated Diver
Gavia arctica

A much scarcer passage and wintering bird than the Red-throated Diver, Black-throated Divers are consequently recorded with much less frequency in the Hull area. The first record was of an inland bird, found by a wildfowler on the bank of the River Hull at Dunswell on 1st February 1956. The bird, a first-winter female, was still alive but in a poor condition. The wildfowler took it to H. O. Bunce, the East Riding recorder for the Yorkshire Naturalists' Union at the time, but its fate is unknown. The next record, again of an ailing bird, came on 21st January 1963 when members of the Hull Scientific and Field Naturalists' Club found one on the Humber tideline in east Hull. The intensive coverage of Saltend and the Hull docks by S. L. James and

1

others in the mid 1980s gave the best insight yet into the occurrence of Black-throated Divers on our stretch of the Humber. The first were three flying upstream on 17th January 1985, with a very obliging bird in St Andrew's Dock from 2nd to 5th February. There were no more records until November of that year when one flew upstream on 4th. Another was circling back and forth on 9th November and one to four were observed flying past on four more dates to the end of the month. The last of the year was on 27th December, with just one in 1986 on 27th February. It is noticeable that virtually all of these Humber records were of birds flying upstream. The timing of Black-throated Diver sightings off Hull and Saltend is pretty much the same as that for Red-throated Divers, with the majority being in November and then the very occasional sighting into late winter.

Great Northern Diver
Gavia immer

The Great Northern Diver, as its name suggests, is a species of the far north with several hundred pairs nesting in Iceland, although the main range lies in North America. It is a rare winter visitor to British waters, occasionally inland, and there are just two, possibly three, records from the Hull area. In 1985 S. L. James saw a winter-plumaged Great Northern Diver flying upstream past Saltend on 16th November before landing on the Humber off Barton. Three days later James saw what may have been the same bird flying downstream past Saltend. The only other sighting concerns an adult watched by B. Richards as it drifted downstream past Saltend on 9th November 1998. As with many species that occur mainly on the Humber in our area, it is likely that other Great Northern Divers have been missed due to infrequent observation.

White-billed Diver
(Yellow-billed Diver)
Gavia adamsii

On 18th February 1953 Messrs Bunting and Stathers, of Paull, were out for a walk along the Humber bank when they discovered an ailing large bird on the tideline at the mouth of Hedon Haven, just down-stream of Saltend. The bird was an adult White-billed Diver, an Arctic species that winters off the Scandinavian coast, and it was in a very bad way. Exhausted, slightly oiled and having rather grimy plumage, it was probably incapable of flight and had no doubt sought refuge in the sheltered estuary. Despite its rescue the bird died shortly afterwards and the details of the find appeared in the monthly journal *British Birds* (Volume XLVI (1953), p. 214-5), with whose kind permission they are reproduced here. This bird was only the 13th of its kind ever recorded in Britain up until that time and, in light of its extreme rarity, it was preserved as a museum specimen after death. A photograph of the specimen appears in Mather's *The Birds of Yorkshire* (1986), plate 55.

Little Grebe
Tachybaptus ruficollis

The Little Grebe, or Dabchick to give it its old name, is the commonest grebe in the Hull area though it was apparently not always as numerous as it is today. Despite several wintering on East Park Lake during the 1940s there are no early breeding records. A single pair that bred at King George Dock up until 1962 were the only ones recorded within the old city boundary during that decade, although birds were resident and breeding at Thwaite Hall Lake in Cottingham in the 1980s and probably for many years before. Indeed, the presence of calling birds in 2000 suggests that breeding still occurs at Thwaite Hall. Breeding was proved at Saltend Marsh in 1985 when a pair and two young were seen in June and July, with two pairs suspected of breeding the following year. Up to four Little Grebes were regularly visiting the ice-free docks in winter during this time, as they probably still do, while birds also occur along the Holderness Drain in spring and autumn. Counts on the drain include two near the docks in September 1985, seven at Marfleet in November 1988 and two at North Bransholme in November 1993.

Four Little Grebes were seen at the Bransholme Sewage Works in late September 1976 but there were no more records from that site until the 1990s, when numbers increased as the decade progressed. Up to three were present in 1992, rising to a maximum of six the following year and 16 in the late summer and autumn of 2000. Recent years have seen the highest numbers tending to occur here in August and September, with a few birds often present from June to December and others occasionally dropping by in late winter and spring. A pair attempted to breed on the Bransholme Sewage Works reservoir in June 1992, building a precarious nest on a floating mat of algae. Strong winds a week into incubation washed the nest away although two pairs were successful in 2000, with broods of two and three young being seen in August.

Oddly perhaps, Little Grebes are quite scarce on East Park Lake with only one to three occasionally being present during autumn or winter. So, while any sizeable freshwater may attract a bird or two, particularly in autumn and winter, the key sites for the species in the Hull area are clearly the Bransholme Sewage Works reservoir and Thwaite Hall Lake.

Great Crested Grebe
Podiceps cristatus

With its slender neck and body, extravagant summer head plumes and beautiful courtship displays, the Great Crested Grebe is one of Hull's most elegant birds. It is also surprisingly scarce in the area and breeds regularly at only one site, East Park Lake.

Exactly when Great Crested Grebes began nesting in East Park is not clear but they were certainly unknown before the 1980s. In 1994 a pair reared a single chick in the park, though they had probably been breeding here for several years by then. In 1997 a bumper summer saw no less than four pairs hatching six broods between them but only five of the 19 young reached maturity. Just a single pair stayed to breed the following year, 1998, and four stripey chicks were seen in April. The survival rate was low once more, however, and only one chick survived the summer. At least one or two pairs have bred since then and the several well-grown young present in the autumn of 2000 suggest that they might be having more luck these days.

Great Crested Grebes can be seen virtually all year round at East Park, with up to six on the lake in winter, and the incredible courtship can be observed at close quarters from February onwards. During the highly ritualised display the breeding pair spend much of their time 'dancing' face-to-face, copying head movements and fanning their glorious head plumes at each other. One or both birds will occasionally bring some pondweed to the surface and use this in the dance; the birds rear up out of the water, breast to breast with the weed in their bill, and shake their heads ecstatically. The courtship is performed for hours on end all through the spring and is well worth a special visit to East Park just to witness it. Once mating is over the birds build a floating raft of twigs on which to lay their eggs, this being anchored to one of the islands via overhanging branches. When the young hatch, often in April, they can frequently be seen riding on their parents' backs and will usually remain on the lake until early winter.

Great Crested Grebes are quite rare in the Hull area away from East Park although occurrences are increasing. Just one bird was seen in the city during the 1960s, in one of the docks. By the mid 1980s up to six could be found around Alexandra Dock and the eastern waterfront in the early months of the year. Regular watching would no doubt reveal this to still be the case. It is now also possible to find an occasional Great Crested Grebe at the Bransholme Sewage Works during spring or summer, with a pair in June 2001, and a confiding bird was on the Bransholme Fishing Pond in July 2001. Others may be seen in Pickering Park, where one pair bred in 2000.

Red-necked Grebe
Podiceps grisegena

The Red-necked Grebe is a very scarce winter visitor to the Hull area with most records coming from the Humber. The earliest documented record I have comes from 1891 when one was killed near Waghen, the old name for Wawne. The next was not until 1976 when one was spotted on the Bransholme Sewage Works reservoir on 23rd September.

Red-necked Grebes were annual on the Humber during the mid 1980s. One was off Saltend on 18th January 1985, a single was there again on 6th February 1986 and another was at King George Dock on 30th January 1987. The absence of Humber records since then probably reflects a lack of coverage rather than a lack of birds, as the species is seen elsewhere along the estuary in most winters.

On 21st November 2000 I was walking through East Park when I saw a winter-plumaged Red-necked Grebe on the lake near the ornamental bridge. Just a few feet from the bank, the bird allowed close approach between periodic dives. It was still present the following day, though by now it had become quite shy and kept well out near the central islands. Over the course of the following week, however, it was regularly seen near the duck feeding area off Hawkesbury Street. It was last reported on 4th December.

Slavonian Grebe
Podiceps auritus

The first record of the Slavonian Grebe for the Hull area comes from

December 1893 when one was shot on a pond in a former brick pit on the western outskirts of Hull. The hapless grebe joined a Bittern that was shot nearby around the same time, ending up as a stuffed specimen in the collection of a Hull naturalist. The next Slavonian Grebe was a confiding bird on East Park Lake on 5th February 1939, followed by another there between 26th February and 1st March 1954. There have been no documented records in the area since then. Several have probably gone unnoticed on the Humber in autumn and winter, as the species is recorded annually on Yorkshire coasts and wetlands.

Black-necked Grebe
Podiceps nigricollis

There is only one documented record of the Black-necked Grebe in Hull, with a female 'Eared Grebe' being shot on the Humber near the town on 20th February 1864. The specimen went to W. W. Boulton's collection before passing into the hands of T. Boynton of Beverley after Boulton's death. Boynton's collection was later purchased by Hull Museums in the early 1900s. Other Black-necked Grebes must surely have occurred around Hull on the Humber, the docks or the ponds and lakes, as they are not exceptionally rare in Yorkshire. Unfortunately, any such birds either went unseen or unrecorded.

Fulmar
(Northern Fulmar)
Fulmarus glacialis

Since the late 1800s the Fulmar has expanded from its only British breeding outpost on St Kilda to nest on virtually every coastal cliff in the country. Some birds even nest on inland crags up to 15 miles from the sea, although the nearest breeding birds to Hull are at Flamborough. A few also nest on the taller cliffs of Holderness. The spread of the Fulmar during the 20th Century no doubt led to an increase in records on the Humber. Birds are now fairly regular between mid March and mid September as far upstream as the Humber Bridge, though day totals are invariably in single figures.

The first record from the Hull area concerns two birds over the Humber at a place called Grimston Cliffs, west of Hull, on 3rd April 1944. In April 1958 and December 1959

Fulmars were found on returning trawlers in St. Andrew's Dock but where they came aboard can only be guessed at. Another was seen flying over Hessle Road around the same time. Two were on the Humber off Saltend on 19th April 1985 before leaving to the east, with four passing upstream on 19th August and one going the opposite way on 19th September. Singles passed Saltend again on 30th March and 26th April 1986, with one again on 27th. Two passed by on 7th June and day counts of five and two birds were logged in early August. In February 1997 a dead Fulmar was found in a field of winter wheat near North Bransholme, well inland, and it must have been blown in by gales before being killed.

August therefore appears to be the prime month for Fulmars on the Humber, with sightings possible from any waterfront in the Hull area. Spring passage often brings birds our way in April and occasionally as late as June, but I really wouldn't be too surprised to see one gliding over the murky waters at any time of year.

Manx Shearwater
Puffinus puffinus

Like the Storm Petrel the Manx Shearwater is an ocean-going seabird that breeds in large colonies on Britain's west coast. In contrast to the Storm Petrel, however, Manx Shearwaters are frequently seen off the east coast on autumn passage though it is still a rather rare bird on the Humber.

Manx Shearwaters have irregularly been seen heading upstream from watchpoints further down the Humber over the years but all were seen to return seawards a short while later. It looks like hardly any birds make it as far as Paull before turning back, with most of them probably being spooked by the estuary closing in on them way before then. 1986 produced two records from Saltend, however, with one flying downstream on 30th June and another sat on the Humber on 1st September. More recently a lone Manx Shearwater flew downstream past Alexandra Dock on 24th June 1999. These are the only documented records from the Humber in the Hull area.

Manx Shearwaters are very occasionally seen way up the estuary beyond Hull. Birds were reported from Welton, Blacktoft and Whitton Sands in September 1978 and Welton again in July 2001, and they must have passed Paull, Hull and Hessle at some point.

A single record of a grounded Manx Shearwater in Hull concerns a bird picked up alive in the city on 11th November 1959 and taken to the RSPCA, though where it was found and its eventual fate were not recorded.

Storm Petrel
(European Storm-petrel)
Hydrobates pelagicus

Leach's Petrel
(Leach's Storm-petrel)
Oceanodroma leucorhoa

Small, oceanic and largely nocturnal, Storm Petrels are rarely seen on the east coast despite the enormous colonies on the islands of western and northern Britain. They hardly ever come to shore on migration and have been seen over the Humber on only a couple of occasions.

Members of the Hull Scientific and Field Naturalists' Club recorded three Storm Petrels during their investigation into the birds of Hull up to 1967. No details were given, however, but the record of one found alive on St Andrew's Dock on 17th October 1958 was probably included. This bird was taken to the RSPCA for treatment but died the next day. The other records were likely to have been along similar lines, with the most probable scenario being birds found either as tideline corpses or on returning fishing vessels.

Leach's Petrels breed in rock crevices on remote coasts and islands in the north Atlantic, including the British Northern Isles, and winter in the southern oceans. A truly oceanic seabird, it usually takes gales and bad weather to bring Leach's Petrels into the North Sea and close to land in any numbers. Even so, local sightings of Leach's Petrels easily outnumber those of the Storm Petrel, a bird that breeds in huge numbers on Britain's west coast. All of the dated records of Leach's Petrels have occurred in September or October and all have been on or near the Humber.

The first record comes via Nelson (1907) who reported that one or two had been found near Hull up to 1907. One found alive in Hull on 29th October 1952, a late date, was taken to G.H. Ainsworth, a well-known local ornithologist. Ainsworth sent the bird down to Ralph Chislett at Spurn for release but it was very weak and died soon after arrival. On 21st September 1985 S. L. James, S. Brebner and S. Bryan saw a Leach's Petrel flying north over Saltend Marsh towards Hedon Road and Marfleet. It was speculated that this may have been the same bird that had been touring South and West Yorkshire since the 17th, having since found the Humber and a path to the sea. It seemed to be heading in the wrong direction when James and co. saw it, though! Another was seen at Saltend, this time over the Humber, on 30th September 1989. One flying downstream at North Ferriby on 8th October 1989 would have surely passed Hessle, Hull and Paull soon afterwards. Another was at the Humber Bridge on 23rd September 1992, with one more there after easterly gales on 13th September the following year.

Each autumn a few Leach's Petrels are seen elsewhere on the Humber, such as Blacktoft or Sunk Island, and many of these must pass the waterfront between Paull and the Humber Bridge on their travels. John Ward, a regular 'river watcher' at Sunk Island during the 1980s and 1990s, speculated that not all of these Leach's Petrels had been blown up the Humber by strong winds. Others, Ward speculated, had probably unintentionally flown inland over low-lying Holderness during the night and were regaining access to the sea via the Humber. It's an interesting and plausible idea, but in the absence of many inland records over Holderness it is difficult to know for sure.

Gannet
(Northern Gannet)
Morus bassanus

The Gannet is a regular passage migrant on the Humber during spring and autumn, with most occurring during the latter period. It is noticeable that immature birds account for the vast majority of those seen. A Gannet was picked up alive near Hull on 15th October 1958 and was taken to the RSPCA, but where it was found and whether it lived aren't on record. This is the only pre-1980s record but the establishment of a colony at Bempton Cliffs in the 1960s may have been the cause of the increased numbers seen today. Gannets are now frequently seen from Saltend and Paull, particularly in May and September. In 1985 watchers logged 46 on 12th May and 88 on 18th September, though birds usually number less than 10 on any one day. Significant movements of Gannets can occasionally be seen from any vantage point overlooking the estuary, however, with three flocks passing Victoria Dock on 19th September 1997 totalling 95 birds.

The building of the Humber Bridge in the late 1970s came as a nasty surprise to Gannets flying upstream and they seem very reluctant to pass under or over the obstacle. On seeing the Bridge they often fly up and down at the bend of the estuary, off Saltend, as if confused and unsure of exactly what to do. Groups of two and nine Gannets approaching the Bridge on 19th and 20th September 1997 all turned back and flew off downstream, as did a trio of immatures on 20th September 1999. On 1st October 1998 E. Clubley watched three immature birds flying upstream towards the Bridge. On reaching it, they circled around for a while before deciding to go back the way they had come. Shortly afterwards Clubley saw two more Gannets approaching from the west; these birds also circled at the Bridge for a while before biting the bullet and flying underneath it, this being the first such instance witnessed by Clubley in 17 years. It is possible that these two Gannets had just crossed Britain from the Irish Sea and were therefore much more desperate to carry on and reach open water than westbound birds are to fly up an ever-narrowing estuary.

Cormorant
(Great Cormorant)
Phalacrocorax carbo
Two races of Cormorant occur in the Hull area, the native British race (*Phalacrocorax carbo carbo*) and the Continental race (*Phalacrocorax carbo sinensis*), which has begun to breed in Britain in recent decades. In general adult Continental birds tend to have whiter heads in spring, though dis-

tinguishing the two races in the field with absolute certainty is probably impossible.

In the 1960s the Cormorant was a rare winter visitor to Hull and mainly on the Humber around the eastern docks. In the 1980s birds were seen at the docks and along the Humber in every month, with up to 40 in winter and a peak of 49 reported in January 1985, while up to 10 were regularly seen roosting and loafing on the cranes around the eastern docks. Cormorants can still be found at Saltend and on the Humber, particularly in winter, though numbers seem to have decreased a little.

Cormorants are occasionally encountered on inland waters in the Hull area and the Holderness Drain at North Bransholme was a favoured spot in the early 1990s. From September until March up to four birds could be seen resting on the wooden pylons near Carlam Hill Farm or fishing in the drain at this site, though they were much scarcer towards the end of the decade. A small bird showing characteristics of the Continental race was sat alongside a darker British bird on 23rd February 1990. The Bransholme Sewage Works also attracts a

Cormorant or two in late autumn, invariably in first-winter plumage, and they occasionally fish on the River Hull. On 21st November 2000 a first-winter Cormorant was nervously fishing in East Park Lake but soon departed as human visitors arrived. During the very cold spell around Christmas 2000 I regularly saw a Cormorant in flight over Stoneferry, no doubt after fishing in the ice-free River Hull.

Any moderately sized water that holds fish may tempt down a passing Cormorant, probably in late autumn or winter, though they are still persecuted by anglers in the belief that they can empty whole waters of their fish. While this is nonsense there's no denying that a well-stocked fishpond is nothing less than a bird table for a fish-eating bird, so there is little surprise that they occasionally take advantage.

Shag
(European Shag)
Phalacrocorax aristotelis

Much rarer in the Hull area than its close cousin the Cormorant, Shags are most likely to be found on the Humber in very small numbers from autumn to spring. The Hull Scientific and Field Naturalists' Club recorded three off Hull between 1960 and 1966, with another found walking along a city street on 3rd March 1965. Regular watching from the eastern docks in the mid 1980s revealed the presence of one or two birds in autumn and winter, with three together on 6th November 1985. An immature bird passed downstream at Paull on the unusually late date of 18th May in 1986 and one was back as early as August in 1986. Documented sightings dried up after that time as regular watching and reporting decreased, though a first-winter bird off King George Dock on the 16th November 1998 indicates that it is still possible to find Shags on the Humber.

Bittern
(Great Bittern)
Botaurus stellaris

Bitterns are rare winter visitors to the Hull area and those that do occur are more likely to be immigrants from the Continent rather than members of the tiny British breeding population. Bitterns appear to have been rare around Hull since at least the late 19th Century; a dead bird on sale in Hull market in December 1890, presumably killed locally, was notable enough to be reported in *The Naturalist*. A Bittern was killed near a brick pond on the west side of Hull in November 1893 and ended up as a mounted specimen in the house of a Mr J. Hane. J. R. Lowther reported a Bittern having been shot at the side of a ditch near Beverley in late December 1899. Back then "near Beverley" could mean as far south as present day North Hull, so this record may have been in the modern day Hull area as dealt with here.

The first live record, but only just, was of one picked up starving and exhausted on the shore at Paull on 12th January 1913. A small invasion occurred during that month and five more were killed in the district of Paull alone. On 9th March 1940 another ailing and emaciated Bittern was caught at Hedon but it died shortly afterwards. The next was seen somewhere within the city boundary on 12th November 1966, with no exact location given. One was flushed from Saltend Marsh on 16th February 1985 before flying off over the Humber towards Lincolnshire. Another was seen flying up the River Hull over the city on 16th November 1991.

November to January seem to be the best months for finding a Bittern in the Hull area, with reedy or swampy areas bordering the River Hull or the Humber estuary being the most likely places. The secretive nature of the Bittern means that more must have occurred without being recorded,

particularly when the species was more common in Britain during the mid 19th Century. Indeed, it is highly likely that Bitterns bred in the carrs and marshes that covered much of the area north of 17th and 18th Century Hull. The name of a farm house that stood at that time, now long since gone, just north of the Hull area near Meaux paid tribute to the continuous booming of Bitterns that bred in nearby marshes. The house was called Butterbump Hall, the term 'Butter-bump' being an old East Riding country name for the Bittern, and Nelson (1907) tells us of an old couplet that locals recited: - "When the Butterbumps cry, Summer is nigh!"

Little Bittern
Ixobrychus minutus

Nelson's *The Birds of Yorkshire* (1907) lists one alleged occurrence of the Little Bittern for the Hull area, with W.W. Boulton of Beverley stating in 1880 that one was killed at Cottingham "several years ago". Thomas Boynton of Bridlington bought the specimen after Boulton's death and it was in his collection up until 1905 at least, when it was reported to Nelson.

Night Heron
(Black-crowned Night Heron)
Nycticorax nycticorax

Night Herons are rare wanderers to Britain from their scattered colonies on the Continent and at least four have been recorded in the Hull area. The first was an immature male shot on Cottingham Common, between Cottingham and Dunswell and now covered by North Hull housing estate, by a gamekeeper called Martin way back in 1837. The specimen went into the possession of W. W. Boulton of Beverley before being bought by Sir Henry Boynton and then passing onto the Burton Agnes Museum sometime before 1907.

The next was not for another 150 years, when a second-summer bird settled at Swine from 28th April 1987 until at least 2nd May. Incredibly this bird was joined by a second Night Heron, in first-summer plumage, on 30th April and one of them was still present on 7th May. The first-summer bird was later seen at Easington and Kilnsea in May. The next Hull record, claimed on 5th May 1990, was deemed to have been not proven by the British Birds

Rarities Committee and was subsequently rejected. No exact location was given for this bird but it is probably the same undated record I have received for East Park around that time. The most recent record was beyond contention, however, when a first-summer bird was discovered roosting on an island in East Park Lake on 27th March 1996. It is noticeable that all of the dated records have occurred between late March and early May and all have been sub-adults.

Little Egret
Egretta garzetta

A Little Egret was shot near Paull in March 1826. It was later bequeathed to Chester Museum in a display case bearing the label "Shot March 1826, near Paull, Humberside, Yorkshire". The specimen was apparently forgotten about in Yorkshire until it was 'rediscovered' by Thomas Hudson Nelson at the turn of the last century. Nelson inspected the case himself and was as sure as he could be that it was a genuine Yorkshire record, with the case label apparently being written in one hand and all at one time. The dubious nature of many 19th Century specimens, however, due to the underhand methods some early collectors employed to build their collections, meant that the origin of the Paull Little Egret was soon called into question. In 1901 J. H. Gurney wrote to *The Zoologist* on the subject and implied that the word 'Yorkshire' had been added to the case label at a later stage and going on to state that, in his opinion, the bird was the same one documented to have been sold at Southampton in 1826 and was probably shot there. Mather discusses these exchanges in his 1986 *The Birds of Yorkshire*, pointing out that whether 'Yorkshire' was added to the label at a later date or not is pretty irrelevant seeing as Paull and Humberside are definitely not near Southampton and definitely are in Yorkshire. It is hard not to agree. As there seemed to have been nothing on the case itself to suggest it *was* from Southampton then I think it is fair to assume that the record is genuine. This is the only record for the Hull area, though others have been seen in Yorkshire over the years and the species has recently colonised southern Britain. As the population of breeding and wintering birds increases and spreads then it seems likely that more Little Egrets will visit the Hull area sooner or later.

Grey Heron
Ardea cinerea
There is no record of Herons ever having nested in the Hull area, though Nelson (1907) states that they may have nested at Swanland, just outside the range of this book,

"many years ago". Writing of the birds to be seen from his garden near Pearson Park in 1901 John Nicholson mentioned that Herons were occasionally seen flying over Hull "en-route to the heronry at Wassand", this presumably being Wassand Hall at Hornsea Mere. While Herons no longer breed at Hornsea Mere a colony of around 50 birds currently nest near Driffield and this may be the source of some of the birds seen around Hull.

The Grey Heron was apparently very rare in the Hull area in the 1960s, probably as a result of poisoning by the agrochemicals that had so badly affected birds of prey. Only two were seen in the first half of that decade. Numbers had recovered somewhat by the late 1970s and a few Herons could be found feeding on the tidal creeks on the Humber shore in spring and autumn. By the mid 1980s sightings were still very irregular over most of the Hull area and a pair flying north over Cottingham on 15th July 1985 was a notable record. Birds were more frequent at Saltend Channel and, in hard weather, St. Andrew's Dock at this time with regular dawn flights of up to five birds passing over the Humber to feed on the Lincolnshire side. One or two were seen most months along the Holderness Drain at North Bransholme from 1989 and birds were only absent there during midsummer. Three were roosting in a waterlogged field nearby on 16th August 1992, having been feeding on the spoils from dredging operations on the drain. By the late 1990s Grey Herons were being reported from many areas around Hull, with Saltend having one or more throughout the year and others seen from Victoria Dock in most months. Herons have also been recorded over East Park and at the Bransholme Sewage Works as well as from the flooded fields along Priory Road.

Although the nearest breeding site is many miles to the north it is now possible to see a Grey Heron at any time of the year except midsummer, usually in flight en-route to fishing grounds along the Humber. Increasingly the occasional Heron can also be found feeding along some of the larger drains or trying their luck at one of the several ponds, lakes or marshes scattered about the Hull area.

Purple Heron
Ardea purpurea

On 15th July 1986 A. S. Pepper reported seeing an adult Purple Heron soaring over Hedon Road before descending towards Saltend Marsh and being lost from sight. This record was never submitted to the national or local rarities committees for adjudication, and some consider it unsafe.

White Stork
Ciconia ciconia

The White Stork, popular in European folklore and legend, used to breed in Medieval Britain but was driven out many centuries ago. A few wanderers from southern and central Europe are seen in Britain each year but the situation is clouded by escapees from bird gardens and wildlife parks. Most of the Hull area records have been of birds in flight, all are very recent and most possibly refer to free-flying birds from the Harewood House Bird Garden near Leeds, possibly even the same bird.

On 25th May 1998 a White Stork was seen flying over Hull and another was spotted soaring over the city on 14th July 1999. On 19th April 2000 an adult was observed from a garden to the west of Hull as it drifted south near the Humber Bridge. This last bird in particular spent much of the spring of 2000 touring the region and is generally thought to have had its origins at Harewood House. On 4th April 2001 a White Stork was discovered on flooded grassland on Anlaby Common, off Hull Road. As with the other records for this species the possibility of the bird being an escapee loomed large, though it was unringed and in good condition. It was still present at dawn the next day and was watched from First Lane as it fed on frogs, but it was gone by the afternoon. Further investigation revealed that the bird might have been present since 2nd April and its photograph appeared in many of the national birdwatching magazines the following month.

Mute Swan
Cygnus olor

It is unclear whether the Mute Swan is a native British bird or whether the Normans, or perhaps the Romans, introduced it from the Continent. The species is now established throughout Britain but has never been common in the Hull area

due to the restricted number of water bodies large enough to support it. Mute Swans were first introduced to East Park in 1902 and they were still mainly restricted to the larger parks in the 1960s, where they bred irregularly. This is largely the case today though breeding can perhaps be described as regular at several sites.

East Park has a pair of breeding Mute Swans each year but they only ever manage to raise one or two cygnets at best from the usual clutch of six eggs. A pair also bred on the Barmston Drain behind Beresford Avenue, on Beverley Road, for most of the 1990s. This pair often attracted unwanted attention, however, with the male being shot while the female sat on the nest in May 1994. In 2000 a pair here were again attacked as they nested, this time by stone-throwing youths, but a family group seen nearby later that summer indicates that they escaped unharmed. Breeding has also occurred at Pickering Park on many occasions and, for the first time, a pair raised three young at the Bransholme Sewage Works in 2000.

The reservoir at the Bransholme Sewage Works often holds the largest numbers of Mute Swans in the Hull area, with birds seen regularly during winter in the 1980s. Up to eight birds wintered at this site in the early 1990s with an unprecedented 34 in October 1997. Pairs or family groups regularly visit the Holderness Drain at North Bransholme, occurring in every month except midsummer though again they are not always left unmolested. Just before Christmas in 1995 a web of Nylon fishing line spanned the drain in what seemed like a bizarre attempt to snare a pair that had arrived a few days before. A week later a plastic bag containing the head, wings, feet and feathers of an adult Mute Swan was found dumped nearby. It seems a Christmas turkey isn't good enough for some people.

Mute Swans often become scarce in late summer as many birds leave to undergo their moult at traditional gathering places such as Hornsea Mere. Numbers build again from September and an extra pair or two can be found at East Park, on the larger drains and ponds or even on the Humber until they leave to find nesting sites in March. Breeding birds will not tolerate any other Swans on their stretch of water and violent fights can be witnessed during April and May as the males slug it out for territory.

Bewick's Swan
(Tundra Swan)
Cygnus columbianus

Bewick's Swans are irregular winter visitors and passage migrants in East Yorkshire. Flying thousands of miles to Britain from their breeding grounds on the Eurasian tundra, sightings have always been rather rare in the Hull area. A flock of 23 was on the Humber off Paull on 8th November 1970, with two adults flying up and down the estuary off nearby Saltend on 18th November 1985 before eventually leaving to the east. The following month saw 10 adults and three immatures on the Humber off Saltend on 2nd December. More recently, five flew south over Anlaby on 12th October 2000 and seven were over the Humber Bridge on 21st December. It is noticeable that all of these records concern birds on, or on their way to, the Humber in autumn or early winter.

Whooper Swan
Cygnus cygnus

Whooper Swans are winter visitors to Britain from Iceland and they tend to stick to traditional wintering grounds, such as the Ouse Washes in Cambridgeshire, but can also be seen outside of these areas on occasion. Unfortunately the Hull area does not hold a regular wintering site for Whooper Swans and those that are seen are usually just passing over en-route to somewhere else.

The largest number of Whooper Swans ever seen in the Hull area occurred on 6th November 1981 when Brian Fendley witnessed an incredible flight of over 150 birds passing over Kirk Ella. Eleven on the reservoir at the Bransholme Sewage Works on 10th December 1984 was a rare stopover, while a one-legged bird in the company of a Mute Swan on the Holderness Drain, North Bransholme, in December 1991 was a curious record. Swans are one of the few birds that cannot survive with one leg as this renders them unable to walk or take off due to their great weight. The origins of this cripple are therefore a mystery and human interference cannot be ruled out.

In November 1996 David Turner witnessed 10 Whooper Swans flying over the Carr Lane Nurseries in East Hull. A tame bird, probably an escapee from a wildfowl collection, toured the Hull valley during 1997, being present at East Park until 5th March before being seen at Bransholme Sewage Works and elsewhere in East Yorkshire throughout the summer. The bird returned to East Park in September and stayed until 2nd January 1998. Three flying upstream at the Humber Bridge on 6th November 2000 were probably using the estuary to guide them inland to wintering sites in South and West Yorkshire.

November or December therefore seems the best time to look out for wild Whooper Swans as they pass through the Hull area, with any lone birds seen outside this time, particularly during the summer, highly likely to be feral.

Black Swan
Cygnus atratus

The Black Swan is a resident of Australia and New Zealand but many are kept as ornamental wildfowl in Britain and despite their sedentary nature some birds nevertheless succumb to wanderlust, with sporadic breeding not unknown among feral birds. There is just one record for the Hull area, however, with a single bird appearing on the Bransholme Sewage Works reservoir during very cold weather in December 1984.

Bean Goose
Anser fabalis

There are just three records of this goose, which hails from the Eurasian taiga region, occurring in the Hull area. The first was a dead bird picked up on Hessle Foreshore on 15th January 1950, though the tide may have carried it from anywhere. The next was a bit more lively and was flying east at Saltend in the company of 30 Pink-footed Geese on 4th April 1985 before flying back west a few minutes later. The only other bird was in East Park on 28th January 1987 though, as with any unusual waterfowl in East Park, the spectre of a captive origin hovers over this record.

Bean Geese are just about annual as winter visitors or passage migrants in East Yorkshire so it is likely that others have been missed in the Hull area or mistaken for the similar Pink-footed Goose, possibly along the Humber or in flight over the city.

Pink-footed Goose
Anser brachyrhynchus

During much of the 20th Century the Humber estuary was a major haunt of the Pink-footed Geese that came from Iceland and eastern Greenland to winter in Britain. Up to 15,000 birds roosted on the upper estuary overnight and fed on the surrounding fields throughout the winter. The wild geese heard during winter nights over John Nicholson's Hull town house at the beginning of the 1900s were almost certainly Pinkfeet, and in October 1956 a memorable flight took place over Hull as large flocks of birds, numbering many hundreds, rose from the Humber and crossed over the southern half of the city on a broad front.

The geese were still common winter visitors over Hull during the 1960s, with small skeins regularly seen over the western suburbs and occasionally elsewhere. Around that time, however, changes in farming practices in the principal feeding grounds on the Wolds meant that Humberside was becoming less attractive to Pinkfeet. In addition changes in Scottish agriculture, mainly the conversion of large areas of pasture to arable, meant that many Pinkfeet didn't bother flying the extra few hundred miles to the Humber. Up to 2,000 birds were still wintering around the Humber in the 1970s but the flock was halved by a poisoning incident in 1975 when around a thousand birds died after eating contaminated wheat. Numbers then declined rapidly during the 1980s and by 1990 just a few hundred were returning to the Humber each year.

The decrease in the local wintering population of Pink-footed Geese was reflected in the decrease in the number of skeins seen over the Hull area. A flock of 65 flying east over Saltend on 18th November 1985 and three flocks totalling 265 flying over on 27th December were notable records. A skein of 80 flew southeast over North Bransholme early one morning in October 1989 and a large skein, 250-strong, flew east to the north of Wawne on 5th March 1991. By now skeins were becoming quite infrequent and the species was best described as a passage migrant in the Hull area rather than a winter visitor. Few were seen during the early years of the 1990s, while 90 flying south over Victoria Dock on 25th November 1997 and 91 at Low Paull on 10th October 1999 were the only skeins reported in those years. An impressive 200 passed over the Avenues area of Hull on 5th February 2000 and this was followed by 170 flying southeast over the Bransholme Sewage Works on 21st October. This latter skein was seen to lose height a little as it passed over the city towards Saltend but as with many of the flocks these days, it was felt that the birds were probably heading for The Wash. Later that winter 260 flew south over Cottingham on 10th December, this being the largest single flock seen for many years and it was almost matched by the 250 that passed over Anlaby on 10th February 2001. A few days later, on 14th, another 70 flew west over the city centre.

One or two Pink-footed Geese are occasionally seen at East Park, with a pair on the lake on 16th November 1993, a single the following May and another during the last quarter of 1997. Their relative tameness means that these birds were probably feral. The first wild Pink-footed Geese are usually seen over the Hull area from mid October, with a peak during November and the last around mid March.

White-fronted Goose
(Greater White-fronted Goose)
Anser albifrons

All of the White-fronts reported in the Hull area have either been identified as or presumed to be birds of the Eurasian race, *Anser albifrons albifrons*, rather than members of the more westerly-wintering Greenland race, *Anser albifrons flavirostris*. One of the rarer geese in the Hull area, sightings are probably less than annual although it is a little more frequent elsewhere along the Humber.

Described as a very rare winter visitor in 1960s Hull by the Hull Scientific and Field Naturalists' Club, there were just three sightings between 1960 and 1966 including a small nocturnal party passing over on 12th December 1965. On 28th December 1984 four birds were on a floodwater pool at Willerby Carr Farm, north of Wold Road. There was a good run of records in the mid 1980s at Saltend and around the eastern docks when there was regular coverage of this area. The first was an adult at Saltend on 26th March 1985 while another flew northeast there on 18th December and seven were near the docks on 22nd February 1986. Six were at Saltend on 6th April and another four birds were near the docks again on 14th. A more recent record involves a first-winter bird at East Park on 11th April 1997, though its origins are perhaps a little more open to question.

The White-fronted Goose is therefore a rather rare, usually brief, winter visitor to the Hull area anytime between December and mid April. The Humber shore is by far the most likely place to see one.

Greylag Goose
Anser anser

Greylag Geese probably bred quite naturally in the wetlands of the Hull area before drainage and hunting eradicated them from the region several hundred years ago. The species was then absent from the Hull area, except perhaps for the odd vagrant flock in winter, until the middle of the 20th Century when the Hull and District Wildfowlers Association introduced a small group onto East Park Lake. Several escaped in 1964 and toured the county, being seen on the Humber and Hornsea Mere, and this or other releases for shooting or ornamental purposes in the 1960s probably seeded the current feral population in the city. In 1967 just five were present in East Park in February and seven in December, while 165 were counted there on 15th January 1970. Breeding numbers remained low, however, well into the 1980s. By this time small flocks were present elsewhere in the area, with six in Pearson Park on Valentine's Day 1982 and up to 12 at Thwaite Hall Lake, Cottingham, where breeding occurred in 1984 and 1985 despite the taking of eggs. In 1986 a pair was suspected to have bred near Paull and other pairs were roaming as far as North Bransholme in the spring of 1989.

By the 1990s the population at East Park was well established and, along with the flock at Hornsea Mere, formed one of the largest subpopulations of feral Greylag Geese in England. In May 1993 the breeding flock at East Park numbered 95 adults and 57 young, while in May of the following year 207 adults had 47 young in tow. By 1997 the number of goslings hatched had reached 84 from 15 pairs, though only 34 young were hatched from five pairs the following year. The first goslings appear in April and most of the broods tend to hatch within a few weeks of each other.

Hybridisation with other goose species is regular in East Park, with three Greylag x Canada Goose goslings reared in 1993 and up to seven such birds being present in recent years. Since the early 1990s a small number of Swan Geese (*Anser cygnoides*) have become incorporated into the Greylag flock. A total of 15 such hybrids had 11 goslings in May 1993, though the continued cross-hybridisation with Greylag Geese meant that only one Swan Goose x Greylag Goose hybrid could be picked out by October 2000.

A clear pattern of the seasonal flux in numbers at East Park became established during the 1990s. The low point, generally less than 100 birds, occurs in March, though this was as low as 11 in 1998. Numbers then build in April and May to a peak of up to 350 in June and July as adults from around the city gather to join the breeding flock and moult their flight feathers in relative safety. By August the number typically falls to around 230, slowly decreasing to fewer than 150 by February before dipping below 100 again in March.

Away from East Park, several pairs of Greylag Geese can also be found nesting at Pickering Park and 22 young were seen in June 2000, while over a hundred adults are often present. Small numbers of Greylags often roam the Hull area in the autumn and winter months; Saltend saw a flock of 21 flying northeast on 6th August 1985 and 30 flew west there on 19th August 1986, with single figures passing over from November to May around the same

time. A flock of 16 was at North Bransholme on 4th November 1993 and up to five were around the Priory Road fields in early 1996. One or two Greylag Geese have also turned up at the Bransholme Sewage Works with flocks of Canada geese in autumn, flying from the parks in order to feed on the arable fields bordering the city.

Relations between Greylags and the human visitors to Hull's parks are not always cordial. Letters occasionally appear in the local press berating the geese for fouling the grass, while in 2000 police investigated an incident in which a man throttled an over-enthusiastic Greylag Goose to death after it bit his daughter as she fed the ducks in Pickering Park.

Snow Goose
Anser caerulescens

Snow Geese breed from Greenland across Arctic Canada and into Alaska, wintering in southern USA and Mexico, and are often recorded in Britain. While some of these records are of genuine transatlantic vagrants others are clearly escapees from captivity. Several small feral flocks also exist in Britain with the nearest of these being a group of white-phase birds based at the York University campus. The first record for the Hull area may well pre-date the York flock, but it too was almost certainly feral. In 1975 a white-phase adult Snow Goose was seen on 11th January and again on the 1st February at Hedon, with presumably the same bird later being seen at Spurn and Hornsea. White Greylag Geese have occasionally created confusion and one at the Bransholme Sewage Works was claimed as a Snow Goose in 1993. A white Greylag Goose, however, never shows the dark wingtips of a white-phase Snow Goose. The other Hull record also concerns clearly feral birds, with two Snow Geese being present in Pickering Park in December 2000.

Ross's Goose
Anser rossii

A Canadian species, Ross's Goose resembles a small white-phase Snow Goose and all British records are considered to have probably been escapes from wildfowl collections. One bird that certainly was of captive origin was an adult at East Park on 29th May 1997.

Swan Goose
Anser cygnoides
A native of Siberia and China, Swan Geese (also known as 'Chinese

Geese') were introduced to East Park during the 1960s and two were present in February 1967, with four the following December. During my visits to East Park in the early 1990s I noticed that several of the *Anser* geese were hybrids between Swan Geese and Greylag Geese. The presence of family parties where both parents where hybrids proved that the hybrids were fertile, and I counted 15 adult hybrids and 11 goslings in the park on 5th May 1993. All 26 were still present that July.

Subsequent visits throughout the 1990s showed that the Swan Goose characteristics, notably the knob above the bill and the dark crown, were gradually being bred out of the hybrids as they cross bred with pure Greylag Geese and by October 2000 I could only pick out one bird with noticeable Swan Goose features.

Canada Goose
Branta canadensis
The Canada Goose was introduced to Britain from North America in the 17th Century to grace St James' Park in London. The first birds to appear in Hull were introduced to East Park from Ripley, near Harrogate, by the Hull and District

Wildfowlers Association in the 1950s. A small feral population was well established in the park by the 1960s, with two pairs breeding in 1967 and the resident flock hovering around the 20 mark. As early as 1962 there were enough Canada Geese to act as a source for other introductions at Brandesburton, Rise, Walkington and Wauldby. In 1963 another 12 birds were taken from East Park and released on Hornsea Mere.

Canada Geese were breeding at East Park and perhaps Pickering Park throughout the 1980s. Numbers were never reported but were probably not more than a handful of pairs at each site. Birds were occasionally seen at Thwaite Hall Lake in Cottingham during this time and by the late 1980s large flocks were flying out of East Park to feed on autumn stubble fields around the outskirts of Hull. Late in the afternoon of 7th October 1989 over 100 Canada Geese were feeding on freshly sown wheat at North Bransholme before leaving noisily to the south after being shot at. In the early 1990s flocks were occasionally visiting the Bransholme Sewage Works in autumn and winter, with 1992 seeing up to 32 in August, 116 in September and 44 in November. Eighteen birds

were present on two dates in August and October the following year. These birds sometimes had a couple of Barnacle Geese in tow, hinting at the East Park origins of the flock. Summer visits to this site by Canada Geese were very rare – a crippled bird stranded since 1991 attracted only the occasional companion in May or June until its death three years later.

Nesting starts at the beginning of April and by the end of the month the first goslings have appeared. In May 1993 a crèche of 23 young were accompanied by 23 adults in East Park and 18 young were raised the following year. Just one pair was breeding successfully by 1997, with the single brood of eight young containing two Greylag goslings. This unusual mix must have been the result of a Greylag Goose laying in a Canada Goose nest or an adoption soon after hatching. Both Greylag goslings survived their adoption, however, though only five of the Canada goslings fledged.

Midsummer during the 1990s saw very large numbers of Canada Geese arriving to moult in the relative safety of East Park. In July 1993 a total of 341 birds were present on the lake, this being the highest count recorded in the Hull area. This was nearly matched the following year when 321 were counted in June. Overall, numbers occurring in East Park have increased slightly since the early 1990s and generally follow a clear seasonal pattern. Lowest counts are usually in spring when the birds are nesting and become territorial. At this time of year, between March and April, around 20 to 50 birds may be present with numbers building during May to maybe 100 by early June. The main summer build-up occurs from mid June to peak at anywhere between 100 to over 300 in July, though just 35 were present during July 1997. Birds then leave en masse after the moult, and by August fewer than 10 may be present on some days. Numbers slowly creep back up in September and October to between 120 and 240 in November. Over 100 are usually present for the remainder of the winter but more than double this total may occur from time to time until birds begin to disperse again at the end of February.

The large numbers of Canada Geese that congregate in East Park are not totally benign, however. In 1998 I looked into the impact that waterfowl were having on the fertility of the lake and discovered hugely elevated nutrient levels in the water. Calculations and observations pointed to waterbirds as the primary source of the additional phosphorous and nitrogen, with Canada Geese being the main culprits (Broughton, 1998). This was party due to the Canada Goose's habit of roosting on the water rather than on land, thereby adding much more nutrients to the lake than the more numerous, but land-roosting, Greylag Geese.

While East Park is the main site for Canada Geese in the Hull area they are also commonly found at Pearson Park and Pickering Park. Up to 60 were present at the former in January 1999 and breeding is occasional at the latter, with one pair rearing six young in 2000. Numbers in Pickering Park are usually lower than at East Park and rarely exceed 100 birds, although 180 were counted in December 2000. There is probably a high degree of interaction between all of the main Hull parks. Wandering flocks or individuals may sometimes be seen elsewhere as the birds move between waters or feeding areas. Twelve flying east at Victoria Dock on 18th February 1997 were possibly not local birds, though 144 at the Bransholme Sewage Works on 14th November 1998 certainly were. Hybridisation with Greylag Geese sometimes occurs and three or four such birds have been present at East Park since the early 1990s at least, with up to seven in 1998.

Hull's Canada Geese, in common with all of those in Britain, are thought to be birds of one of the larger of the dozen or so races from North America. In 1985, however, S. L. James saw a dark, 'small race' Canada Goose drifting west up the Humber at Saltend on 4th February. B. Fendley saw what may have been the same bird, which he assigned to the race *Branta canadensis minima*, at Saltend on 16th November. This bird may have been a genuine trans-Atlantic vagrant but the apparently lengthy stay and the intermittent appearance of a similar bird at East Park and Hornsea Mere from November 1985 onwards could indicate a more suspect origin.

Barnacle Goose
Branta leucopsis

The Barnacle Goose has a surprisingly limited world distribution, breeding only in eastern Greenland, the Arctic islands of Svalbard and Novaya Zemlya and, very recently, on Gotland in the Baltic. Greenland birds migrate via Iceland to winter in Ireland and western Scotland, Svalbard birds pass through Norway to winter on the Scottish Solway Firth, while those from Novaya Zemlya winter in the Netherlands. It is birds from this last population that are most likely to turn up in a wild state in the Hull area.

A flock of 57 flying southeast over North Bransholme on 8th November 1993 were heading in the right direction for Holland and could have been genuine wild birds correcting themselves after crossing over to Britain. The Barnacle Geese most commonly seen around Hull, however, are from the small but increasing British feral population. Members of the Hull and District Wildfowlers Association released several Barnacle Geese onto East Park Lake in the early 1960s. Two were present on 4th February 1967, with one still there in December, and small numbers were present throughout the 1970s at least. A flock of over 100 feral birds have wintered at Hornsea Mere since the 1980s, spending their summers at Flamingoland in North Yorkshire, and this may be another source of some of the birds seen around Hull. A feral flock of up to 30 birds based at Whitton on the south bank of the Humber, upstream of Hull, since at least the mid 1990s may also account for some local sightings. In any event, feral Barnacle Geese are now a regular sight around Hull. One flying down the Humber off Saltend on 18th June 1986 was certainly feral, as were a pair among a mixed flock of Canada and Greylag Geese at the Bransholme Sewage Works on 29th August 1992.

A single Barnacle Goose was at East Park on 7th July 1993 and 12 were present during November, including at least eight immature birds. Three were back again in March 1994. In early 1997 up to 15 were present in East Park until March, when all but one departed. Thirteen arrived back to join the lone bird in late September, with a further three boosting the number to 17 from October. This small flock seems to have established a regular migratory pattern whereby they arrive to winter at East Park in September or October and leave in February or March to spend the summer elsewhere. At least one bird usually remains all year round. The winter flock numbered 16 in January 1998, being accompanied by a hybrid Barnacle x small race Canada Goose, before leaving for the summer. A trio of Barnacles returned in August before increasing to 14, plus the hybrid, from the end of September to the year end. The flock numbered eight in November 2000 before growing to 15 by December. The three birds in Pickering Park on 16th December were almost certainly part of this flock, while a party of 11 passing the Humber Bridge on 16th November 2000 may have been Whitton birds, perhaps on their way to East Park.

The East Park Barnacle Geese are clearly breeding and summering somewhere else, maybe elsewhere in Yorkshire or maybe at Whitton. The size of the wintering flock at East Park seems to have increased slightly during the 1990s and this trend looks set to continue. We may yet see Barnacle Geese establish themselves around Hull in the same manner as the familiar Greylags and Canadas.

Brent Goose
Branta bernicla

The smallest of the regularly occurring geese in Britain, a sizeable flock of Brent Geese winters at the mouth of the Humber on both the Yorkshire and Lincolnshire sides. These birds are of the dark-bellied race, *Branta bernicla bernicla*, but are rarely recorded further up the Humber and I can list only a handful of documented instances.

Boylan (1967) reported two Brent Geese flying over the city centre on 16th March 1965. The next record was not for another 19 years, when one was at Saltend on 12th December 1984. Dedicated observation at Saltend in 1985 revealed one flying upstream on 2nd February, two on the following day and six going downstream on 6th. Another flew west on 18th and a trio flew up and down offshore the next day before eventually leaving to the east. A flock of 20, the highest number recorded in the Hull area, was on the Humber off Saltend on 6th February 1986 and nine were there again on 16th. Another was at Saltend on 6th October 1998 and five flew west over Hedon Haven on 20th September 1999. One flying up river on 20th October 1999 did an abrupt U-turn on reaching the Humber Bridge.

Others must have surely passed through the Hull area over the years, particularly at Saltend. The lack of regular watching and reporting since the 1980s means that the Brent Goose probably appears to be somewhat rarer in the Hull area than is actually the case.

Ruddy Shelduck
Tadorna ferruginea

In the 1881 *Handbook of Vertebrate Fauna of Yorkshire* W. Eagle Clarke mentions a Ruddy Shelduck killed at Cottingham in the mid 19th Century and seen by H.B. Hewetson. Nelson seemed unconvinced of the reliability of this record in his 1907 *The Birds of Yorkshire*. As with the similar record of Little Bittern there are good reasons for being cautious over such unsubstantiated claims but, again, there is no justification for dismissing it out of hand. It is simply another one of those cases where we shall never know for sure.

Shelduck
(Common Shelduck)
Tadorna tadorna

Shelducks are characteristic birds of the Humber mudflats and can usually be found at Saltend and west of St. Andrew's Quay throughout the year at low tide. In 1844 Thomas Allis wrote that Shelducks used to, and occasionally still did, nest in rabbit burrows a little north of the Humber banks, taking their young onto the estuary as soon as they are able to travel. The Humber banks in the Hull area were very likely to have been involved, at least occasionally. Shelducks were familiar to the Hull game dealers at the beginning of the last century although they don't seem to have been popular table birds. In the winter of 1901 a few Hull game shops started displaying Shelducks in their windows just for ornamentation, an introduction of the 'exhibit' trend that started in London. This suggests that nobody really bought them for the meat.

A few pairs of Shelducks bred in the Hull area throughout the 20th Century. Two adults and six ducklings were seen in a field near Marfleet in June 1942 and breeding was probably occurring near the eastern docks in the 1960s at least. Gibbons *et al.* (1993), meanwhile, recorded breeding in all 10 km squares covering the Hull area between 1988 and 1991.

The Saltend mudflats are the main location for Shelducks in the Hull area and general numbers have remained fairly constant since the mid 1980s, although monthly counts do fluctuate on an annual basis. Around 50 to 100 birds are present from January to March, with passage birds inflating this to as many as 200 in April and May. Summer sees a decrease to as few as 20 or 30 from June to October before a build up to between 50 and 100 again from November onwards. Again, I emphasise that numbers can be very variable; a maximum of nine in August 1998 compared with 450 in August 1999! This last figure accounted for around 15% of all Shelduck present along the entire length of the Humber at that time. The summer drop in numbers is explained by most birds moving away to breed, with those still present being non-breeding birds or failed breeders. Later in the summer most birds usually prefer to gather further down the Humber at Foulholme Sands to complete the annual moult. Numbers at the western foreshore, off Clive Sullivan Way, are tiny by comparison and often struggle to reach double figures at any time of year.

Traditionally, the whole of the northwest European population of Shelducks, including all of the British birds, migrated to the Heligoland Bight on the German coast to complete their wing-moult. The birds are flightless during this period, hence the need to migrate to a safe place, and outbound flocks were regularly seen flying down the Humber in July and early August. In the late 1970s, however, small numbers of Shelducks began staying on the Humber to moult, as at other British estuaries, and by 1980 there were up to 1,000 flightless birds loafing and feeding on Foulholme Sands (downstream of Paull) each July. The 450 birds present at Saltend in August 1999 indicates that this habit has possibly spread further along the estuary, though they may have just been some of the Foulholme birds coming up on the tide.

Shelducks are fairly regular on inland floodwaters and lakes in Hull and the surrounding area, particularly in April and usually in pairs. These birds are possibly looking for nesting sites. Extensive floods at North Bransholme in the spring of 1994 seemed to encourage a pair of Shelducks to consider nesting in one of the abandoned rabbit warrens nearby. They were seen on and off from late April to mid June, with a third bird joining them towards the end of their stay. No tangible evidence of breeding was forthcoming, however.

Back in 1967 four Shelducks were resident on East Park Lake throughout the year, these presumably being released from captivity in common with many other species on the lake at that time. On 22nd October 2000 I was pleasantly surprised to see a splendid male Shelduck near the duck feeding area at East Park. I was even more surprised when he joined in the scrum for bread with the other waterfowl, showing no wariness at all. The bird was still present at the year's end, though in light of his tameness a captive origin must be considered possible. This does not necessarily have to be the case, however, if one considers how readily the migratory Pochards and Tufted Ducks will come to bread once they see the local Mallards benefiting from it. You can never really be sure at East Park!

Muscovy Duck
Cairina moschata

This South American species is frequent as a feral bird in Britain and small numbers have been present in East Park in recent years. Four were seen on 2nd January 1998 and three were at the duck feeding area off Hawkesbury Street during November 2000. These birds are probably resident. Small numbers have been seen elsewhere in East Yorkshire and it is likely that lack of recording masks other sightings and breeding records.

Mandarin Duck
Aix galericulata

The male Mandarin Duck is spectacularly beautiful almost to the point of gaudiness. After becoming established in Britain during the 20th Century the feral population in this country now exceeds that in its native Far East, where it is endangered. Small numbers of Mandarin Ducks, probably wing-clipped or pinioned, were released onto East Park Lake during the 1950s and 1960s. Some could still be seen throughout the 1970s but they subsequently disappeared. It is not clear if breeding occurred there or whether the adults and any progeny

eventually flew off, were returned to captivity or simply died. Whatever the case, no free-living birds occur in the park today. A wing-clipped pair were released onto the Queen's Gardens pond in the mid 1980s and, supplied with a nest box, they bred and reared several young during one season. The family remained until the autumn but then disappeared and, again, it is unknown whether they flew off or were taken into captivity.

Wood Duck
Aix sponsa

The Wood Duck is a colourful North American relative of the Mandarin Duck that is also popular in British wildfowl collections. Escapees and deliberately released birds have not established themselves with the same degree of success as the Mandarin Duck, however, and a pair on East Park in 1967 were probably recent releases that quickly disappeared.

Wigeon
(Eurasian Wigeon)
Anas penelope
The Wigeon is mainly a scarce passage and winter visitor to inland

areas around Hull, although passage flocks may be seen more often as they pass by on the Humber. A flock of 14 moving upstream off Saltend on 14th December 1984 was the highest day count for the latter half of that year. A total of 300 were logged on 4th January 1985 and counts of between six and 36 were made on five other dates that month. A party of 10 were on the Humber there a few weeks later and a pair was on Saltend Channel in late May.

There was another big passage off Saltend the following autumn. A respectable 196 were logged on 23rd September and 149 on 13th November. A further 247 passed by on 16th, with 164 on 19th and 267 on 16th December. All were flying upstream. Even larger numbers of Wigeons, totalling over 1,000 on any one day, have been observed purposefully moving up the Humber in autumn from various watchpoints further down the estuary. All of these birds undoubtedly pass the waterfronts of Paull, Saltend and then Hull and Hessle as they progress upstream.

The larger inland waters and any flooded fields are likely to attract a Wigeon or two in passage periods and in winter, though usually only briefly. Several were noted on East Park Lake in March 1940, with seven on 4th February 1967 and eight in December. One to two were seen on the Priory Road fields in the early to mid 1980s, including a pair on floodwaters there on the very unusual summer date of 4th June in 1983. Another pair was on floodwaters at North Bransholme on the more typical date of 23rd October in 1992.

Away from the Humber the Bransholme Sewage Works has perhaps provided more records than anywhere else in the Hull area in recent years. One or two have visited that site between October and April in most years since the early 1990s. East Park still hosts the occasional Wigeon, too, with one from December 1997 to January 1998, though the high level of disturbance here means that any birds soon move on once the park opens.

American Wigeon
Anas americana

Breeding in North America and wintering down to Central America, the

American Wigeon is a rare vagrant to Britain. East Park has hosted an American Wigeon on no less than two occasions, with the first being an adult male seen on 17th and 21st March 1984. Curiously the second record also concerns a March adult male, this time on the 24th in 1986. It is possible that both of these records concern the same bird which, having made the ocean crossing during a previous autumn, had established a spring migratory flight on this side of the Atlantic and used East Park as a stop-over point. This sort of pattern is often seen in other stranded North American ducks, such as Ring-necked Ducks, that return year after year to favourite seasonal haunts. As our similar Eurasian Wigeon is rather rare in East Park and, indeed, uncommon elsewhere in the Hull area, all Wigeons are clearly worth a second look.

Gadwall
Anas strepera

Gadwalls were rather scarce in Yorkshire until the middle of the 20th Century and the species was still virtually unknown in the Hull area as recently as the 1960s. The only Gadwalls to be found locally at that time were apparently released onto East Park sometime before 1967, with two being present in February of that year and one in December. A few were recorded at Saltend in 1985. A male on 23rd February left to the north, a pair headed west offshore on 12th September and another pair were on the Humber off West Wharfe on 23rd. A male was there again on 30th December.

The only moderately regular site for Gadwalls around Hull today is the reservoir at the Bransholme Sewage Works, and even here they were apparently not recorded until 1993. Between four and six were present during January of that year, with just one remaining in February and March. There were no more until November when a pair returned for the winter. Numbers increased at this site during the mid 1990s with between 13 and 15 from February to April 1997, a singleton in July and then nine in September increasing to 14 by October. A total of 19 were present at the Bransholme Sewage Works in October 1998 and the maximum for 2000 was 40 on 3rd March, a record Hull count. Gadwalls are always somewhat unpredictable in their occurrence, though, and only three were present in the latter months of the year. In spite of their fickleness it is likely that visits to this reservoir between September and April will reveal at least a few Gadwalls among the Mallards and it is good to see that numbers are generally increasing.

Gadwalls may very occasionally be found on other ponds or lakes in the Hull area, with up to four in East Park in the autumn and winter of 1997 and a first-winter male on 7th and 12th January 1998. A pair was on the Bransholme Fishing Pond on Christmas Day 2000.

Teal
(Eurasian Teal)
Anas crecca

The Teal has been familiar to Hull people for centuries and was very much on the menu in days gone by. In 1560 a proclamation was made in Hull that set the price of 'Teall' at tuppence each, half that of a Mallard. They must have been very common in all seasons on the marshes and carrs that surrounded the town back then. The smallest duck, Teals are now winter visitors and passage migrants in the Hull area and occur more widely and in greater numbers than one might imagine.

The Saltend mudflats and the tidal creeks that feed them are undoubtedly the main site for the species in the area and may, in fact, hold up to 80% of the Teals on the whole north bank of the Humber. Large numbers occur in midwinter although counts fluctuate depending on the weather, with more birds in cold spells. Several hundred birds winter in the Old Fleet and Hedon Haven channels, flanking either side of Saltend, and then can easily be seen from the embankments as they emerge to feed on the mudflats at low tide. Comparative spot-counts on the Saltend flats over the years include 420 in January 1985, 350 in January 1986, 500 in January 1989, 202 in January 1997 and 200 in January 1999.

After being virtually deserted from June until August the Saltend flats begin to see small arrivals of Teals from early August. Sixty on 25th August 1985 was typical for the time of year. Passage birds can also be seen winging past over the Humber at this time, with 262 moving west on one day in September 1985. Numbers build on the Saltend mudflats throughout the autumn, as demonstrated by a count of 400 in early November 1989 growing to 535 by 26th and 550 on 22nd December. A decade later and the situation was similar, with a handful in October 1998 increasing to 150 in November and 725 on 24th December. This last count is the largest congregation of Teals recorded in the Hull area and represents half of the population of the entire Humber estuary. On 22nd December 2000, meanwhile, I counted 330 at the mouth of Hedon Haven alone. After the peak counts of midwinter the number of Teals at Saltend steadily falls from late January onwards. Counts fell from 420 in January 1985 to 270 in February, 180 in March, 50 in April and none in May. A flock of 200 birds in January 1999 decreased to 150 in February and then to less than 20 in March and April. Over 400 were recorded on 15th March 1981, however, probably due to spring passage.

Away from Saltend small parties of Teals are regular but unpredictable throughout the Hull area anytime from early September to late April, with the majority between November and March. The boggy ponds, ditches and drains on the Priory Road fields, southeast of North Bransholme and east of Bransholme are favoured stopover sites for groups of up to nine birds, although a flock of four or five is more usual. Larger areas of water also attracts the occasional flock of Teals from autumn through to spring. Nine were on the Bransholme Sewage Works reservoir on 10th April 1993, this being a large count for that site. Another four were at East Park in mid November 1997. Thwaite Hall Lake in Cottingham also seems a likely place, but restricted access means records are patchy.

Saltend is really the only site in the Hull area where Teals can be guaranteed in season. To hear the evocative whistles of these wild and wary birds coming off the flats as you walk the Paull embankment on a misty morning really does stir the soul.

Mallard
Anas platyrhynchos

The Mallard is the commonest duck in Britain, indeed Europe, and the Hull area is no exception. Mallards can be found wherever there is sufficient water around Hull, from the parks to the Humber shore and all manner of drains, wet dykes, ponds and flooded fields inbetween. Most Hull folk are familiar with the Mallard, as few children have not paid a visit to Queen's Gardens or the Hull parks to feed the ducks.

The earliest reference to the Mallard in Hull comes from the 1560 *Wildfowl at Hull* manuscript, which set the price of a "Mallerde" at fourpence. The tidal creeks along the Humber and the extensive marshes, carrs and meres that surrounded Hull back then were teeming with Mallards and other wildfowl. Duck decoys (elaborate duck traps) at Meaux, Sunk Island, Watton and Scorborough probably supplied the Hull markets. Boylan (1967) described the species as a resident and common winter visitor in

1960s Hull, with breeding occurring in several dykes and drains. There was a large roost on the Humber and winter counts of up 500 birds were made on East Park Lake. East Park counts from other sources around that time give 575 birds in February 1967 and 300 in December of the same year. Up to 200 birds can still be found wintering on East Park Lake, with a similar number at Pearson Park Pond and in Pickering Park. Up to 50 birds winter on the Queen's Gardens ponds and perhaps 100 do so on Thwaite Hall Lake, Cottingham. Breeding commonly occurs on all of these waters and many of the birds are extremely tame and will gladly take food from the hand. Passage birds at East Park and Thwaite Hall are much wilder and keep well away from the public. The Bransholme Sewage Works supports large numbers of Mallard, with a wintering flock of up to 120 birds between October and March. Several broods are reared there during the summer, although counts rarely exceed 40 birds between May and July. Up to 50 now frequent the newly created Bransholme Fishing Pond, with 20 or more much wilder birds regularly being flushed from the marshy ponds in the surrounding fields. Breeding is regular there, too, and I have counted 45 on the nearby stretch of the Holderness Drain in winter. Pairs or small groups of Mallards may often be found in many ditches, drains or flooded fields throughout the Hull area and breeding is not uncommon in quiet stretches of water.

The Humber estuary was once internationally important for the number of Mallards that spent the winter on its shores, mudflats and tidal creeks. A decline since the 1970s means this is no longer the case, though large numbers can still be found around Saltend. Wintering flocks there have regularly exceeded 100 birds since the mid 1980s and up to 350 have been counted in recent years. Numbers fall steadily during February and March until less than 20 remain by May. This is a result of the wintering birds returning to the Continent and local birds moving away to breed. A small peak of perhaps 50 birds is frequently noted in June as the males gather to prepare for moulting after the rigours of courtship. Numbers then fall again in July as the birds move away to a quiet stretch of water to complete the flightless phase of their moult in safety. A rapid post-breeding influx then follows in August and September, and the figure may be close to 100 again. Counts usually peak in November as the Continental birds arrive once more, mingling with the Teals in Hedon Haven and Old Fleet Channel to wait for the rich mudflats to be exposed by the tide.

Gatherings of Mallards are much smaller elsewhere along the Humber shore away from Saltend. Up to 50 birds may be found on the western waterfront (off Clive Sullivan Way) in winter but 32 was considered a good number at Hessle Haven in mid October 1999.

Pintail
(Northern Pintail)
Anas acuta

One of the most attractive native ducks, the Pintail is unfortunately rather uncommon in the Hull area. In the 1960s the Hull and District Wildfowlers' Association released a few Pintails onto East Park Lake - two males seen in February 1967 and a pair in December were almost certainly feral. Resident birds were still present well into the 1970s but they eventually died out.

Intensive coverage at Saltend and the eastern docks in 1985 and 1986 produced seven winter records of singles and pairs flying along the waterfront, all from August to March. Up to three were in King George Dock in the winter of 1986. Extensive floodwaters, caused by heavy rain, on farmland to the east of North Bransholme in the spring of 1994 attracted several Pintails; six, including a drake, were seen dabbling in the shallow pools on 25th March while a pair were seen again on 30th April.

A pair of Pintails in Pearson Park in 1996 were possibly feral birds in light of the location. In the same year a female was in East Park from mid April to mid May and again from mid November to mid December. A drake was then present in East Park on 25th February 1997 and, after he was joined by a female on 27th, the pair were present intermittently until 7th April. This seems a rather long stay for supposedly wild Pintail. It is quite possible that the Pearson Park and East Park records for 1996 and 1997 involve the same two birds. Another long-staying female was at the Bransholme Sewage Works from 8th January to 9th March 2000.

This collection of records indicates that Pintails are rather scarce passage migrants and winter visitors in the Hull area, most regularly as fly-bys on the Humber but occasionally inland on flooded fields or lakes. The origins of long-staying birds in heavily disturbed areas such as the Hull parks must, however, be considered questionable.

Garganey
Anas querquedula

The Garganey is the only duck to occur in Yorkshire that is actually a summer migrant rather than a winter visitor. It is also quite scarce in the county and is only a passage migrant in the Hull area, with just two relatively recent records. On 6th September 1993 I found a well-marked juvenile male Garganey on the reservoir of the Bransholme Sewage Works. It was still present the next day when I was able to take some fuzzy photographs of it while it sat on the bank, occasionally displaying the characteristic wing pattern that clearly separates it from certain plumages of the very similar Teal. It was last seen on 18th September after quite a lengthy stay. Early on the morning of 22nd May 1997 Brett Richards located a pair of Garganey on East Park Lake, but they left soon afterwards.

Shoveler
(Northern Shoveler)
Anas clypeata

The Shoveler is one of the less common of the regular ducks in the Hull area. After an increase in local numbers during the early 1990s the species has recently become scarce once more.

Just two Shovelers were seen in Hull during the first six years of the 1960s, probably at East Park, and two were present there on 4th February 1967, with three on 16th April. The species was described as a very scarce winter visitor at that time and it remained so into the 1980s. Intensive coverage at Saltend then revealed it to be not only a very scarce passage migrant on the Humber but also a sporadic breeder. On 16th August 1984 regular watchers at Saltend were very surprised to find a pair of Shovelers with a single duckling on a sheet of water known to them as 'First Pond'. All three disappeared on 1st September and breeding was never recorded in the Hull area again. Passage and winter records from that period involved a pair in St. Andrew's Dock in February 1985 and a male on Saltend Marsh on 9th December. A total of five passage birds passed Saltend in April and May. A female was on Saltend Marsh on 31st July 1985, with two on 2nd August. Autumn passage offshore was represented by a total of 12 birds between mid August and mid October that year. There were just four passage records in 1986 - three birds in March and one in August.

The scarcity of Shovelers continued until the early 1990s when small numbers started to frequent the Bransholme Sewage Works. Nine were present on 23rd February 1992, with seven still there on 7th March. None were seen again until August of that year when two birds arrived, increasing to six on 20th September. An influx in October saw a record total of 27 on the Sewage Works reservoir but only three were left by the end of the month. Numbers rose again in November to a peak of 11 on 29th before dropping back down to two by Christmas Eve. The good run of records spilled over into 1993 when up to 16 were still at the Sewage Works during January. Four to six remained into February, with a maximum of two in March and then none until one to three were back in July and August. The unprecedented numbers of the previous autumn were not matched, however, and a lowly peak of five was the best count between October and December. Hardly any Shovelers have been recorded from the Sewage Works since then and a pair in February 1997 is the only recent record.

Shovelers are very occasionally seen on the park lakes, with a female at East Park on 20th January 1998, but never in any numbers and never for long. The Bransholme Sewage Works probably still provides the best chance of finding Shovelers in the Hull area, most likely in October or November when an influx of migrants swells the British population. Alternatively, a vigil over the Humber in spring or autumn may offer a brief view of a passing bird or two, though I flushed a pair from floodwaters at North Bransholme in April 2001.

Red-crested Pochard
Netta rufina

In October 2000 a drake Red-crested Pochard was a surprise find on East Park Lake. This species is no more than a rare visitor to Britain from Continetal Europe. As with many of the more attractive waterfowl, however, the chances of this individual being an escape from captivity were not ruled out by the finder. Cynicism later proved to be the order of the day; when the bird was seen again at close range in November it was noted to be lacking most of its right wing. I later learned that the bird had been present since at least July 1998 after being released from the aviaries some time before.

Red-crested Pochards were being released onto East Park Lake as early as the 1960s and three birds were present on 4th February 1967. The presence of a hybrid Mallard x Red-crested Pochard the following December indicates that the introduced birds were eager to breed but were rather limited in their options.

Pochard
(Common Pochard)
Aythya ferina

Often found side by side with the Tufted Duck, the Pochard is a regular and fairly common winter visitor and passage migrant on the larger freshwaters of the Hull area. Most of our wintering Pochards come from central Europe and Russia, with the first arriving in early September. Numbers often peak in November before dropping a little from December to February. There is usually with a second peak in early March as passage birds move back through the area. Numbers plummet towards the end of March and by mid April virtually all Pochards have left. Very small numbers, maybe just one to three, can sometimes be found during the summer months and these are probably non-breeding birds of the resident British population. In some years small groups of moulting males can be found during late June and July and, again, these are probably British birds rather than early immigrants. In 1996, however, breeding actually occurred on East Park Lake when a female and three young ducklings were seen on 3rd June, although only one chick survived to full size.

Pochards have been winter visitors to East Park Lake since it was first built and up to 30 could be found in November or December during the 1960s. This site still attracts the largest regular flock in the Hull area. An apparent increase since the sixties means that 40 to 50 is now the usual peak count, with 55 on 13th November 1998 being the highest recorded tally there. While a few Pochards can be found on Pickering Park Lake now and again the only other regular site in the Hull area is the reservoir at the Bransholme Sewage Works. Numbers rarely exceed 25 at this location, with 10 to 20 being more usual and exceptionally as many as 40 at peak times. This was not always the case, however, and between 1980 and 1986 passage birds were noted here on only two occasions. There is probably some interchange between East Park, Bransholme Sewage Works and other East Yorkshire lakes, as numbers at each site often fluctuate from day to day.

The largest number of Pochards ever seen in the Hull area occurred on the Humber in the mid 1980s when a huge flock discovered wintering off the south bank of the estuary was visible from Saltend. After a count of 40 birds in early February 1985 the flock increased to 300 by the end of the month. The following year a phenomenal 525 were recorded there on 8th February. These figures were in stark contrast to the usual Saltend counts of up to 30 or so (though more often less than 10), recorded on passage from September to April.

Ferruginous Duck
Aythya nyroca

An adult male Ferruginous Duck was reported from Bransholme, almost certainly the Sewage Works, on 10th October 1976. Another drake frequented East Park Lake from 23rd January until 19th March 1987, with what may have been the same bird again the following year from 2nd to the 9th April. While Ferruginous Ducks breed across southern and eastern Europe they are also quite common in captivity as ornamental waterfowl, so the origin of the Hull birds remains open to question.

Tufted Duck
Aythya fuligula

While the 'Tufty' is the commonest diving duck in Britain it is usually outnumbered by Pochards in the Hull area, though both are found in more or less the same habitat and can usually be seen side by side. Tufted Ducks do not breed in the Hull area although small numbers nest elsewhere in East Yorkshire. The wintering birds that visit the city may either be local or from northern and eastern Europe, as ringed birds recovered elsewhere in the county have hailed from as far afield as the Baltic states.

The only regular sites for Tufted Ducks in the Hull area are East Park and the Bransholme Sewage Works, with infrequent appearances on Pickering Park. Up to 50 were wintering on East Park Lake during the 1960s, this being roughly double the winter peak recorded in the late 1990s. Maximum counts have also decreased at the Bransholme Sewage Works since the early 1990s, with up to 30 in 1993 comparing to 15 in 1997 and 19 in 2000. Numbers have always fluctuated at both of these sites due to local movements but counts elsewhere in the county suggest that a real decline has taken place since the early 1990s at least.

The number of Tufted Ducks on the regular waters starts to build from early September, with the autumn peak occurring in late October or November as immigrants flood into the country. Numbers drop a little from December onwards as many migrants move on, with maybe 15 to 20 at East Park and 10 to 15 at the Sewage Works. A second peak is often noted in late February or March as birds return on their outward journey. April sees a rapid decline as the migrants leave and the British birds move out to find a breeding site. There are only a handful of non-breeding birds left in the area during May and early June. Failed breeders and post-breeding males return to East Park and the Bransholme Sewage Works as early as mid June. Up to half a dozen may be found at these locations throughout the rest of the summer until the autumn build-up begins again.

Small numbers of Tufties are sometimes seen at other lakes in the Hull area, such as Thwaite Hall in Cottingham, and two males were on the Holderness Drain at North Bransholme in May 1993. The highest counts of Tufted Ducks recorded in the Hull area were the result of a very unusual flock present on the Humber off Saltend in February 1985. Tufted Ducks aren't normally too keen on brackish or salt water but an incredible 320 were counted here on 5th February, with 220 still remaining on 28th of that month.

Scaup
(Greater Scaup)
Aythya marila

Scaups are infrequent passage migrants and winter visitors to the Hull area from breeding grounds in Iceland and Scandinavia. Some may also come from as far away as western Siberia. Predominantly sea-going ducks, Scaups are best looked for on the Humber where they are occasionally seen moving upstream or loafing offshore from late autumn to spring. Numbers and dates vary but flocks are usually between 10 and 30 strong with the majority of sightings occurring from November to February. Nelson (1907) quotes a letter from Francis Hoare, dated 1880, in which Hoare states that after north-easterly gales he had known Scaups to come up the Humber as far as Paull bight, below Hull, in large numbers and sometimes stay all winter. Hoare went on to say that he himself had killed great numbers there.

A large movement of Scaups was recorded on 6th November 2000 when 204 birds flew upstream past the Humber Bridge. The fact that many of the Humber records concern November flocks flying westwards is intriguing in that it suggests that the birds are purposefully moving inland, maybe with the intention of crossing over to the Irish Sea. Loafing Scaups are occasionally seen from the waterfronts; a flock of 12 females were off Hessle on 1st February 1947 and a group of six were seen there on 7th February 1986. Seventeen were off Victoria Dock on 19th November 1997. Larger numbers can sometimes be found off Saltend and a build up during early 1985 peaked at 52 on 6th February before decreasing to eight by 26th. A flock of 57 were back again on 20th November. Eleven on 6th February 1986 grew to 51 by 8th before dropping to just one by 26th.

Scaups are very rare on inland waters in the Hull area but they were apparently more frequent in the past. On 3rd March 1940 a female on East Park Lake was followed by a drake on 7th, with two there on 12th

December 1942. Between 1960 and 1966 members of the Hull Scientific and Field Naturalists' Club recorded no less than nine occurrences of Scaups on East Park Lake, mainly during harsh winter weather. A bird was also seen on a disused pool at the Clough Road gas works. An impressive flock of 17 males were on East Park Lake on 15th September 1969, this being the largest inland count in the Hull area. More recent inland records have been few and far between. A male was at the Bransholme Sewage Works on 12th to 13th April 1982, with a female on East Park Lake on 15th January 1988, a juvenile male at Bransholme Sewage Works on 17th September 1991, a female on East Park Lake again on 12th December 1999 and another there on 24th.

Eider
(Common Eider)
Somateria mollissima

Members of the Hull Scientific and Field Naturalists' Club were only able to record one sighting of the Eider duck during their informal survey of the birds within the old Hull boundary between 1960 and 1966, though no further details were given. A flock of eight were spotted flying downstream past Paull on 9th April 1981 and regular watching at and around Saltend in the mid 1980s resulted in many more records and a better indication of the status of the Eider on the Humber. A flock of nine passed Saltend on 8th November 1984 with up to 14 in mid January 1985 and three males loafing offshore on 3rd February. Birds were regular in November, with five passing by on 13th and up to 13 on most days until 22nd. A total of 45 moved upstream on 19th and the last bird of the year was on 16th December. The following year saw one off Saltend and Hull on 5th January and 6th February respectively, while eight males moved upstream on 8th February. Three more headed upstream off Saltend on 15th November 1986 and two were off the eastern docks in late January 1987. Regular watching and recording in that area dried up in the late 1980s and consequently so did the sightings.

More recent records of Eiders in the Hull area include four on the Humber off Victoria Dock on 20th October 1997. Several flocks moving up and down the estuary there on 19th November added up to an impressive 150 birds. Four were seen off Saltend on 6th October 1998 and 13 were loafing on the Humber off St Andrew's Quay, with 80 Common Scoter and a couple of Velvet Scoters, on 20th December 2000.

Eiders are therefore infrequent and rather unpredictable winter visitors on the Humber in the Hull area, usually in small numbers and anytime from October to April. Regular passage upstream off Hull is not thought to occur and there are no records from any inland locations around the city.

Long-tailed Duck
Clangula hyemalis

Rare inland, these seaducks breed across the Arctic tundra and along the coasts of Scandinavia and Iceland but winter in dense flocks off the coasts of Northern Europe. Occasional along the Yorkshire coast, Long-tailed Ducks appear to enter the Humber only rarely. A bumper year in 1985 had a record nine moving upstream off Saltend (in the company of Common Scoters) on 16th November and singles from the 18th to 20th. A pair on 22nd November increased to a trio on 23rd before dropping down to a single on 26th. Comparison with records from this area the following year indicate how extraordinary 1985 was; 1986 had just one bird flying downstream off King George Dock on 2nd March and another going the same way on 22nd December.

Late autumn at a deep inland water in the Hull area may also reward the regular observer with a very occasional Long-tailed Duck. A female on the Bransholme Sewage Works reservoir on 7th November 1991 was followed by a first-winter male from 2nd to 12th November 1999.

Common Scoter
(Black Scoter)
Melanitta nigra

Common Scoters are, as their name suggests, common seaducks on the Yorkshire coast and birds are frequently seen over the Humber from vantage points in the Hull area. It has been recognised for several decades now that there is major late summer and autumn cross-country movement of Common Scoters from the east coast to the west, and vice versa, across Yorkshire. The Humber is the main route inland for the migrating flocks and Hull is therefore very well placed to enjoy the annual spectacle.

The main movement begins in late July and usually lasts throughout August, with flocks of up to several hundred birds at a time making their way upstream past Paull, Hull and Hessle. Later in the autumn, from September to November, flocks can still be seen moving up the Humber though many return seawards. These may be feeding flocks or just jittery birds that can't bring themselves to pass under the Humber Bridge. Daily counts at this time can be among the most impressive of the year, such as the total of 1,153 that flew west past Saltend on 16th November 1985, though most flocks number less than 50 birds. By December the flocks are more infrequent but they are a little more likely to be found loafing on the Humber rather than just flying past. It is worthwhile looking through such congregations of Common Scoters to see what else they might contain; a flock of 80 off St Andrew's Quay on 20th December 2000 also held two Velvet Scoters and 13 Eiders.

Velvet Scoter
Melanitta fusca

There are five records of the Velvet Scoter from the Humber in the Hull area, the species being an uncommon wintering bird in British waters. On 18th January 1985 three were seen moving upstream with Common Scoters off Saltend, with two males going the same way on 12th May and another downstream on 23rd November. A drake was spotted off Hessle on 14th November 1998 and two were located among a flock of Common Scoters and Eiders off St Andrew's Quay on 20th December 2000. Others have surely passed by unseen, either drifting on the tide or commuting along the estuary.

Bufflehead
Bucephala albeola

First seen at Hornsea Mere on 8th December 1996, a female Bufflehead spent most of January 1997 there before being refound on East Park Lake by Brett Richards on 27th January. The bird then moved to the reservoir at Bransholme Sewage Works from 10th February until 18th April before wanderlust took hold again and she moved back to East Park, staying from 22nd April until 1st May. Still not settled, she finally moved back to Bransholme Sewage Works the following day before disappearing on 27th May.

The tiny Bufflehead, superficially similar to a small Goldeneye, is an extremely rare visitor to Britain from North America. There are only eight accepted records. The species is also frequent in European wildfowl collections, however, and many birdwatchers were therefore keen to determine the origins of the Hull bird. After much scrutiny it was noticed that she carried a black ring on one leg that bore the numbers 1 and 11 above 4 and 13. As this kind of numbering system is apparently not used by any of the major organisations studying wild birds the general opinion leaned towards the duck being a probable escapee from captivity.

Goldeneye
(Common Goldeneye)
Bucephala clangula

Boylan (1967) described the Goldeneye as a very rare winter visitor to Hull with just four records between 1960 and 1966, probably on East Park Lake. Bonavia (1990) recorded it as being occasional on the Bransholme Sewage Works reservoir from January to March between 1980 and 1986. Large numbers were recorded on the Humber at this time, with 168 off Saltend in February 1985, 165 off the eastern docks in January 1986 and 126 still

being present in early February. These gatherings were considered to be unusual, with numbers on the Humber generally being in the low single figures and occasionally up to 35. A record flock was present on the Humber off St Andrew's Quay in December 2000, however, peaking at 380 towards the end of the month.

Single Goldeneyes, very rarely two, were seen on the Holderness Drain at North Bransholme between November and March in the early 1990s and up to three occasionally visited the Bransholme Sewage Works around the same time, as they still do. East Park has also produced a few winter records but Goldeneyes are less frequent here than at the Sewage Works.

The status of the Goldeneye in the Hull area can therefore be described as a rather scarce but regular winter visitor to inland waters. It is invariably seen in single figures and may appear any time from November to March. Large flocks may be present on the Humber in some years.

Smew
Mergellus albellus

The drake Smew is one of the most attractive of all the ducks. The erratic and infrequent appearance of the species in Britain, often when freezing conditions in Continental Europe force them westwards, makes them all the more enigmatic and special to birders. Around the turn of the 20th Century Smews were reputed to be regular on the River Hull in the general area of Beverley and this probably extended south to Dunswell and Wawne. The beautiful drakes were especially prized by bird-stuffers and many were shot.

There were no documented records for the next 80 years, but January 1985 saw an influx into the Hull area when cold weather in Europe brought flotillas of Smews to Britain in what was a bumper year. The first arrivals were a drake on the Holderness Drain at North Bransholme on 15th January, another on the Humber off Saltend and a 'redhead' (female or immature male) on the old Prince's Dock (pre Prince's Quay) the same day. On 21st and 22nd January there were three drakes on the Holderness Drain at North Bransholme, with an amazing four drakes there from 23rd to 26th. They must have brightened up that part of Hull no end. The drakes were joined by two 'redheads' on 23rd February, making six birds in all. That was it for 1985, except for a 'redhead' flying upstream past Saltend on 21st February, although a drake was in St. Andrew's Dock on 15th February the following year.

Three Smews were seen flying east at Paull on 16th January 1987 and singles were on East Park Lake on 2nd, 3rd and 7th February that year. January 1991 saw another big influx

into Britain with up to 150 birds involved across northeast England. Hull played only a small part, however, with one flying west past Victoria Dock on 7th January and another two drifting down the River Hull onto the Humber on 20th.

Any relatively deep water in the Hull area, be it fresh or saline, may therefore produce a Smew during an influx. If birds begin to be reported from northeast England then a visit to East Park, the Bransholme Sewage Works, the docks or any vantage point over the Humber and the channels flowing into it could well be rewarding, especially if your prize comes in the form of an exquisite monochrome drake.

Red-breasted Merganser
Mergus serrator

The Red-breasted Merganser is a scarce wintering bird on the Humber but probably occurs in the Hull area in most years. Regular watching over the Humber off Saltend in the mid 1980s showed that one or two birds could usually be found, on and off, between November and February. There were eight records in 1985 but just one in

1986. On 19th March 1987 three birds were in King George Dock and another three were seen at the Humber Bridge on 6th November 2000. Small numbers are regularly seen flying upstream further down the Humber at sites such as Sunk Island and these birds surely pass Hull on their way inland. Red-breasted Mergansers have never been recorded on inland waters in the Hull area so a vigil on the shores of the Humber between late autumn and spring offers the best chance of catching up with one.

Goosander
Mergus merganser

While perhaps 3000 pairs of Goosanders breed on the fast flowing rivers of upland Britain, the small number of birds that winter in the Hull area are just as likely to be immigrants from Europe or Scandinavia. Goosanders used to be very rare around Hull and the only chance of seeing one was the occasional bird passing on the Humber during a hard winter. The species was virtually unknown away from the estuary up until the 1980s, with a pair spending three days on a small pool in the Priory Road fields in March 1983 being very unusual. Four were on the Holderness Drain at North Bransholme on 17th January 1985, with six on 19th and singles on 20th January and 24th February. Those prepared to spend many cold hours watching wildfowl passing by on the Humber could expect to see more Goosanders, if only fleetingly, with 11 flying past Saltend on 18th January 1985 and 43 there the next day. This movement was due to birds being displaced by a hard freeze on the Continent and was no doubt responsible for the North Bransholme birds and the scattering of Smews recorded at the same time. Single figures were noted passing Saltend again in February and March 1986.

In the early 1990s the occasional Goosander was reported from the Bransholme Sewage Works and around that time birds began to spend the winter on East Park Lake. On 9th March 1994 three males were loafing near the easternmost island in the lake and seven birds were present in January 1997. This number increased to 12 the following month, the largest gathering reported in the city, before the last three were seen on 14th March. The following winter saw a male returning in mid November 1997 and staying until December. On 19th November 1997 three flew up the Humber past Victoria Dock while up to two were back at East Park from January to March 1998, with three there on 10th March and the last bird on

20th. November and December 1998 again saw just one or two present on the lake, while only one was seen in January 1999. Another was present from December that year into January 2000. The first bird to return to East Park in late 2000 was a female, also alone, on 1st December. She was present until the year end. Another female was on the Bransholme Fishing Pond on Christmas Day and two males were in East Park in mid February 2001. While the numbers are often very small, it is nevertheless quite possible to see a Goosander on East Park Lake in most winters and this is probably the best place to look for them in the Hull area. The first birds tend to arrive from mid November to early December and the last ones leave around the middle of March, with the showy males often being in the majority.

Ruddy Duck
Oxyura jamaicensis

The Ruddy Duck is an American species that escaped from the famous Slimbridge wildfowl collection in the 1950s and established a feral population in the English Midlands.

By 1990 there were over 3,500 Ruddy Ducks breeding in Britain and the birds had spread far and wide. In the early 1980s Ruddy Ducks started breeding just 9 miles, as the crow flies, from northern Hull at Hornsea Mere. Nesting also occurred at Tophill Low, north of Beverley, in 1993. Sightings in East Yorkshire away from these two sites have always been very rare, however, despite counts at Tophill Low reaching 70 in recent years.

The first definite record from the Hull area is of a pair of males at the Bransholme Sewage Works on 28th July 1992. A female was on East Park Lake on 17th April 2000 and a pair were present from 28th April to 8th May. A female was at the Bransholme Sewage Works on 3rd August the same year. While others may well have occurred and not been seen or reported, the Ruddy Duck is nevertheless a rather rare visitor to the waters in and around Hull. At one time it looked as if it was only a matter of time before the species was regularly encountered wintering in East Park or the Bransholme Sewage Works, or even breeding on Thwaite Hall Lake. This now seems very unlikely due to the eradication campaign begun in the late 1990s. The Ruddy Duck is very closely related to the endangered European White-headed Duck and the two species are so similar that they interbreed to produce fertile hybrids. The fear was that Ruddy Ducks would spread to the Continent, as they began to do, and 'breed out' the small population of White-headed Ducks to the point where the latter became extinct. As a result British Ruddy Ducks, the source of the European birds, are now being killed in order to remove the species from Europe. Consequently, any Ruddy Ducks seen in the Hull area in the next few years could well be the last.

Honey Buzzard
(European Honey Buzzard)
Pernis apivorus

During the 1960s members of the Hull Scientific and Field Naturalists' Club recorded seven unidentified Buzzards over Hull, being unable to assign any of them to either Rough-legged or Common Buzzard. All of these birds were seen on spring or autumn passage and I can't help wondering, if they were that unsure of their Buzzards, whether they had adequately eliminated Honey Buzzard. Perhaps they thought this species to be too unlikely?

The first definite record of a Honey Buzzard in the Hull area is of one flying over the Humber Bridge on 14th September 1993 after easterly gales. This remained the only cast-iron sighting until the incredible autumn of 2000, when a strong easterly airflow swept migrating Honey Buzzards off their southerly route over central Europe and brought an unprecedented influx into Britain. From 19th September until well into early October at least 1,000 Honey Buzzards arrived on the British east coast, many of them making landfall in Yorkshire, and they quickly penetrated inland. The big movement through our region took place between 20th and 22nd September and around 15 individuals were seen in the Hull area. The first was a single bird drifting west over Bilton at 9.45 a.m. on 20th. A flock of eight unidentified buzzards, almost certainly Honeys in the circumstances, passed over Skidby that afternoon. The next day saw two landing in trees just west of the Humber Bridge, one later heading off south over the Humber. On the morning of the 22nd another was seen crossing the Humber from the direction of Hessle, with three more moving south past the Humber Bridge during the course of the day. How many more passed through unseen can only be guessed at, but southbound birds were so numerous in eastern counties during that period that scanning literally any patch of sky for long enough was likely to produce a passing Honey Buzzard or two. Events such as this are, in all probability, a once-in-a-lifetime occurrence and the Honey Buzzard has now returned to being an extremely rare passage migrant in the area.

Black Kite
Milvus migrans

Common across much of Europe and Asia, the Black Kite is only a rare visitor to Britain but a couple are seen most years. Up to three have occurred in the Hull area, though not without controversy. On 8th July 1979 H. O. Bunce saw what he identified as a Black Kite from his garden in Skidby. Although seen rather briefly as it was being mobbed by crows, Bunce had been the Yorkshire Naturalists' Union bird recorder for the vice county covering East Yorkshire for 14 years up to 1974 and was therefore a very experienced and respected observer. Indeed, Bunce had seen another Black Kite the previous spring along the River Derwent but, despite these credentials, the Skidby record was judged to be unacceptable by the British Birds Rarities Committee on the presumed grounds of brevity. To many people, however, including J. R. Mather in his 1986 *Birds of Yorkshire*, the identification appears sound. The next record was less controversial. On 26th August 1986 S. L. James and a companion watched an adult Black Kite come in from over the Humber before passing north over West Wharfe at Alexandra Dock. This record was accepted by the British Birds Rarities Committee. The final record concerns a report of a Black Kite over Victoria Dock on 2nd May 2001, although further details were not available at the time of writing.

Red Kite
Milvus milvus

The Red Kite has one of the most chequered histories of any British breeding bird. England's most common raptor until the 18th Century, they were familiar scavengers in many towns and were protected for their valuable role in keeping the streets clean of refuse. Red Kites were even a favoured falconry quarry for noblemen. By the early 20th Century, however, there were just four or five birds left in the whole of Britain and these were confined to the remote Welsh hills. The Red Kite was pushed to the brink of extinction in the name of game and livestock preservation, and the Victorian zeal for shooting and vermin control very nearly wiped them out. In fact, the rather feeble Red Kite mainly eats carrion and earthworms and does not attack gamebirds or lambs at all.

The Hull area, along with much of England, probably lost its Kites sometime around the mid 18th Century. The only ones seen after this time would have been the very occasional Continental immigrants that may have wandered up the Humber in winter, although none were officially recorded around Hull. While the Welsh population slowly increased under protection during the 20th Century it became clear that they would never recolonise their full British range on their own. This led several conservation agencies to begin a reintroduction programme in the 1990s by releasing Swedish, German and Spanish Red Kites into the Chilterns, Scotland and the English Midlands. In July 1997 a farmer saw what he described as "a big hawk with a forked tail" over Wawne Common, northeast of Wawne itself. This may well have been a Red Kite from one of the reintroductions, as some of these birds wandered far and wide. The reintroductions were so successful, however, that it was decided to bridge the gap between them by reintroducing the species to Yorkshire.

On 7th July 1999 a group of young Red Kites were released from their pens at Harewood House near Leeds, where they had been reared after being taken from nests in the Chilterns. One bird, bearing an orange-red wing tag on the left wing and a black tag on the right wing, remained at Harewood until early September before moving into East Yorkshire. The bird, known as 'Orange/Black 4' after its wing tags, gradually worked its way over to Risby Park (just north of Skidby) on 3rd November. Incredibly, Orange/Black 4 was seen in the company of a second, untagged, Red Kite that day. This untagged bird was probably a youngster reared in the wild by reintroduced birds in the Midlands. The two of them were seen on and off around Risby Park until Christmas Eve before moving north out of the Hull area. The movements of Orange/Black 4 could be tracked using a radio transmitter attached to its tail, however, and this showed that the bird wandered as far west as Market Weighton and as far east as Burton Constable. In early February 2000 there were at least four Red Kites lingering in the area between Hull and Beverley, these being Orange/Black 4 and another wing-tagged bird from Harewood with an untagged bird accompanying each of them.

Wandering Red Kites from the Yorkshire reintroduction scheme and the offspring of these birds when they begin nesting, as well as birds from further afield, are likely to be seen more frequently in the Hull area once a Yorkshire population becomes established. It cannot be long now before these magnificent birds are seen regularly over the outskirts of Hull and the surrounding villages.

White-tailed Eagle
Haliaeetus albicilla

Early on the morning of Sunday 14th November 1999 a very large bird of prey was seen soaring over Swine. It was the immature White-tailed Eagle, the 'flying door', that had been discovered wintering further east on the Burton Constable estate earlier that month. Standing two and a half feet tall with a wingspan of eight feet, the eagle had become something of a local media celebrity during its two-week stay at Burton Constable and many hundreds of birdwatchers went to see it. Half an hour after being seen at Swine the eagle was back at Burton Constable, this being its only recorded visit to the Hull area. Three days after leaving Burton Constable, however, what was presumably the same bird was seen on the opposite side of Hull at Welton on 22nd November. It is therefore possible that it passed over the Hull area again, unseen.

Despite a reintroduction programme in western Scotland it is more likely that the Burton Constable eagle was from Scandinavia; small numbers migrate from that region to winter on the southern North Sea coast and the odd one or two are reported from eastern Britain in most years. What was probably the East Yorkshire bird was later rediscovered in north Norfolk where it spent the rest of the winter in the loose company of an adult eagle.

The only other record of this spectacular species sadly comes from less enlightened times. In his 1809 *British Birds*, T. Bewick remarks that a White-tailed Eagle was shot at Hessle "a few years ago". At this time native birds were still nesting in northwest Britain, being more common than the Golden Eagle in many places, so the doomed Hessle bird could just as easily have been a British wanderer as a traveller from overseas.

Marsh Harrier
(Eurasian Marsh Harrier)
Circus aeruginosus

The Marsh Harrier only recolonised Britain in the latter half of the 20th Century after being exterminated by the ignorant persecution of gamekeepers and collectors a century before. The population has increased over the last 30 years and there are now several pairs on the upper

Humber. Marsh Harriers are also increasing as passage migrants in the East Riding and, as a result, one or two are probably occurring annually in the Hull area these days.

The first modern records coincided with the increase on the Humber in the 1980s. An all-dark bird was at North Bransholme on 16th May 1985 and a female was observed flying south over the Humber at Saltend on 4th April 1986. Another female was at Saltend on 14th and 16th May 1986 and an adult male was flushed from Saltend Marsh on 5th October. On 23rd July 1996 I was walking my dog in the field where the Bransholme Fishing Pond now lies, between the housing estate and the Holderness Drain, when I noticed a large bird of prey slowly quartering a reedy pond in the next field. It was a second-year male Marsh Harrier, but was lost to view as it left to the northeast. Around 4pm on 30th April the following year I was at the Holderness Drain just upstream of the Great Culvert Pumping Station, merely half a mile from the previous year's sighting, when I saw another Marsh Harrier flying low along the drain close to Carlam Hill Farm. This time it was a full adult male, a very impressive bird, and I watched for ten minutes as it gained height before passing overhead and flying off over East Hull at great height. On 22nd September 2000 a Marsh Harrier flew south over the Humber close to the Humber Bridge, with four Honey Buzzards and an Osprey also crossing the estuary there the same

day. On the evening of 5th April 2001, meanwhile, observers looking in vain for a White Stork that had been reported on Anlaby Common were given some compensation in the form of a Marsh Harrier overhead.

Hen Harrier
Circus cyaneus

The Hen Harrier is a scarce and infrequent winter visitor to the Hull area. Recorded sightings are actually quite few and far between, though several wandering Hen Harriers probably go undetected as they quarter the more remote fields and ditches each year. Most birds are seen close to the Humber and in the more open ground around the outskirts of Hull. They may turn up anytime from September to April, with a distinct trend for midwinter records.

A 'ring-tail' Hen Harrier, the generic term for female and immature birds, was at the Holderness Drain on North Bransholme on 14th December 1984. It or another was seen again from 2nd to 15th January and 12th to 15th March 1985. Another ring-tail flew along the Humber at Saltend before roosting in Saltend Marsh on 29th September 1985, remaining in the area until 5th October. More recent sightings include a ring-tail near the Humber Bridge on 9th February 1997 and another drifting northwest over Saltend on 31st December 2000. There are also several undated records for Saltend since 1985.

Montagu's Harrier
Circus pygargus

The only acceptable Hull area record of this rare passage migrant and summer visitor is of a single bird seen at Paull by S. M. Lister on 7th June 1986. An undated record of a Harrier in Hull between 1960 and 1966 could not be assigned to either Montagu's Harrier or Hen Harrier by the observers, but was more likely to be the latter.

Sparrowhawk
(Eurasian Sparrowhawk)
Accipiter nisus
Few birds have gone through such a roller-coaster of fortunes in the 20th Century as the Sparrowhawk. In the early part of the century it was fairly common around Hull, as it was over most of Britain, despite the relent-

less persecution of gamekeepers. In 1901 John Nicholson noted that Sparrowhawks sometimes hunted in his garden near Pearson Park, as they no doubt did throughout the area.

Our own birds were supplemented by European immigrants in winter, with one ringed at Wassenaar, Holland, in August 1938 being found dead in Hull on 21st January 1939. This bird was already migrating when it was ringed so its birthplace was likely to have been even further afield. In the 1950s, however, pesticides such as DDT and Dieldrin were working their way through the food chain and killing birds of prey wholesale. The Sparrowhawk population crashed and they completely disappeared from most of eastern England. By the 1960s Sparrowhawks were so rare in Hull that one present in Northern Cemetery for two weeks in October 1963 was a very notable occasion. In fact, the only other Sparrowhawk to be seen in Hull that decade was a flyover bird on 14th December 1966. Both of these birds were probably passage migrants. Despite a ban on the deadly pesticides they continued to linger in the environment, accumulating in Sparrowhawks' bodies up to lethal doses or rendering their eggshells so thin that they cracked before they had chance to hatch. Throughout the 1970s the situation remained the same around Hull, with the only Sparrowhawks to be seen being the occasional migrant. One such bird flew west over the city on 26th September 1972.

The upturn in fortunes came at the end of the 1970s, with the arrival of a Sparrowhawk at Kirk Ella in October 1979. The bird was seen again in December and there were more sightings in nearby Kerry Woods in August 1980, April 1983 and August 1984. One was also seen at Andrew Marvell School on 13th February 1980. Up to two birds were hunting at Saltend at the end of 1984, with two in June 1985 and three different birds from August to December. Birds were also seen at Saltend throughout 1986, including a pair in February, but there was no evidence of breeding. Between 1981 and 1986 sightings were becoming increasingly common at Willerby Carrs and Priory Road fields in winter. In November 1985 a pair were present at Kirk Ella. Sightings continued to increase in the west of the Hull area and by 1989 Sparrowhawks were regularly seen in that district. Birds were also spreading into East Hull and became a regular sight at North Bransholme by 1988, although they often disappeared between April and September to breed in some unknown location.

In 1991 I was shown a Sparrowhawk egg that a lad had taken from a nest full of chicks at the Humber Bridge Country Park. The egg couldn't be 'blown' and clearly contained a now dead chick almost ready to hatch. Aside from strongly pointing out the mindless ignorance of the lad's act there was little more of benefit that could have been done. Around the same time I was brought a dead juvenile bird that was found at Ings Plantation, where Kingswood is now being built. The expansion continued, however, with the first birds arriving at Hedon Road Cemetery in the early 1990s and breeding occurring in the vicinity from 1995 onwards. Recent breeding has also been recorded around the railway sidings behind Calvert Lane and the Bransholme Sewage Works Plantation/Haworth Hall area. Breeding is probably occurring in East Park and many of the woods and copses around the outlying villages. A pair was displaying over the Humber Bridge Country Park in April 1999, indicating continued breeding at this site.

By the mid 1990s it was possible to see a Sparrowhawk almost anywhere from Queen's Gardens to Hessle, Wawne, Paull and all areas inbetween. In the winter of 1996 no less than three different Sparrowhawks, recognised as an adult male, adult female and juvenile male, were raiding my North Bransholme bird table. Their cunning and determination was often breathtaking and several experiences are worth repeating. One afternoon the familiar alarm calls of the garden sparrows alerted me to a female Sparrowhawk clinging to a chickenwire fence that bordered a neighbour's privet hedge. On the other side of the wire was a Dunnock, too scared to break cover. The Sparrowhawk was hanging by one foot as it reached through the wire with the other to make repeated lunges at the potential victim. The Dunnock eventually escaped after about five minutes of frantic dodging. On another occasion I opened my front door to be greeted by a Robin flying directly at me at head-height, only to disappear over my shoulder and into the front room. In hot pursuit, about three feet behind it, was a Sparrowhawk that made a right angle turn at the very last second. It was so close I felt the draft from its wings on my face. The Robin was later released unharmed. Finally, early one winter morning I had been quietly waiting at a bus stop (the lamp post type without a shelter) across the road from my garden when, around a foot from my head, a Sparrowhawk darted past, flew 30 feet across the road and into my garden whereupon the small birds exploded in panic. The Sparrowhawk had actually used me, in conjunction with the lamp post, as cover to screen its approach across open ground and launch a surprise attack.

Common Buzzard
Buteo buteo
Common Buzzards were exterminated from lowland Yorkshire by the mid 19th Century. By 1900 they were very rare birds around Hull, with those that did occur being just occasional passage or winter migrants. In November 1905 a gamekeeper shot a Common Buzzard with a 4 feet 2 inches wingspan as it flew over Woody Carr near Wawne. That was the only bird reported from the Hull area in the first half of the 20th Century. Others probably went unrecorded, however, and there were seven records of unidentified Buzzards over Hull between 1960 and 1966. These birds were described as either Common or Rough-legged Buzzards although, in my opinion, Honey Buzzard was not eliminated either. Common Buzzard was probably the most likely in many or all cases, however.

On 23rd July 1972 a Common Buzzard flew north over Kirk Ella. This was a very odd midsummer date that raises a few questions about exactly where this bird had come from. Another unidentified Buzzard was seen over Wyke Junior High School in West Hull on 13th September 1979; the time of year was right for either a Honey Buzzard or Common Buzzard but probably too early for a Rough-legged

Buzzard. Again, Common Buzzard was more likely but we'll never know for sure. On 18th January 1986 S. L. James and others watched another Common Buzzard making its way slowly east over the Saltend area.

Common Buzzards, having been banished from lowland England for so long, have made notable inroads into eastern counties since the late 1990s. Small numbers are now breeding sparingly in many eastern areas and it has been suggested that the East Yorkshire Wolds may have been hiding a pair or two in recent years. Breeding has also been suspected in mid Holderness. It is pleasing to say that Buzzards look set to reclaim their long-lost territory throughout the region within the next few decades, as long as they are left in peace.

Rough-legged Buzzard
Buteo lagopus

There is just one definite early record of this very rare winter visitor from Scandinavia in the Hull area, with one being taken near the borough of Hull in late autumn 1903 during an influx of Rough-legs into Britain. Boylan (1967) reported seven unidentified buzzards over Hull between 1960 and 1966, however, which he was unable to assign to either Common or Rough-legged. The former is much more likely in all cases.

Osprey
Pandion haliaetus

Ospreys originally bred throughout Britain but persecution led to extinction from their final Scottish outpost in 1916. They returned to breed in Scotland in the 1950s and now number over 130 pairs. An English reintroduction scheme at Rutland Water and a naturally colonising pair in the Lake District both produced their first young in 2001. Ospreys are summer migrants from West Africa and most Scottish birds, as well as many from Scandinavia, move south through Britain before crossing over to the Continent.

Ospreys have been seen migrating over the Hull area on many occasions and increased in frequency as the Scottish population grew.

Occurrences are probably annual now. Spring records began with one at Saltend on 6th May 1990, with another flying west over Kirk Ella on 31st March 1994 and then one over Bricknell Avenue on 17th April 2001. There was a midsummer record of one flying east at Saltend on 4th July 1986.

All autumn records have been in September. One was over Kirk Ella on 18th September 1976 and I watched another from my window on 22nd September 1991 as it circled for ten minutes over fields east of North Bransholme before heading off south over Hull. One flew west over the Humber Bridge on the morning of 9th September 2000 and another flew south there just under a fortnight later on 22nd. In addition, there are two or three undated records from the city centre and Witham areas of Hull since the 1970s. An interesting event concerns an ailing immature Osprey, almost certainly a Scandinavian bird, coming aboard a trawler off Scotland in August 1963 and remaining on board until it reached Hull. It was taken into care before being released. An Osprey may be spotted migrating anywhere over the Hull area in both passage periods, from late March to early June and late August to early October, and they can occur literally anywhere. Several of the records given above have been seen from the gardens or windows of lucky observers, only going to show the benefit of keeping a sly eye on the skies wherever you are during migration time.

Kestrel
(European Kestrel)
Falco tinnunculus

The Kestrel was the Hull area's most common bird of prey for much of the last century but has probably been overtaken by the Sparrowhawk in recent years. Kestrels are still common in the area, however, often seen hovering over any patch of rough grassland, carr, drain or railway embankment from the outlying farmland to the industrial quarter of Hull. The usual prey is small mammals, especially in the outlying areas, but in the more urban habitats they are not averse to catching small birds in a Sparrowhawk-style ambush.

Kestrels were breeding in Wincolmlee and the Hull parks in the 1960s and were regular at Northern Cemetery in autumn and winter. Other pairs have been breeding around the eastern docks and Hedon Road Cemetery since the 1970s, usually on a disused water tower, and they are present all year in this area. What may have been another pair was breeding around Saltend in the mid 1980s and it is still possible to see Kestrels there.

There were several pairs around Cottingham and northwest Hull in the 1980s, including the Sutton Fields Industrial Estate, and nesting was regular in the roof of the Kinnersley factory into the early 1990s at least. Even now, hunting birds are frequently seen over the rough grassland off Cleveland Street, especially around the motorcycle track, despite recent development and the loss of grassland in that area. Up to three pairs breed in old Carrion Crow nests or tree holes to the east of North Bransholme, with a regular pair at Carlam Hill Farm, another at High Bransholme Farm and often another around Castle Hill Farm. There is still much excellent habitat for them on this eastern fringe, with plenty of rough grassland and small copses. A pair bred on top of the Reckitt and Coleman building, on Dansom Lane, in 1990 and 1991. They were found to be using pockets of rough grassland for catching voles and mice, although half of their diet consisted of Blackbirds, House Sparrows and Starlings. I occasionally saw what was probably one of this pair diving at Feral Pigeons and Starlings at the top end of Holderness Road. Other recent nesting sites include the Bransholme Sewage Works, Priory Road fields, Hall Road area, the Priory Sidings off Clive Sullivan Way, Humber Bridge Country Park, Hull's Avenues and Dunswell Road in Cottingham. A pair at this latter site in 1999 delayed construction workers who wanted to remove the old pylon they were nesting on.

Breeding is therefore widespread throughout the Hull area and one should not be too surprised to find a Kestrel nest in any part of the city or the surrounding farmland and villages.

There is some evidence that our local Kestrels are joined by passage migrants in spring and autumn, with up to six noted at Saltend during April and September in the 1980s. Elevated numbers of Kestrels can also be seen in July when the young leave the nest and family parties gather on a pylon or tree. Patient observation is often rewarded by views of the youngsters clumsily practicing their hovering, a skill it appears to take some time to learn!

Red-footed Falcon
Falco vespertinus

Up to 10 Red-footed Falcons, vagrants from eastern Europe, occur in Britain in an average year and they always quicken the pulse of their lucky finders. One such observer near the Humber Bridge on 19th August 1987 was disappointed, however, as the record was not accepted by the British Birds Rarities Committee.

Merlin
Falco columbarius

The nearest breeding Merlins to the Hull area are to be found on the North Yorkshire moors and the Pennines, and they only visit the low ground in our region during the winter months. At this time of year the native stock is supplemented by birds form Northern Europe and Iceland that visit East Yorkshire in variable numbers. Merlins are rather easy to overlook, however, being fast, low-flying and looking superficially like a kestrel from a distance. Occurrences are rather poorly documented around Hull due to birds being overlooked, unreported or sightings being lumped in with accounts for Holderness or East Yorkshire as a whole. Most Merlins in the Hull area appear to be seen between September and April but they are rather unpredictable in occurrence and can nowhere be described as regular or common. Any open ground may attract them, from the farmland to the estuary shore.

Just one Merlin was reported in the old Hull boundary during the 1960-66 Hull Scientific and Field Naturalists' Club survey. The next report did not come until 1983 when one was seen at Willerby Carrs on 22nd January. A female carrying prey flew from Saltend over the estuary on 13th January 1985 and another was at Wold Road on 31st January. An immature male was at Saltend from early February to early April. A female was back in the Saltend area from late September 1985 to early March 1986, while a male flew in from the south on 22nd November 1985. Another male was seen near Saltend in February and March 1986, with a female again in September and December and two on 27th of the latter. One was at Kerry Woods, Kirk Ella, on 19th September 1992 and it was a good autumn at North Bransholme that year, with a large stubble field near Carlam Hill Farm attracting flocks of Linnets that, in turn, brought in the Merlins. The first was a lone bird seen flying east on 3rd September, while two females or immatures were over the stubble field on 23rd October. One bird remained throughout November.

An immature was perched in an area of burnt rough grass at High Bransholme, near the Great Culvert Pumping Station on the Holderness Drain, on the exceptionally early date of 12th August 1996. It left to the southeast in the direction of Saltend. A male was seen in much the same place on 20th November 1998 and a female was at Saltend in October and November. Two were there on 10th December and one was seen the next day. Saltend seems to be the most regular site for Merlins in the Hull area, with the combination of rough grass, open fields and shoreline being classic winter territory.

Hobby
(Eurasian Hobby)
Falco subbuteo

Around 1872 W.W. Boulton regarded the Hobby as being a fairly frequent summer visitor to the Beverley area, having received several locally-killed birds from the River Hull over the years. They were no doubt occurring as passage migrants in the modern-day Hull area at the same time. As with virtually all other birds of prey, however, Hobbies were shot on sight by gamekeepers and farmers and soon became very rare. This culture of killing anything with a hooked beak in the name of 'pest control' continued well into the middle of the 20th Century. Hobbies were not reported again in the Hull area until 1980, when one passed over Kerry Woods at Kirk Ella on 23rd June. One was chasing House Martins at Hull Marina on 29th July 1985 before departing to the west and another spent two hours at Saltend Marsh on 21st August the same year. One passed over Saltend and Paull on 18th May 1986 with others at Saltend on 21st June, 19th August and 6th September. A Hobby was also seen perched at Kerry Woods on 20th May that year. Yet more were at the eastern docks on an unspecified date in 1987 and "in Hull" on 25th August 1988. On 3rd September 1991 I saw an unmistakeable Hobby pass overhead at the Bransholme Sewage Works and, two days later, I saw what may have been the same bird chasing Swallows over North Bransholme.

A Hobby spent over a month around Bransholme in the summer of 1993. I first saw it as it swooped low over the reservoir at the Bransholme Sewage Works in hot pursuit of House Martins on 20th June. On 3rd July it was seen hanging on the wind over the plantation between the Sewage Works and Thomas Clarkson Way. I watched it for an hour as it picked insects off the leaves and chased any passing bird from Woodpigeons and Swallows to the resident male Kestrel. On 11th July what was probably the same bird was seen sat on a tussock near the Holderness Drain at Low Bransholme, east of Noddle Hill Way. It flew off in the direction of Bransholme Sewage Works. On 24th July it was seen for the last time as it flew northwest over North Bransholme. On each occasion the bird was noted to have a distinctly brown tail, possibly denoting a female or immature. On 12th May 1994 I was lucky enough to see another Hobby, chasing Swallows again, over playing fields off Bellfield Avenue in East Hull. On 12th May 1997 a Hobby was seen over scrubland in West Hull with another at Kerry Woods again on 23rd September.

Mid May to late June appears to be the most likely time to come across a spring Hobby in the Hull area, with autumn birds occurring from August to late September. The occasional Hobby may be seen during midsummer, however, and this might encourage one to believe that the recent northward creep of breeding birds in Britain might spread to the Hull area at some point in the future. In the meantime, Hobbies are undoubtedly increasing as passage migrants in the Hull area and it is well worthwhile keeping a close look out for this most graceful of British falcons.

Gyr Falcon
Falco rusticolus

Sadly this huge and spectacular falcon has never occurred in a totally wild state in the Hull area, although there are two records tempered with human interference. The first was in October 1954 when a probable Gyr was at large in Hull after escaping from captivity. The bird was later seen at Beverley and Flamborough, on both occasions with a tether around its leg. It probably survived in the county for quite some months and is included here for completeness. The second was a wild bird that was brought into Hull on board a ship on 11th August 1964. The bird, a juvenile, alighted on board in the Bear Island region of the Arctic and was either captured or fed by the crew until it reached Hull. It was then taken to the Hull RSPCA who released it at Bempton on 12th August.

Peregrine Falcon
Falco peregrinus

Most people have heard of the Peregrine and to see one hunting is one of the most impressive sights in the natural world. The power, speed and agility of their stooping dives (which can reach 180 mph) and level-pursuits really does leave you open-mouthed and wondering how anything can escape when they mean business. Indeed, I have only once seen a Peregrine beaten by its quarry.

Peregrines occur in the Hull area more often than one might imagine and there are records going back to the late 19th Century. The first documented occurrence appears to have been that of an adult bird shot at Sutton in early 1895. In the last week of October 1924 a pair were frequenting the area around Paull and eastwards to Stone Creek. The female of the pair was seen to make several kills, including a Curlew and a Partridge, with the smaller male in attendance. On 21st December 1930 a male was killed at Sutton but records almost totally dried up by the 1960s - legal protection was removed during the Second World War in order to give safer passage to homing pigeons and the toxic effects of pesticides in the 1950s and 60s finished off most of those that were left. Despite these pressures a Peregrine was seen over Hull some time between 1960 and 1966 and an adult was observed over the Hull University campus, Cottingham Road, on 28th November 1973.

As with the Sparrowhawk, the recovery was well under way by the 1980s and Peregrine records increased in the Hull area as a result. An adult male was at Saltend on 12th January 1985 before leaving to the northwest over Hull, with an immature male there from 20th January to 5th March. An immature male flew upstream past Saltend on 28th December that year and what was possibly the same bird was chasing Feral Pigeons over Hull city centre on 29th January 1986. Later that year a juvenile flew past the Saltend Chemicals Plant on 26th July. Other Peregrines were seen over Hull on 17th March and 20th December 1987. On 19th March 1994 I was observing a flock of Golden Plover in a flooded field at North Bransholme when they exploded into the air in sheer panic as an immature Peregrine dived low into them from the east. As the plovers scattered the Peregrine circled for a while before leaving in the direction of Saltend. I don't know about the Golden Plovers but it certainly set my heart racing! A Peregrine was at Saltend on 21st May 1996 and on 25th July a juvenile flew upstream over the Humber just west of the Humber Bridge. As with the 1986 juvenile this bird posed an intriguing question as to its origins and birthplace. Another Peregrine flew west over Victoria Dock on 5th January 1997 and an adult caught a Black-headed Gull over my North Bransholme garden on 23rd August 1997 before carrying it off southeast. Visitors to Pickering Park were no doubt similiarly impressed by the bird flying overhead on 28th August 1998. The Humber bias was apparent once again when a Peregrine was seen attacking a Herring Gull over the Humber Bridge in November 1998. Another was at Paull on 10th January 1999.

The majority of Peregrine sightings in the Hull area have occurred in winter but late summer records are not unusual. The only time when it is rather unlikely to see one is during early summer when they are away breeding on their cliffs and crags.

While many of the more recent local sightings have been around the estuary a significant number of Peregrines have been seen inland over built-up districts. Records are increasing and their current status is probably best summed up as scarce winter visitor and passage migrant.

Red-legged Partridge
Alectoris rufa

This distant relative of the native Grey Partridge was introduced to Britain in the 18th Century. It remained rather uncommon until the 20th Century, spreading north through Yorkshire during the first few decades of the 1900s. Red-legs reached Hull around 1910 after a decade of expansion through the East Riding and breeding was reported close to the city in that year. By the 1960s Red-legs were resident and breeding around the northwest suburbs of Hull, roughly where Orchard Park lies today, and one was even found wandering down Spring Bank. Birds were also seen around Kirk Ella and Carr Lane in the late 1970s and early 1980s and had probably been present there long before that.

Red-legs were probably breeding around Cottingham in the 1980s and no doubt before, but were less common than Greys. A pair or two were also nesting around the eastern docks around the same time and a pair of adults with three young were behind the ferry terminal on King George Dock on 18th September 1985. Singles were seen all over the eastern waterfront during this period, from the tidal barrage at Sammy's Point to the chemical works at Saltend, with a covey of nine at Saltend Marsh on 13th November 1985. Breeding was also occurring in northeast Hull by this time. As a boy in the late 1980s and early 1990s I occasionally found the egg shells of Red-legged Partridges in the fields around North Bransholme, though I rarely saw more than one or two pairs of adult birds. Red-legs can still be found there, with two males calling at the Holderness Drain near Carlam Hill Farm in October 2000, but the largest recorded covey contained just seven birds on 14th November 1992. In the summer of 1990 an adult Red-legged Partridge was picked up, apparently uninjured, in the fields where Kingswood is now being built. It was very docile and was thought to have maybe been a recent release for shooting purposes. After a night in an aviary it was very flighty and flew past my head and out over Bransholme as I opened the door the following morning. It was later recaptured and released in the more suitable surroundings of High Bransholme Farm.

Paul Milsom's study of the birds on Priory Road fields in 1995/6 found larger numbers of Red-legs than at Bransholme and confirmed their continued presence around Cottingham. Up to 12 were regularly seen on Willerby Carrs and others were noted on the Loatleys and West Gengs fields. A pair of adults with a couple of juveniles in July 1995 suggests continued breeding there. The Priory Road fields are probably the best place to find Red-legged Partridges around Hull, with this northwest corner being the stronghold since they first arrived in the area a century ago.

Grey Partridge
Perdix perdix

Very sadly the Grey Partridge is in deep trouble in Britain. Once one of the most common birds in the lowlands, numbers have tumbled to less than half of those in the 1970s. The population seems to be in freefall, with a major reason being modern intensive farming depriving the chicks of vital insect food. Several authors have questioned whether the Grey Partridge is in the process of following the Corncrake to near-oblivion in Britain. The decline is in the opposite direction to that of the Corncrake, however, with eastern England, including East Yorkshire, remaining something of a stronghold.

At the beginning of the 20th Century Grey Partridges could often be heard calling from the fields on the margins of northwest Hull. On 14th December 1901 a lone bird was seen flying over gardens on Park Grove, off Prince's Avenue, between two open spaces. Gamekeeping and predator control in the estates surrounding Hull probably meant that overspilling Grey Partridges were pretty common in the area up to the Second World War at least. Even during the 1960s they were reported to be breeding in small numbers in the Hull suburbs themselves. This was probably in the arable fields and rough undeveloped ground around places such as Sutton and Stoneferry, before the building of the massive housing estates in the 1970s. The expansion of Hull merely pushed the Grey Partridge back to the fringes of the new developments and it remained a resident just within the new city boundary and beyond, as it is today.

Grey Partridges seem to prefer a mix of arable land and rough grassland and anywhere where these elements combine in the Hull area is likely to hold birds. Numbers around Cottingham and the Priory Road fields have remained fairly constant since 1980, despite the crash in the national population taking place during the time, with coveys of up to a dozen birds regularly seen in winter. A survey by the Cottingham Bird Club of the 10 km square centred on Cottingham (TA03) in December 1983 found 30 birds, but there was no mention of breeding between 1980 and 1986. Paul Milsom's survey of the Loatleys, Gengs and Pickhills fields, south of Cottingham, between 1995 and 1996 found coveys of between two and eight birds throughout the year and a maximum of 12 in December. Milsom also suspected that up to two pairs were breeding in the area. In the mid 1980s birds were present in all suitable weedy habitat along the eastern waterfront, from Sammy's Point (the site of 'The Deep') to Saltend. Favoured areas included rough ground near the Holderness Drain at the eastern docks, Saltend Marsh and the Saltend Chemical Works site, with coveys of up to half a dozen birds being seen almost daily in these areas. Small groups still occasionally wander up the old Hull to Withernsea railway line in southeast Hull as far into town as the Hedon Road Cemetery, indicating the continued presence of a small population around the eastern docks. Indeed, M. Flowers saw a small covey at Victoria Dock in March 1997.

Two to three pairs of Grey Partridges were breeding within the city boundary throughout the early 1990s between North Bransholme and the Holderness Drain. Male birds, giving the characteristic call that sounds for all the world like a squeaky door hinge, were noticeable here between February and May when pairing was taking place. Coveys made up of family groups or amalgamations of families were regularly seen between September and January, usually numbering between three and eight birds in size.

Late autumn and early winter is when the largest counts of Grey Partridge occur in the Hull area as birds gather together and winter has not yet taken its toll. Notable counts at North Bransholme included 24 from three coveys on 31st October 1992, 21 a month later and 40 on 17th December 1993. Two coveys of 10 birds each were a mile and a half away near Swine in August 1997, indicating the continuing survival of Grey Partridges east of Bransholme. Grey Partridges have the largest clutch of any European bird and a pair with 10 half-grown young were at Bransholme on 2nd August 1992, while an adult at Saltend had 12 chicks in tow on 21st August 1997. It was at nearby Paull where the largest gathering of Grey Partridges in the Hull area, an impressive 67, was recorded on 27th September 1986. While the national decline has yet to bite hard around Hull, numbers as large as this seem rather unlikely in the years to come.

Quail
(Common Quail)
Coturnix coturnix

Quails are scarce visitors to the Hull area, as in the rest of Britain, and are only occasionally heard calling from weedy arable fields in spring or summer. In 1994 a male was heard giving its characteristic 'wet-me-lips' call from a field of linseed on Wawne Common, north of Hull, from the 8th until at least 20th July and it was flushed on one occasion. By imitating the song it was possible to draw the bird within 20 feet of the sitting observer, though it never left cover to show itself on the ground. The following year another male was heard calling from a weedy field of wheat at Carlam Hill Farm near North Bransholme. It was present from at least the 25th until the 30th of June, calling persistently during warm weather.

There is another anecdotal and undated record from near North Bransholme during the late 1980s and others have no doubt visited the cereal crops or fields of rank grass around the city outskirts in other summers, possibly staying to breed. A Quail that set up home near Cottingham in 1947 didn't get the chance, however; it was shot.

Pheasant
(Common Pheasant)
Phasianus colchicus
Introduced by the Normans or perhaps even the Romans, Pheasants are such a familiar sight in the countryside of East Yorkshire that it is easy to forget that they are not native. Pheasants are still bred for the shoot on many estates surrounding the Hull area, such as Risby and Burton Constable, and there are also rearing pens in many of the woods and copses around Wawne, Swine and Cottingham. The sound of shotguns across the fields in September and October is a familiar one to residents in the outskirts of Hull and the villages. In addition to these released birds, many of which probably don't live long or wander far, there is a healthy wild population of Pheasants in many parts of the Hull area where organised shooting does not occur.

The rough grassland and arable fields around Bransholme and East Hull, with their hedgerows, marshy areas and copses, holds many Pheasants. At least five males crowed each April and May between North Bransholme and the Holderness Drain in the 1990s and females with young were a familiar sight from June to August. A loose group of 22 Pheasants were in this area on 27th December 2000. It is not uncommon to see the occasional bird picking over grassland just yards from the houses of North Bransholme, or even among the shrubbery on roundabouts. Pheasants are also common around Cottingham and the Priory Road fields, with 10 together at the latter site in December 1995. One was in a garden on the edge of Kirk Ella on 16th December 1989 and birds are occasionally seen in nearby Kerry Woods. In the mid 1980s at least three females were rearing young in the swath of land bordering the Humber from Sammy's Point, at the mouth of the River Hull, to Saltend. A total of 16 young were reared here in 1985, with birds favouring the areas around Saltend Marsh, Holderness Drain and Victoria Dock. The latter has since been developed for housing.

Pheasants will freely wander quite deeply into built-up areas if there is a corridor of sufficient cover to draw them in, with the railway lines and the banks of the river and drains being good examples. Several lone cock Pheasants have been seen in the Hedon Road and Preston Road Cemeteries after wandering up the old Hull to Withernsea railway line. There were seven sightings in dense cover in the Avenues in 1996, birds that had no doubt wandered down the Hull to Beverley line and then further along the east-to-west freight line. The occasional Pheasants in the scrubby corners of the Bransholme Sewage Works probably found their way there via the banks of the River Hull. Pheasants are quite tolerant of development as long as they have cover to retreat into and I regularly saw them strutting round the newly-created cul-de-sacs of Kingswood before the landscapers moved in.

Most of the male birds seen in the Hull area are of the Chinese races, the white-collared *torquatus* group, although a few resemble the nominate *colchicus* group from southwest Asia which lack the white collar.

Golden Pheasant
Chrysolophus pictus

A common aviary bird, the Golden Pheasant also occurs in very small numbers in a feral state in several areas of Britain. Golden Pheasants have been part of the East Park menagerie since at least the 1980s, being kept in the aviaries and also in the open-topped animal enclosure. Although some of the birds in the latter are pinioned and flightless others certainly are not and two timid males rushing into the shrubbery some distance away from the enclosure on 9th March 1994 had clearly 'jumped the fence'. It is possible that such escapees could live for some time in a wild state either in the Park or beyond it if they decided to roam, though the densely urban area surrounding East Park and the attentions of urban foxes or cats means that freedom is probably short-lived for these birds.

Water Rail
Rallus aquaticus

The Water Rail was no doubt a fairly widespread breeding bird throughout the marshes and carrs of the Hull area before wholesale drainage in the 18th and 19th Centuries, though Nelson (1907) mentions that they were common on the sedgy margins of the River Hull. Now apparently just a winter visitor around Hull, I have not once heard of breeding in the area although their skulking nature may mean they have been overlooked.

The earliest report of a Water Rail in the Hull area concerns an injured bird found walking down a street near East Park on 15th October 1951 that was taken into Malet Lambert School and later released. Another quirky report comes from October 1953 when a Water Rail was brought into Hull on a ship after coming aboard off Portugal. It was fed by the RSPCA before being released locally

but, as Mather (1986) puts it in his *The Birds of Yorkshire*, a trip in the other direction would have been more beneficial to it! Another at Albert Dock in 1954 may also have had an unorthodox journey into the city.

The very severe 1962/3 winter produced a flurry of Water Rails in the Hull area as starvation forced birds out into the open to feed on any unfrozen watermargins they could find. A total of 10 birds were recorded by Boylan (1967) at this time, mainly close to the city centre on the Barmston and Cottingham drains and the now filled-in stretch of the Foredyke Stream that ran from Bransholme to New Cleveland Street. A couple of Water Rails even resorted to foraging among the waders on the West Hull foreshore. As Saltend Marsh became established on The Growths (reclaimed mudflats between King George Dock and Saltend) in the early 1980s one or two Water Rails regularly passed though between October and late March, sometimes staying for several weeks at a time. During the early 1990s I saw single Water Rails creeping though dense cover alongside Old Main Drain at North Bransholme on four occasions during the winter months. What may have been the same long-staying bird possibly accounted for three of those sightings between late November 1993 and mid February 1994. Saltend was still attracting Water Rails up in the late 1990s. At least one bird present between April and July 1998 maybe indicated a breeding attempt, this being the only report of summering that I have come across in the Hull area. Others at Saltend were seen in the more typical months of November and December.

Any watery habitat around Hull with lots of marginal cover may, therefore, attract an occasional Water Rail anytime from October to late March, very rarely at other times. Their secretive nature means they are unlikely to advertise themselves and are thus surely under recorded. Just how many skulking birds go unseen in the reed beds fringing the River Hull or hidden among the herbage of the many drainage channels, large and small, throughout the area can only be guessed at. On the basis of the above records, however, the species appears to be a regular, if thinly distributed, winter visitor to the Hull area.

Spotted Crake
Porzana porzana

Spotted Crakes possibly nested in the marshy ground bordering the River Hull and elsewhere up to the late 1800s, though there are no spe-

cific records for our area. The only documented occurrence of a Spotted Crake around Hull concerns an immature killed by a cat in a garden in "the heart of the manufacturing district of Hull" on 5th September 1917, this being reported in *The Naturalist* soon afterwards. Besides being extremely shy and unobtrusive, the Spotted Crake is also very rare in the East Riding these days so the chances of seeing one in the Hull area are rather slim.

Corncrake
(Corn Crake)
Crex crex

During the 20th Century the Corncrake underwent one of the most spectacular declines of any British species, with the blame being placed firmly at the feet of modern agricultural methods and the resultant habitat loss. Corncrakes are summer visitors to Britain from wintering grounds in sub-Saharan Africa and they were once common throughout the country. Rarely seen, they were nonetheless well known to country people due to their nocturnal calling, a dry double rasp that gave the bird its scientific or Latin name of *Crex crex*. The birds bred in hayfields and meadows and it was a switch to mechanised cutting of hay, cutting earlier in the season for silage and the conversion of many meadows to arable crops that sent the population into freefall; nests were crushed, adults killed in reapers or their meadows were ploughed up. The British breeding population is now largely restricted to the Hebrides where traditional hay meadows persist, although a handful of pairs occasionally nest elsewhere.

Writing in *The Naturalist* in 1901, John Nicholson described the birds that could be seen around and about his Hull townhouse near Pearson Park when it was just two or three streets from open country, and he noted the Corncrake among them. Nicholson spoke of how the rasping call could be heard in summer, saying nothing to contradict the assumption that the species was a regular member of the local avifauna. The Corncrake bred not uncommonly in the meadows and hayfields throughout the Hull area, particularly northwards along the River Hull, during the first decade or two of the 20th Century. It was noted to be getting scarcer in the East Riding as early as 1907 and by the 1940s the Corncrake was extinct within the Hull area. They were also very rare throughout the East Riding by then, with around four calling males around Beverley being the only ones left. Once regular breeding had ceased later that decade the Corncrake was reduced to being only a rare passage migrant in East Yorkshire, mainly on the coast, and it remains so today.

The only records of the Corncrake in the Hull area in the latter half of the 20th Century concern several remarkable sightings from the private grounds of Holderness House, the Georgian mansion at the corner of Laburnum Avenue and Holderness Road, in the inner suburbs of Hull. The former Assistant Head Gardener at Holderness House saw what he identified as a Corncrake skulking around the paddock on 8th July 1986. The bird was seen again on the 13th and 16th July and may have been summering in the grounds. Interestingly, a Corncrake was reportedly heard calling throughout the breeding season of 1986 in a secret location in the east of Yorkshire. Calling was heard again in 1987, with breeding suspected, and that year a bird was photographed "in a garden" at the site. These records may refer to Holderness House. Incredibly, the same Holderness House gardener reported another Corncrake in the grounds on the 1st and 2nd August 1997.

Moorhen
(Common Moorhen)
Gallinula chloropus

The Moorhen is a common and familiar species on any stretch of open water in the Hull area that affords it enough cover along the margins for shelter and nesting. Even quite small ponds and narrow ditches will usually have a few birds. The Moorhen is much shyer than its cousin the Coot, but in the Hull parks and Queen's Gardens it becomes relatively tolerant of people and will occasionally take food offered to the ducks.

East Park has long had a contingent of Moorhens among its waterfowl and Boylan (1967) put the usual figure at 20 to 30 during the 1960s. Twenty-five were counted in February 1967 and this is still about right for a winter count today. In the 1980s Bonavia (1990) described the Moorhen as being a "common breeding resident wherever there is water present" in the dykes and ponds around Cottingham and northwest Hull as well as on the River Hull itself. I have often seen Moorhens on the river as it passes through northern Hull but never with young, assuming that the strong tidal flows were too much for such delicate chicks to cope with. Bonavia's area of concern stretched as far as Beverley, however, so perhaps Moorhens have more luck on the higher stretches of the river

where the current is weaker. At least three pairs were breeding on Saltend Marsh in the mid 1980s and the 15 or so birds present in winter often moved onto St. Andrew's and Alexandra Docks when the marsh froze.

In the early 1990s a pair or two usually bred on the sludge pits at the Bransholme Sewage Works. I counted as many as 22 there in February and March 1992, but the pits have now been filled in and Moorhens are quite scarce there these days. In the same period up to 10 pairs could be found breeding on the Old Main Drain, Holderness Drain and marshy pools east of North Bransholme, with the squeaky calls of the young coming out of the reeds from mid May to August. Young Moorhen chicks are often very naïve, as well as extremely cute, and they will sometimes come to people if the parent birds are out of sight. Chicks of this age are very vulnerable and I have seen them in the possession of local boys who seemed to be enchanted by their new pet, not knowing they would invariably be dead of starvation within a day. Throughout the 1990s breeding has occurred in the Pickering, Pearson and East Parks and at least one pair still breeds in Queen's Gardens. Four young were seen there in April 1999. Several pairs also nest at Thwaite Hall Lake in Cottingham and I counted around 30 birds there in December 2000.

During calm, warm nights in spring and early summer Moorhens occasionally take to the skies and go on aerial display flights, circling high over their territories while uttering a repetitive, almost mechanical "kip...kip...kip" song. This can go on for half an hour or more and the strange calls fade in and out as the bird circles towards you and then away again, but it is oddly hypnotic. Another slightly quirky habit of the Moorhen is its tendency to dive when surprised and then seemingly disappear as the observer waits for it to resurface. I have seen them do this several times and at first I was perplexed over how they appeared to completely vanish. On one occasion, however, the mystery was solved when I saw a Moorhen dive below the surface of a small pond at Bransholme and spotted a red beak under the water at the spot where the bird had dived. Looking more closely, the bird was among weed at the bottom of the pond and, thinking it might be trapped, I reached into the water and fished it out. There was nothing wrong with it and I concluded that it had simply been sitting tight on the bottom and waiting for me to leave. On another occasion I saw a Moorhen dive below the surface of Foredyke Stream as I appeared on the embankment. This one had a different strategy, and a trail of cloudy water and bubbles showed that it was walking along the bottom of the drain completely hidden from view. A minute or so later it popped its head up at the far bank some 10 metres away before creeping off into cover. Such observations go to show that even the common birds have the power to surprise you.

Coot
(Common Coot)
Fulica atra

Bold, aggressive and noisy, the Coot is present in the Hull area wherever there is sufficient open freshwater with enough depth to enable them to dive. They will also nest on quite shallow pools if there is sufficient cover for them to hide in when danger threatens. Coots may also be found on the Humber in winter.

East Park is probably the best place to see Coots in the Hull area with several breeding pairs, a fairly large wintering population and confiding resident birds. They were not always so frequent in the park, however, and Boylan (1967) states that they were only scarce winter visitors during the 1960s, adding that they had bred but the implication being that this was unusual. They have been anything but scarce for as long as I can remember, with five pairs tending 13 young in May 1994, between 30 and 50 birds throughout 1997, 63 in January 1998 and 75 in October 2000. Breeding also occurs in Pickering Park, albeit in lesser numbers than East Park. There has apparently been no breeding in Pearson

Park or on Thwaite Hall Lake in recent years, although two pairs were present at the latter site during 1984 at least.

Up to three pairs bred around Saltend in the mid 1980s, at 'First Pond' and on the Saltend Marsh, with up to 10 birds on and off. Up to two secretive pairs bred on the shallow reedy pools between Foredyke Stream and Bransholme Road, east of the Bransholme housing estate, throughout the 1990s. The creation of the Bransholme Fishing Pond at this place in the late 1990s provided a more suitable habitat for the local Coots and up to four birds quickly took up residence there. A juvenile in July 2001 confirmed that the pond was now a new breeding site. In 1992 three pairs attempted to breed on the Bransholme Sewage Works reservoir, building their precarious nests on the concrete ramparts of the sluice gates. Choppy waters whipped up by the wind, combined with a lack of anything to anchor the nest to, led to all the nests being washed away and the Coots subsequently gave up. Two pairs tried again the following summer, however, and kinder weather conditions during the egg stage allowed the chicks to hatch safely in July, with five young eventually being reared to maturity.

Coots are more abundant and widespread around Hull in winter while passage birds also inflate numbers in spring and autumn. A total of 32 were at the Bransholme Sewage Works in September 1976 and 26 were counted in March 1993. In December 1962, during the big freeze, 26 Coots were seen among waders on the ice-free mud of the West Hull foreshore. Another freeze in February 1986 pushed 65 onto the Humber near the eastern docks. During less severe winters during the 1980s the breeding birds from Saltend Marsh would relocate to St. Andrew's and Alexandra Docks during cold snaps. Strangely, however, I have never seen Coots on either the Barmston or Holderness Drains or the River Hull.

Crane
(Common Crane)
Grus grus

Cranes are huge, stately birds with a bugling voice and an impressive wingspan. They possibly bred on the carrs of East Yorkshire in medieval times, as hinted at by the village name of Hutton Cranswick (i.e. Crane's Wick), but they are now very rare vagrants after flying off course on their annual migrations to and from Scandinavia and northern Europe. They seem to be occurring in Britain more frequently of late, however, and have recently begun to breed again in Norfolk. They are still a rarity in East Yorkshire and just four have been claimed for the Hull area.

On 16th May 1986 an adult Crane was observed by M. Lambert as it flew down the Humber past Saltend, with an immature seen on the mud-flats there by another observer 11 days later. Neither of these records was submitted to the regional or national Rarities Committees, how-ever, and the adult bird at least was allegedly not specifically identified as a Common Crane. There is an out-side chance that it may have been an escaped Demoiselle Crane, a couple of which have turned up in Yorkshire over the years, though Common Crane is probably more likely.

On 10th May 1987 K. and M. K. Rotherham saw a Common Crane at Willerby, this record being accepted by the Yorkshire Naturalists' Union Rarities Committee. Another was in fields between Paull and Thorngumbald on 14th November 2000.

Around 11pm one May night in 1996 I was walking back to my student digs in The Lawns, Cottingham, when I heard some obviously large birds giving trumpeting calls over-head. I cannot be sure, but they sounded very much like Cranes to me, perhaps two or three of them. Cranes are daytime migrants, how-ever, so one would not expect them to be on the wing well after dark at 11 pm. It is possible though that a small band of migrating Cranes may have gone astray on their spring migration and found themselves over the North Sea as the sun set.

Faced with no other option, they would have been forced to carry on flying through the night before reaching England and passing over Cottingham in the darkness. Yet again, as so often happens in birding, there's no way of knowing for sure.

Little Bustard
Tetrax tetrax

The Little Bustard breeds from Iberia, through France and Eastern Europe to Kazakhstan and it is a very rare vagrant to Britain. On 20th November 1956 an adult female Little Bustard of the eastern race, *Tetrax tetrax orientalis*, was shot in a field of barley stubble undersown with trefoil near Preston, north of Hedon. Incredibly a first-winter male of the western race was shot outside of the Hull area at Aldborough, only six miles from Preston, just ten days before. That these two very rare birds from oppo-site ends of the species' range and two different continents managed to make it to our island and settle down in more or less the same place at the same time is truly mind-boggling. What is especially sad though is that both birds were shot. This was not the unenlightened Victorian age of the 'sportsman naturalist' and those responsible really should have known better. Both birds were sent to A. Hazelwood of Bolton Museum for racial identification, this being confirmed by Colonel R. Meinertzhagen, and both specimens were residing at the Bolton Museum when John Mather inspected them prior to his 1986 *The Birds of Yorkshire*.

Oystercatcher
(Eurasian Oystercatcher)
Haematopus ostralegus

The Oystercatcher used to be known as the Sea Pie, 'pie' meaning black and white and not in the culinary sense. Oystercatchers were nevertheless very much on the local menu in days gone by. Inventories for Lord Percy's castles at Wressle and Leconfield (north of Beverley) in 1512 mention "Sea-Pyes" as being served for "Princypall Feestes" and these were probably acquired from the Humber via Hull. Nelson himself, in his 1907 *The Birds of Yorkshire*, is able to provide tasting notes for the Oystercatcher, stating

that the young birds are excellent eating in early autumn but the older ones are a bit fishy.

Boylan (1967) relates that the Oystercatcher was a scarce passage migrant and very rare breeding bird within the Hull boundary during the 1960s, with 10 records and one breeding pair. This pair was summering on The Growths, then an expanding area of reclaimed mud-flats just east of King George Dock, and they were first noted in 1960. Breeding was first confirmed in 1964 when a nest was found on the cinder ballast, the eggs being conspicuous against the dark substrate though the sitting adult was well-camouflaged. The addition of dredging waste in 1964 made the site more gravely and the pair returned to breed in 1965, when another pair also nested at Paull. Pairs bred at The Growths and near Paull into the early 1970s, with singles and pairs occasionally being seen over nearby Hedon Road, although The Growths was abandoned by the late 1970s. A breeding pair appeared on the railway sidings at Hessle in 1988, returning to nest there for at least the next two years, and a pair was present around Saltend throughout the summer of 1999 but breeding was not proven.

Oystercatchers are still predominantly passage migrants in the Hull area and numbers have changed little since Boylan's time. Regular watching at Saltend in the mid 1980s revealed peak counts of around a dozen birds in May, July and August, with single figures on and off throughout the rest of the year. Things were pretty much the same in the late 1990s, with a maximum of 13 at Saltend in May 1998 and up to six now and again at other times. Birds may turn up anywhere along the Humber, however, and I saw a mobile flock of a dozen of so roaming around Hessle Foreshore in late July 1996. Some were immatures and they may have been reared locally.

Oystercatchers occur inland with some regularity and are more likely to turn up in bizarre situations than most other waders. Two were on Willerby Carrs on 3rd March 1983 and one was feeding in a ploughed field at North Bransholme on 23rd October 1992. In 1993 I heard the unmistakeable piping call of a lone Oystercatcher passing over North Bransholme in the middle of the night on no less than three occasions, these being in May, July and September. Another was seen on the Bude Road playing fields, near Sutton Park, on 27th November the same year. In January 1997 Michael Flowers saw an unseasonal Oystercatcher probing for earthworms in a snow-free patch of ground in Hedon Road Cemetery. It must have been starving. On 20th February 1998, meanwhile, an Oystercatcher was doing its best to dodge traffic on Leads Road, East Hull, as it pecked for food on the tarmac! On that basis I wouldn't be surprised to find an Oystercatcher anywhere in the Hull area, though spring or autumn along the Humber offer the best opportunities of seeing them.

Avocet
(Pied Avocet)
Recurvirostra avosetta

In 1837 the Avocet was exterminated as a British breeding species when the last nest was flooded and robbed on the upper Humber at the mouth of the River Trent. Avocets only returned to breed on the Humber in 1992, at Blacktoft Sands, having recolonised the country in East Anglia fifty years earlier. The Avocet was recorded from the Hull area on just a handful of occasions during its long absence as a Humber breeding species. It is now best described as a very scarce passage migrant along our stretch of the estuary.

The first 20th Century record was of a single adult spotted by wildfowlers on the mudflats at Paull in mid August 1955. On 25th March 1984 E. W. Clubley saw two at King George Dock, while S. L. James saw another roosting with Curlews at Saltend on 1st December the same year. B. Richards saw two more at Saltend on 23rd May 1989 and a party of three were seen there on 23rd April 1998. Breeding colonies are now firmly re-established on the Humber. In autumn 2000 over 300 Avocets were present on the estuary, with colonies at Read's Island and Blacktoft Sands having a total of 71 breeding pairs between them that summer. With the recent increase in the region it is likely that more Avocets will occur in the Hull area in the future. The most likely place to find them is the Saltend/Paull mudflats during spring or autumn migration.

Little Ringed Plover
(Little Plover)
Charadrius dubius

The Little Ringed Plover, or LRP as it is often called by birdwatchers, only colonised Britain in 1938 and the first Yorkshire record was as recent as 1947. The date of the first bird to occur in the Hull area is not recorded for posterity, but none were found nesting anywhere in the East Riding in 1950. None of the 10 pairs nesting in the county in 1972 were in the Hull area, despite two pairs displaying near King George Dock (probably The Growths) in May 1970. A couple were seen on the Saltend mud in 1985, one in mid April and the other mid May, but none were seen in 1986 and they appear to be very infrequent there to this day.

Shallow floodwater pools on fields to the east of North Bransholme were the best place to find Little Ringed Plovers in Hull from the mid to late 1980s, with the first being two on 29th June 1985 and three on 23rd July. One was back at North Bransholme on 24th April 1987, with two on 5th May, and breeding was confirmed when B. Richards saw four tiny chicks on 14th June. Three survived until 6th July at least and the last bird was seen on 27th. The nest site was just south of the Foredyke Stream, between North Bransholme and the Holderness Drain, and while a second pair was also present nearby it is not clear if they bred. A pair returned in 1988 and up to three birds were present between 19th April and 22nd June, but any breeding attempts apparently failed. The site was now becoming a little overgrown for Little Ringed Plovers, who prefer barren, stony ground alongside water, and just a single bird returned in 1989 on 9th May.

That was it as far as North Bransholme is concerned and they have not been seen there since. Indeed, Little Ringed Plovers have been very scarce around the whole of the Hull area since that time. The only other records to reach me are of one at the Bransholme Sewage Works on 13th April 2000 and a juvenile at Castle Hill Farm, between Sutton and Swine, in late July. This last bird raises hopes that breeding may have occurred locally that year. The Little Ringed Plover is nevertheless best described as an uncommon passage migrant and sporadic breeder in the Hull area. I am sure, however, that if suitable habitat were created for them then the nesting birds would soon return.

Ringed Plover
Charadrius hiaticula

Much more common in the Hull area than the Little Ringed Plover, the Ringed Plover is also more restricted to the Humber and the immediate vicinity. In 1967 Boylan stated that the Ringed Plover was merely a "scarce passage migrant" on the foreshores in the old Hull boundary but numbers were much higher at nearby Saltend. Breeding was also occurring in the Hull area soon afterwards, with three pairs on The Growths (east of King George Dock) and another pair on the shore near Hessle in 1970 being the first proven breeding in the upper Humber. Two pairs were also present on The Growths in the summer of 1979 and a clutch of four eggs was found there on 29th May 1985, although the site was known as Saltend Marsh by then. A pair with two young were seen on Victoria

Dock on 16th August 1986 but breeding seemed to dry up during the 1990s. R. Eades then saw an adult bird acting suspiciously on an area of rubble off Wellington Street, at the eastern end of Albert Dock, in late March 1999. Return visits by Eades were rewarded by a pair displaying in mid April and an adult sitting tight, probably on eggs, by early May.

Ringed Plovers are much more abundant in the Hull area as passage migrants and winter visitors and concentrations at the primary site for them, Saltend, can be very high. Spring passage is usually heavier than in autumn but peak numbers are quite variable. The build up at Saltend occurs in late April when the late winter population of typically less than 50 birds grows to as many as 400 by mid May before invariably dropping to less than 20 by mid June. Many of these May birds are of the smaller and darker Arctic race, *Charadrius hiaticula tundrae*, sometimes numbering several hundred, but they have generally moved on by the second week of June.

Counts at Saltend start to creep up again from mid July, with perhaps 50 birds by the end of the month. August sees another influx as both nominate and *tundrae* birds pass through again on their way south. Up to 260, more typically 150, can be found at Saltend by the end of the month. Many more are scattered along the whole shoreline at low tide, up to the Humber Bridge and beyond. Numbers remain high, if not still increasing, into September but the proportion of *tundrae* among them is generally much lower than in spring. The autumn passage is often much more protracted than that of the spring, however, and while numbers are falling by October there can still be well over 100 into November. The late autumn period is nevertheless characterised by fluctuation. The peak November count in 1984, for example, was just 10 while the following year it was almost 150. This trend carries on until the following spring, albeit with ever decreasing numbers, with anything between five and 50 birds remaining by mid April. The following week sees the first passage birds arriving and the build up begins once more.

The Ringed Plover, then, is a common passage migrant on the Humber shore, especially at Saltend, but is very rare inland; I saw one or two at North Bransholme around 1990 but have received no other such reports. A visit to Saltend at any time of the year will produce at least a handful of Ringed Plovers, although the shoreline off Clive Sullivan Way typically holds less than 10. Breeding, on the other hand, is possibly an annual occurrence in the Hull area somewhere within sight of the Humber, but in this respect the species is clinging on by a little more than a toehold.

American Golden Plover
Pluvialis dominica
On 8th September 1998 B. Richards identified a moulting adult of this species on the Saltend mudflats.

This is the only record from the Hull area of this rare North American wader and it was duly accepted by both the Yorkshire Naturalists' Union and the British Birds Rarities Committees.

Pacific Golden Plover
Pluvialis fulva

Like the American Golden Plover this species is rather similar to our European Golden Plover and also hails from North America, breeding farther west than *dominica* from Alaska and into Siberia. Yet again the Humber shore between Paull and Saltend proved its worth when a Pacific Golden Plover was spotted there on 7th July 1993. The bird remained on the Humber for much of July, mostly around Read's Island farther upstream, and this was its only visit to the Hull area.

Golden Plover
(European Golden Plover)
Pluvialis apricaria

The plaintive call of the Golden Plover is a familiar sound to anyone walking through farmland surrounding Hull or along certain sections of the Humber shore between late July and April.

Golden Plovers were regularly caught for the table in the old days and in 1560 the price in Hull was officially set at a penny each. At Christmas time in 1900 heavy rainfall attracted an unusually large number of Golden Plovers to floodwaters on farmland around Paull, with the local farmers taking the opportunity to make some easy cash by netting the flocks of Plovers and accompanying Lapwings to sell for food. This was the first time the practice had been carried out in the area in living memory, though farmers elsewhere in Holderness left the birds alone so that they could clear the fields of harmful insects.

Flocks of Golden Plovers were common on the fields of the northern and western suburbs of the city in the 1960s, a time when the land between Sutton and Wawne was mainly inhabited by sheep, and large flocks of birds have frequented the arable and wet fields along Priory Road between Hull and Cottingham for many years. A flock of 875 was present there on 27th November 1983, 1,000 were at Well Lane (north of Willerby) in January 1984 and 850 were at Haltemprice Farm the following March. In 1996 numbers at Priory Road rose from just 10 in September to over 1,000 by late October. Another favoured location since the 1970s has been the arable fields between Bransholme and Swine village, particularly those at Carlam Hill Farm when heavy rain creates pools of floodwater. A flock of 500 there on 22nd January 1994 rose to around 1,000 a fortnight later and remained so well into March. Over 640 were still present in early April though the last few dozen left on 27th of that month. One of these birds, sporting very wide white wing-bars, was seen throughout the previous week and indicated that the same individuals were present day after day.

Golden Plovers are usually in the company of Lapwings during winter and a mixed flock of around 1,000 was near Swine on 12th December 1999. Smaller flocks of 50 to several hundred Golden Plovers can often be found on almost any ploughed field or freshly sprouting arable crop throughout the Hull area from autumn onwards, though they do not seem very keen on rape fields.

The inland flocks appear to be based on the Humber, returning there to roost or feed when the mudflats and sandbanks are exposed. Flocks have frequently been seen arriving at Bransholme from the direction of Saltend around high tide, sometimes carrying on northwards to fields beyond Wawne, and very large numbers can be encountered at Saltend throughout autumn and winter. A thousand or more begin to gather there from late July and by mid September up to 4,000 may be present, although 7,250 were counted on 21st September 1998. October sees a big influx of Golden Plovers on the Saltend mudflats and 5,000 or more are regular. An incredible 20,000 were estimated to be present on 18th October 1997, however. Up to 10,000 have been logged from November to February although numbers decrease during March and April as birds move off to breed on the moors and bogs of Britain and northern Europe. Very few are left around Hull by late April and they are all but absent in May and June.

As the Humber is the source of the inland birds in the Hull area the numbers found in the fields generally reflects the pattern on the estuary, though they often aren't seen away from the Humber in any numbers until late October or November.

Grey Plover
Pluvialis squatarola

The earliest record of Grey Plovers in the Hull area comes from 1900 when an unusual inland flock was seen at Bilton on 21st December. Boylan (1967) mentions five passage records from the old Hull boundary during the 1960s. The frequent observation at Saltend between 1984 and 1986 showed Grey Plovers to be regular passage migrants in small numbers, primarily in autumn. Peak spring counts at this time were seven in May while in autumn a couple of birds in July typically built up to around 25 in October before decreasing again to perhaps five by December. Single figures were occasionally seen throughout the winter months.

Late 1990s counts at Saltend indicated that the number of Grey Plovers stopping off on spring passage had greatly increased over the previous decade. In 1997 a total of 63 were logged on 20th April and 71 on 28th May, with 94 on 22nd May the following year. The autumn peak for 1998 was just five birds during September, however, with one or two in all other months except June. This is strange, for why Grey Plovers should increase drastically during the spring but then fail to appear in the autumn is a mystery.

Grey Plovers are very rarely reported away from Saltend and the only recent records to reach me are of one flying up the Humber past Corporation Pier on New Years Day

1997 and a flock of 40 heading upstream past Hessle on 25th October 1999.

Lapwing
(Northern Lapwing)
Vanellus vanellus

This is likely to be the most familiar wader to most residents of the Hull area, as it is the most widespread and often most abundant member of the clan throughout the region. Lapwings were mentioned in the *Wildfowl at Hull* pricing list of 1560 under the name "Bastard Plover", with the sum of three-halfpence each being levied on them, and they were still being taken for the table right up to the 20th Century. In 1900 unusually large flocks of Lapwings were gathering in the fields around Paull in the company of Golden Plovers, and the local farmers began taking them with nets to sell on for food. It was the first time they had attempted this in living memory, although it was a well-used tactic for catching waders in general on the extensive wetlands north of Hull in the 18th Century.

At the beginning of the 20th Century it was perfectly legal to take Lapwing eggs for the table before April 15th but there was some concern at the time that this was seriously depleting the local breeding stock. Lapwings were very common back then, however, much more so than today, and the eggers argued that taking the early clutches actually improved the fortunes of the birds as chicks from later clutches were more likely to survive. It is unlikely that many people actually obeyed the law and stopped taking eggs come April 15th, however, and in the spring of 1901 the breeding Lapwings on Saltend Common were completely wiped out by egg collectors. The stoppage of the nearby East Hull shipyards was disastrous for breeding waders on the common as people were now free to wander over it at will, though the building of the chemical works there some years later was no doubt far worse! Come the 1920s there had been a huge decrease in breeding numbers in the East Riding and the species was virtually extinct as a breeder by 1923. Numbers gradually recovered over the following decades as the tradition for gathering eggs waned. By the 1960s Lapwings were breeding not uncommonly in the pasture fields surrounding Hull, right up to the suburbs. Boylan (1967) also tells us that they were very common passage migrants, often being seen over the city centre, and fairly common in winter.

The rapid expansion of Hull during the 1970s as it sprawled over the pastureland of Bransholme and Sutton Fields, combined with the gradual switch from livestock to arable in the remaining farmland, severely restricted the breeding opportunities for Lapwings in the area. A few pairs were breeding on the wet pasture off Priory Road in the 1980s, a pair tried to nest on Saltend Marsh in 1985 and up to eight pairs were nesting on fields just east of North Bransholme in 1989. A few scattered pairs also managed to hold on in other areas, breeding on spring-sown crops which gave them just the right amount of cover to nest in. Things got even worse, however, with the almost complete change to autumn-sowing of crops by the 1990s. By spring time the sward was now too tall and dense and Lapwings were unable to nest on most areas of farmland. By 1991 there were just three pairs at North Bransholme and breeding had ceased at the Priory Road fields by 1995. By the late 1990s the only regular breeding sites within the Hull boundary were on North Carr (east of Bransholme) and south of Carlam Hill Farm (east of North Bransholme). North Carr is permanent grassland while the near-by Carlam Hill field is regularly flooding arable land that is often left uncultivated until late in the spring. Up to five pairs now regularly nest at Carlam Hill with perhaps two more on North Carr. I was pleased to find 13 pairs between them in April 2001, however, after the very wet winter had created many shallow floodwater pools and left the fields too water-logged to sow crops.

The tumbling display flight is usually seen over the Carlam Hill fields from the middle of March. The first eggs appear in the last week of March or first week of April and chicks towards the end of the month, though they are rarely left in peace here. Aside from early ploughing and raids by Carrion Crows leading to nest failures, one of the Carlam Hill birds was shot by an airgunner on 5th May 1993. Later that month I watched a pair of Lapwings desperately mobbing a large male Pheasant that was threatening to eat the young chicks. Of 12 chicks seen in April 1994 only two could be found a month later. Despite these depredations the birds seem to return each year if they can find enough bare ground to feel secure about nesting on, and a flock of 23 at Carlam Hill on 26th June 1993 probably represented the whole local breeding population and their fledged young that year. While a few scattered pairs may still manage to rear young outside of the Hull boundary, the only indication of any success in recent years was the sight of four juveniles on floods south of Castle Hill Farm, between Sutton and Swine, on 27th July 2000.

Lapwings are much more common and widespread in the Hull area outside of the breeding season and the first small flocks start to arrive at Saltend in mid July. These are probably local breeders from Yorkshire, with the main build up not occurring until September when large flocks can suddenly appear overnight. Inland flocks begin to appear around then, with the first of 1992 at North Bransholme being 250 on 12th September. This had grown to 300 by 10th October. The first 91 on 10th September 1993 had swollen to 250 by 25th. In 1995 a flock on the Priory Road fields grew from 150 in September to 300 by October.

The numbers at Saltend increase steadily as the autumn progresses. A flock of 30 on the mudflats in July 1984 had grown to 117 by 10th November before jumping to 700 two days later. Numbers reached 900 the following month before climbing to almost 1,400 in January 1985. These late autumn and winter influxes often involve Continental birds that are escaping cold weather in Europe. While these flocks often use the Humber at low tide they are pushed onto open fields throughout the Hull area come high tide. Floodwater near Carlam Hill Farm in January 1994 attracted 350 birds on 8th, this building up to 600 two weeks later. Around 500 were in fields between Bransholme and Swine in February 1998, with up to 2,000 the following winter in November and December. The largest gatherings recorded in the Hull area were reported from Saltend in the winter of 1998; 1,600 on the mudflats on 18th December grew to a whopping 3,000 later in the month before dropping back to 1,600 in January 1999.

Lapwings can clearly be very common in the Hull area during winter and on passage. Flocks can pass over anywhere and virtually any farmland or patch of damp ground may attract many hundreds, if not thousands, of birds. The breeding population around Hull is nevertheless small and threatened. The handful of pairs that persevere in breeding within the city boundary are clinging on by a toehold and could very easily be lost. This would be a great shame as there are not many industrial cities in Britain that can still boast the tumbling display flight of Lapwings in spring.

Knot
(Red Knot)
Calidris canutus

The Knot is mainly an autumn passage migrant in the Hull area, being irregular in spring and rare in winter. Boylan (1967) mentions five passage or winter sightings along Hull's waterfront during the early 1960s, but all other records come from Saltend in the mid 1980s and late 1990s.

The only records for 1984 were two flocks, of 10 and 28 birds, flying upstream at Saltend in mid November. Monthly peaks in 1985 were three in August, 138 in September, 95 in October, 36 in November and one in December. Occasional Knots were seen throughout the winter during periods of hard weather, though 90 flew east on 28th December. The only spring record for 1986 was of three birds on 3rd May and, more recently, the only record for 1997 was just a single bird on 25th May. It is not clear whether this dearth was due to a lack of birds or a lack of birdwatchers.

1998 was perhaps more representative of the status of the Knot at Saltend. Spring passage peaked at seven birds in May and 84 were counted on 26th June, a rather late date. A flock of 62 were back in late September, with 34 in October, three in November and just one in December.

Sanderling
Calidris alba

Sanderlings are lovely little birds that scamper along sandy beaches just ahead of the surf like clockwork toys. They are quite common on the Holderness coast in winter and, coming from the far north, they are often fairly tame and are a pleasure to watch as they chase the waves to pick up titbits. The lack of obviously sandy beaches in the Hull area means that there is not much to tempt Sanderlings away from the coast, though a handful are usually seen on passage each year at Saltend. Boylan (1967) gives just two winter records from Hull's waterfront between 1960 and 1966 but furnishes us with no dates or numbers. As for many of the waders, the only other records come from the two periods of regular observation and reporting from Saltend in the mid 1980s and late 1990s. Numbers changed little between the two periods and both indicate a light spring passage between the last week of April and first week of June, but especially the latter half of May, which peaks at 10 to 15 birds. Autumn passage may begin in early August and lasts until late October, the maximum count being 17 on 16th September 1998. Occasional birds may still pass through as late as November.

Little Stint
Calidris minuta

The Little Stint is a regular passage migrant in the Hull area, overwhelmingly in autumn but in varying numbers. Almost all sightings have been at Saltend. Boylan (1967)

gives one record for Hull's waterfront in the early 1960s and a maximum of 15 were recorded at Saltend on 28th September 1970. The peak count at Saltend the following year, however, was just five on 3rd September.

Lack of observation meant that the Saltend records dried up until 1984, when one was seen in mid August, while 1985 gave the first detailed coverage at that site. The first of that year was one on 18th August and this or another was present until the end of the month, with another in the first week of September, two in the second and third weeks and an impressive 16 on 22nd. Seven could be found until the end of September and six until mid October. The last bird of the year was present until 2nd November. The following year, 1986, saw a spring record of two birds on 17th May, while up to three on and off between 25th July and 12th October showed just how much numbers can vary from year to year.

Lack of coverage and reporting meant records subsequently dried up until the late 1990s. Another spring bird occurred on 1st June 1997 but it was a poor autumn with just single birds on two dates in early September. The spring of 1998 was better than most and singles were present on four dates between 8th and 24th May. The maximum that autumn was 11, all juveniles, on 14th September.

Mid to late September is undoubtedly the best time to look for Little Stints at Saltend, although autumn passage is often protracted and can last from the last week of July to the first week of November. Dozens of birds pass through Saltend in a good autumn but spring passage is much more muted; one should not expect more than a handful of birds to pass through between early May and early June, with most occurring around mid May.

Temminck's Stint
Calidris temminckii

A much rarer passage migrant than the Little Stint, the Temminck's Stint tends to occur in spring rather than autumn. While around half have occurred at Saltend there have also been several inland records.

The earliest record for a Temminck's Stint in the Hull area comes from William Yarrell's 1843 *British Birds*, which states that one had occurred near Hull. The next was not until 1985 when one was spotted at Saltend on 14th May and another turned up on 29th September, this being the only autumn record for the Hull area to this day. An amazing ten days in May 1988 brought no less than four individual Temminck's Stints to shallow floodwater pools on the large field south of Carlam Hill

87

Farm, immediately east of North Bransholme. The first was present between 3rd and 5th May and the second bird, clearly different from the first due to differences in their stage of moult, was present between 8th and 10th. The next day a pair of totally different birds, in almost full summer plumage, were on the same pool, remaining until 12th May. Such a run of records on little more than a few large puddles on an inland field is quite amazing and, needless to say, a Temminck's Stint has not been seen there since.

Attention switched to Saltend again in 1998 when another concentration of sightings challenged the North Bransholme record. The first was one on 24th May, with another on 29th and then another between 1st and 2nd June, but it is not clear if all of these sightings involved different birds. In addition to the above, I have also received an undated record from East Park but I am unable to provide any more details.

May, then, is the prime month for finding a Temminck's Stint around Hull. While Saltend is probably the safest bet one may turn up on just about any flash of shallow water. As the above records indicate, however, they are rather rare and extremely unpredictable in occurrence.

Curlew Sandpiper
Calidris ferruginea
The Curlew Sandpiper is a regular passage migrant in the Hull area and, although numbers vary from year to year, daily counts rarely exceed 10 birds. Autumn passage is usually much stronger than in spring, with September being the prime month to find them probing in the mud among the Dunlin. Most of the records come from the mud-flats around Saltend and Paull.

There are no early records from the Hull area and this is probably indicative of a lack of observers in the early days. The first documented sighting was of 10 birds at Saltend on 28th September 1970. The next were in September 1978, a year that saw an influx of Curlew Sandpipers in Yorkshire, when 16 were at Saltend on 11th and 17 were at Paull on 14th. A single spring bird was seen at Saltend on 17th May 1985 and the following autumn saw unprecedented numbers recorded there, this being the best year on record. The first bird arrived on 20th August with a peak of 67 present by 12th September before numbers fell to 20 by the end of the month, though 42 were counted on 25th. Between one and 13 birds were present throughout October and the last ones were a very late couple on 18th November. There was a light spring passage again the following year and singles were seen on two dates in mid May. The autumn passage between 5th August and 13th October was very poor compared with 1985, the maximum count being just nine.

Things were pretty much the same at Saltend in the late 1990s. 1997 saw the first bird on 29th July with singles on three dates in mid to late August and up to seven in September, the last being on 24th. There was an unusually good spring passage in 1998; the first was on 8th May while 29th had eight and one or two were still around until 6th June. Autumn passage was also a little unusual that year with singles on 21st and 28th July being rather early. A peak of 17 on 16th September was a respectable count and five were still present on 2nd October. Numbers were a little down again in 1999, the latest year I have figures for, with a maximum of just five on 17th September and only one or two on a couple of other days that month. Elsewhere on the waterfront that year, four were on Hessle Foreshore on 11th September.

Prospective wader watchers should therefore head for Saltend or the Paull embankment around mid May to look for the handful of spring migrants passing through in their lovely summer plumage. However, autumn passage between late July and late October, but especially September, would seem to be the best time to find them. You should nevertheless consider yourself quite fortunate if your day count reached double figures.

Purple Sandpiper
Calidris maritima

Bridlington Harbour is the nearest regular wintering site for Purple Sandpipers, birds that are tied to rocky coastlines. The closest thing to a rocky shore that the Hull area has to offer is the boulder base to the Saltend and Paull embankment and the concrete waterfront of the Hull docks. It is places such as these that have occasionally played host to a Purple Sandpiper or two, mostly on passage.

Up to three birds were found at Paull in the 1978/9 winter, although exact dates are not recorded. The next were singles at Saltend on 14th May and 26th September 1985. Two were at King George Dock on 20th January 1987 but, in common with most other Saltend and dockland specialities around Hull, lack of observation and reporting after that meant there were no more records until the late 1990s. On 25th April 1997 a Purple Sandpiper was found in the Victoria Dock area and the most recent report came from Saltend on 5th October 1998.

Reading between the lines, it is probable that Purple Sandpipers are annual visitors to the Hull area on both spring and autumn passage, even occasionally in winter, though numbers are unlikely to be more than half a dozen per year. While the Saltend and Paull areas have produced the lion's share of the records around Hull so far, probably due to greater coverage there, any hard shoreline is likely to prove equally attractive.

Dunlin
Calidris alpina

The earliest allusion to Dunlins around Hull comes from the 1560 *Wildfowl at Hull* manuscript, which listed the price of "stintes" at fourpence per dozen. The Dunlin is a common winter visitor and passage migrant along the Humber shore of the Hull area, with this contingent being part of the 15,000 or so birds that winter on the estuary as a whole in most winters. Dunlins are most abundant during autumn passage from late July to December and the mudflats at Saltend attract important concentrations. Large flocks of 'stints', as Dunlin were still being called, were noted here as early as 1901. Up to 1,500 could be found at Saltend during autumn in the 1960s,

decreasing to maybe 400 in the early months of the year, while over 1,500 were counted along the Humber between Hull and Brough in February 1967. There appears to be some movement between feeding sites within the estuary, with a first-winter bird ringed at Spurn in October 1974 being recaught at Hull five days later.

Most birds have left for their breeding grounds in the uplands of Britain, Northern Europe and the Arctic Circle by mid May, though almost 600 were still on the Paull mudflats on 10th May 1984 and 3,026 were counted at Saltend on 8th May 1998. The mudflats remain very quiet during June and the first returning birds arrive around the middle of July. Saltend numbers peaked at 1,650 in July 1997 before increasing to over 2,000 during October and November. A total of 3,156 were counted on 16th November 1998, this being the highest count reported in the Hull area.

As the passage birds leave Saltend at the end of November numbers decrease and fluctuate until spring. Around 1,000 is a typical count between December and March, though as few as 150 or as many as 3,000 may be present on some days. A spring peak occurs in April as passage birds pass through, when 1,500 or more can again be encountered regularly. Numbers are much lower along the western waterfront, from St Andrew's Quay to the Humber Bridge, with several hundred being more likely than the thousands that frequent Saltend.

Small numbers of Dunlin sometimes visit inland sites in the Hull area, typically an open field with a flood-water pool. These birds are clearly attached to the wader flocks based on the Humber, often being in the company of Redshanks or Golden Plovers, and they have been seen arriving from and leaving in the direction of the estuary. Up to four were regularly seen on the Priory Road fields between January and March in the 1980s and one was seen in a Cottingham garden during very hard weather on 18th February 1985. In 1994 a flooded field at North Bransholme attracted some of the largest inland flocks of Dunlin seen in the Hull area. Up to 95 were present in February of that year, rising to 170 the following month but decreasing to just three in April. This flock was seen to arrive from the direction of Saltend on several occasions, usually around high tide, and seemed to have followed the Golden Plovers inland as the mud-flats flooded. Cold weather rarely affects Dunlins as the mudflats usually remain ice-free, but in the big freeze of early 1963 starving Dunlins at the eastern docks were reduced to eating bread tossed to them by kind dockers.

Broad-billed Sandpiper
Limicola falcinellus
With just a few sightings in Britain each year the Broad-billed Sandpiper is a very rare passage migrant, yet the Saltend mudflats saw a remarkable run of records in the mid 1980s. On 22nd May 1985 S.

Griffiths was looking over the waders on the Saltend mud when two small "stint-like" birds flew in from the Lincolnshire side of the Humber and landed on the mud right in front of him. Griffiths immediately identified them as Broad-billed Sandpipers, almost in full breeding plumage, before telephoning S. L. James who confirmed the identification a short while later. Griffiths and James took detailed

descriptions of the birds and watched them every day until their departure on 29th May. As if this wasn't enough, Griffiths and James found a third bird on 27th, a much greyer bird than the accompanying pair, though this was not seen again. What's more, yet another Broad-billed Sandpiper was seen on 1st June though this may have been one of the previous birds. Nothing like this group of sightings, with a trio together and possibly four birds in all, has occurred before or since in Yorkshire. The only other record for the Hull area is of a single bird, again at Saltend, found by the fortuitous S. L. James on 17th May 1986, which was also present the next day.

Ruff
Philomachus pugnax

The Ruff almost certainly bred on the carrs and marshes surrounding the old town of Hull, places that now make up the suburbs, and was also a common passage migrant until the extensive drainage works of the 18th and early 19th Centuries. Local Ruffs were once great delicacies and Pennant's *British Zoology* (1766) tells us that in the East Riding they were trapped in nets about 40 yards long and up to 8 feet high which were placed in shallow water or on dry ground at an angle of 45 degrees, close to reeds in which the fowler could conceal himself. A stuffed bird, known as a 'stale', attracted the Ruffs under the nets and then the fowler, waiting for his moment, could pull a string and the net would fall. The trapped birds were kept alive to be fattened on bread and milk, hempseed and boiled wheat. If the fowlers were in a hurry to serve up their Ruffs, however, they added sugar, which made the birds "in a fortnight's time a lump of fat". In that state they each sold for two shillings, sometimes two shillings and sixpence. Pennant says that they were summer migrants, coming into the fens at the end of April and leaving around Michaelmas (late September), saying that they laid four eggs in a tuft of grass at the beginning of May and sat for about a month.

Ruffs are now just regular passage migrants on the Humber and also shallow floodwater pools, though never in any great numbers. Spring passage lasts from late March to May, when the ruffed males can be seen. Autumn passage begins in July and lasts until mid October, with the majority of birds at this time tending to be juveniles. The odd wintering bird is very occasionally reported: one was on the Priory Road fields on 2nd February 1984, one was at Saltend from 15th to 20th January 1984 with two on 16th to 18th, and one was at Paull on 21st February 1988. High spring counts include six at Saltend on 27th April 1985 and 14 at North Bransholme on 28th April 1987, though gatherings of more than two or three birds are uncommon. The Saltend area sees similar numbers in autumn and occasional birds alight at West Wharf and Paull, but drainage at North Bransholme means Ruffs no longer stop off there.

Jack Snipe
Lymnocryptes minimus

The Jack Snipe is a rather scarce winter visitor that nevertheless turns up somewhere around Hull in most years. The earliest record is of one at Hessle "in the early months" of 1947. Boylan (1967) gave just one record for Hull itself in the 1960s but suggested that the species "possibly occurs more often". There was a cluster of records in 1985 beginning with one at North Bransholme in late February, another on and off at Saltend Marsh between January and April and a late bird at North Bransholme again from 12th to 18th May.

A singleton was picked out among a large party of Snipes on Willerby Carrs in mid November the same year and another was back on Saltend Marsh in December, remaining until New Year's Day 1986. The only other sighting in 1986 was at Saltend Marsh on 27th April, another latish date. 1987 saw yet more birds at Saltend Marsh and North Bransholme, mainly in December. The remainder of the records come solely from North Bransholme as coverage petered out at other likely sites. Singles were seen there on 11th March 1989, 3rd October 1993 (the earliest autumn date for the Hull area) and 22nd January 1994. All of these last few birds were flushed from a wet field of rough grassland next to the Great Culvert pumping station on the

Holderness Drain, with this field also being guaranteed to produce Snipes in season.

Snipe
(Common Snipe)
Gallinago gallinago

Snipes were no doubt common breeding birds on the carrs and marshes of the Hull area before the land was drained, though the occasional pair still feel the lure of their ancestral breeding grounds and attempt to nest now and again. One such pair settled down to breed at Saltend Marsh in 1985 but without success, and I watched a male performing his 'drumming' display flight over the wet pasture behind the now demolished High Bransholme Farm, near the Holderness Drain in northeast Hull, on 5th May 1991. The outcome of any nest resulting from that occasion is unknown but sporadic breeding certainly occurred in the flooded fields around High Bransholme during the 1980s, until the council filled in most of the marshes around 1990. Most Snipes occur in the Hull area between September and late April and autumn passage sees the largest numbers. Boylan (1967) states that they were scarce within the old Hull boundary during the 1960s but a flock of 75 were seen at the Bransholme Sewage Works in January 1978. Birds were regularly seen on the wet fields off Priory Road during the 1980s, usually in the early mornings when there was less disturbance, and over 100 were on Willerby Carrs on 20th January 1984 and 20th November 1985. Recent counts there have been poor in comparison, with 21 in December being the highest total for 1999.

Accounts from Saltend in the mid 1980s make interesting reading and provide a rough guide to the seasonal waxing and waning of Snipe numbers. Autumn birds arrived early in 1984, the first being in July, though only a handful were present until a build-up to over 20 in October. Up to 35 in early November grew to 74 by 20th before dropping to a maximum of 10 in December. In 1985, the year of the breeding attempt, birds were present in every month except July. Snipes could still be found at Saltend in 1998, with up to five between February and April and returning birds being seen again in September.

Snipes are frequent in the marshy fields southeast of North Bransholme, between Bransholme Road and Foredyke Stream. Numbers fluctuate with the water levels in the fields, while frosts see them off completely, but the wet grassland has been attracting relatively large numbers since the mid

1990s. A site record of 46 on 29th October 1993 was eclipsed by 65 on 6th December 1999, although 20 or more can regularly be flushed during autumn and winter. Snipes may occur on any boggy wet field around the Hull area, however, and a winter walk through the carrs would not be complete without seeing a flushed Snipe zigzagging off towards the horizon.

Long-billed Dowitcher
Limnodromus scolopaceus

The Long-billed Dowitcher breeds in northwest North America through to northeast Siberia and just 215 had been recorded in Britain up until the year 2000. A summer plumaged bird claimed by S. L. James in the Earles Road/West Wharf area at the eastern docks on 9th August 1986 was deemed not proven by the British Birds Rarities Committee. Interestingly, an unidentified Dowitcher species was seen flying over Spurn Point just over two weeks later, so maybe there was a Long-billed Dowitcher hanging around the Humber after all?

Woodcock
(Eurasian Woodcock)
Scolopax rusticola

The strange Woodcock, the woodland wader with crepuscular habits and near all-round vision, is a regular passage migrant in small numbers in the Hull area as well as a scarce winter visitor. A pair nested on the outskirts of Hull in 1942 but this is the only breeding record.

The first Woodcocks of the autumn usually arrive from the Continent around the beginning of October, with the peak occurrence from mid month through November. Lesser numbers of birds are seen throughout the winter until another increase in March before the last birds leave by mid April. Most Woodcock sightings in the Hull area are of birds flushed from a copse, hedgerow or bushy wasteground and they can turn up almost anywhere. A surprising number are also seen in gardens and parks throughout the Hull area, including a late bird over Queen's Gardens on 21st April 1966 and another on nearby Lowgate the following October. Three were seen together in a Kirk Ella garden in February 1988, three more were in the Avenues area of Hull in 1996,

two were in East Park in October 1997 with another in November 1998 and one was seen on a garden lawn in James Reckitt Avenue (East Hull) in March 1998.

The cemeteries in Hull's inner suburbs regularly attract passage Woodcocks, with records coming from Hedon Road Cemetery and Eastern Cemetery, on Preston Road, as well as Northern Cemetery and the ones off Spring Bank West. The railway lines and drain banks that pass through the city also host the occasional Woodcock or two each year. Most probably occur in the hedgerows and copses around the city margin, however, and it is not uncommon to flush two or three quite close together. Six at Saltend on 10th December 1998 is the largest day count recorded in the Hull area and one or two birds are regularly seen here in season. On 8th November 1998 an injured Woodcock was picked up at Bransholme and was seen by a vet before being released at Holmpton. Others are not so lucky, however, and the Woodcock is still a favourite quarry of the rough-shooter.

Black-tailed Godwit
Limosa limosa

In the late 1970s the Black-tailed Godwit was a very scarce bird on the Humber and, despite being present in all months except May and June, the number of birds on the whole of the north bank of the Humber from Spurn to Blacktoft peaked at around half a dozen. Observation at Saltend in the mid 1980s revealed similar numbers, although concentrated at this one site, with up to seven birds on and off during spring passage (April to May) and autumn passage (August to November). In the 1990s, however, there was a phenomenal increase in passage Black-tailed Godwits at Saltend, which became one of the three main feeding areas on the Humber.

By 1998 the peak count at Saltend during April and May was 25 birds, while autumn numbers were going through the roof. On 29th July 1997 there were 155 Black-tailed Godwits on the Saltend mud, this being equivalent to about 10 years worth of records in the 1970s or 1980s! By 15th August, however, there were 274 birds, this growing to 427 on 5th September before dropping to 40 by mid October. Autumn passage was somewhat quieter in 1998, with a peak of around 30 birds between September and November though 73 were counted on 28th July 1998. The numbers kept rising and an impressive 305 were at Saltend on 10th August 2000. The spring flocks are mainly made up of birds of the Icelandic race, *Limosa limosa islandica*, which give way to birds of the nominate race, *Limosa limosa limosa*, in May. Some of these nominate

birds have even recently begun to breed around the Humber, though nowhere near the Hull area.

As with the Bar-tailed Godwit, a visit to Saltend must coincide with low tide if one wishes to see these birds, as they do not roost on the fields around Paull as do many other waders. Instead, the Saltend Black-tailed Godwits fly off to roost at North Killingholme, near Immingham, on the Lincolnshire side of the Humber.

Bar-tailed Godwit
Limosa lapponica

The earliest mention of this species in Yorkshire comes from Pennant's *British Zoology* (1766), in which it is stated that the "Red Godwit" was known to have been shot near Hull. Mainly a passage migrant, it is usually possible to find Bar-tailed Godwits at Saltend in every month of the year, perhaps with the exception of June.

Numbers have remained relatively constant since at least the 1980s, with spring passage peaking at up to 100 birds in May and autumn passage at 200 or more sometime between late July and October, though numbers do vary year on year. The wintering population at Saltend is generally under 20 birds and often less than 10. The spring build up begins in April, but by June there are virtually none left. Birds return from the breeding grounds around mid July, often with a rapid build up through August and into September. Very large numbers can be found on the mudflats at this time, with 190 on 14th September 1985, 290 on 1st October 1996 and 427 on 5th September 1997. Numbers drop rapidly in October and fall back to the wintering levels by November.

During the late 1970s at least, the Saltend Bar-tailed Godwits usually preferred to roost at Cherry Cobb Sands rather than join the Curlews and other waders that make the short trip over the embankment to feed and roost on the fields around Paull. This is possibly still the case, as I have not seen Bar-tailed Godwits on the Paull fields. While Saltend is the prime site for the species around Hull, Bar-tailed Godwits are occasionally reported from elsewhere on the Humber and six were at Hessle on 8th October 1999, but they have never been reported inland.

Whimbrel
Numenius phaeopus

A close relative of the Curlew, the Whimbrel is a scarce but regular passage migrant in the Hull area. Whimbrels are long-distance migrants and the birds that pass through the Hull area are on their way to breed on the bogs and tundra of the far north, including the Northern Isles, or winter on the coast of West Africa. The three passage records between 1960 and 1966 probably demonstrates a lack of observers rather than lack of birds, as small numbers can be found at Saltend, on inland pools or be seen flying overhead from mid April to mid May and mid July to early September.

Whimbrels may be encountered singly or in small groups and overhead flocks are often betrayed by their enigmatic call. Only small numbers pass through on spring passage, with maybe a bird or two on the mudflats at Saltend/Paull or on floodwater or pasture at North Bransholme or Priory Road fields. Occasionally a flock of a dozen or so may pass over anywhere in the Hull area or drop down to rest and feed at one of the aforementioned sites. Many more are seen on autumn passage, with peak numbers occurring in August, and gatherings of 20 or more can be found at Saltend at this time though few occur elsewhere.

Curlew
(Eurasian Curlew)
Numenius arquata

The Curlew has always been a regular passage migrant and winter visitor to the Hull area and can usually be found in all months of the year if one knows where to look for them. Over 100 were counted at Saltend on 15th April 1901 and in the 1960s Curlews were still fairly common off the eastern waterfront, despite the development, and were often heard calling over Hull on spring nights as they migrated overhead. By the late 1970s a small roost had developed on 'The Growths', reclaimed land to the east of King George Dock. Around 100 birds rested here during high tide when water covered their feeding grounds on the Saltend mud. This group represented the highest density of Curlew on the whole of the north bank of the Humber at that time. Counts at Saltend in 1985 were still around the 100 mark in January and February before passage birds inflated this to over 150 in March and April. The figure then dropped to below 40 from May to the end of July as the birds moved out to breed. Autumn passage swelled the

ranks again to between 100 and 170 from August to October and then back to 100 or so until the year end. Saltend is still the best place in the Hull area to find Curlews and numbers appear to have increased during the 1990s and a count of over 300 is now possible throughout autumn and winter, although 400 were present in January 1998. On 22nd October 2000 over 120 Curlews were feeding on the Paull side of the Saltend mudflats and, as the tide came in over the mud, the flock rose to roost in the fields on the other side of the embankment, showing a clear preference for stubble as opposed to the freshly ploughed soil nearby. These Curlews always prefer to roost in stubble fields if possible and they may also feed here as winter deepens. Numbers on the Humber tend to peak between September and March, the minima being between April and June. At this time numbers can fall below 10 birds although they soon pick up again and can be as high as 50 by late July.

It is not unusual to find the odd Curlew further inland in the Hull area, especially during spring and autumn passage. Ten were on the Priory Road fields on 9th September 1983, another flock of ten were just north of Cottingham on 11th November 1985 and 25 arrived from the direction of Saltend to feed on waterlogged stubble at North Bransholme on Christmas Day 2000. Single birds are the norm inland however, and wet fields at North Bransholme or Priory Road attract the odd feeding bird while others may be seen or heard almost anywhere as they fly over.

Curlews were mentioned in the *Wildfowl at Hull* manuscript of 1560 under the name of "Courlewe". The price set down in those days was sixpence each, this being more than for a Mallard, so they must have been either valued table birds, hard to come by or both.

Spotted Redshank
Tringa erythropus

While it is a scarce but regular passage migrant in East Yorkshire, very few Spotted Redshanks are recorded in the Hull area and it remains quite a rare bird. Spring passage in the county, from late April to the end of May, usually involves only a handful of birds and hardly any are seen around the city. One was seen at Paull on 15th May 1965, this being the only one reported that decade, with another spring bird at Saltend on 1st May 1985 and one again on 22nd June 1986. Numbers along the whole of the north bank of the Humber usually reach double figures in autumn passage, which lasts from July to November and peaks in

August, and a couple of birds may occur at Saltend each year at this time. In 1985 singles were at Saltend, on and off, from mid August to mid September, while 1986 saw singles from 2nd to 8th August and again on 13th October. Single figures also winter on the Humber so it is worth double-checking distant Redshanks at almost anytime of year. Lack of coverage is probably the reason for the absence of records and the few birds that do turn up are probably easy to miss among the many Common Redshanks out on the mudflats.

One or two Spotted Redshanks may very occasionally stop off at an inland site in the Hull area, with a floodwater pool on outlying farmland being the most likely scenario. One night in October 1990, just after 10pm, a party of Spotted Redshanks were heard calling as they flew over a house on the outskirts of Bransholme. It was estimated that at least three birds were involved, though it was impossible to be sure. The valley of the River Hull appears to be a migratory flyway for waders moving through East Yorkshire, so other Spotted Redshanks must surely pass unnoticed.

Redshank
(Common Redshank)
Tringa totanus

The Redshank is a relatively common winter wader in the Hull area, where it occurs on the shores of the Humber, inland floodwater pools or damp fields and along the River Hull at low tide.

Several writers remarked on the calling waders that could be heard passing over Hull during the night in the early part of the 20th Century and the Redshank was surely among them then as it is today. Redshanks were breeding on Saltend Common in the early 1900s, before it was industrialised, but the closure of the nearby East Hull shipyards at the end of the 19th Century was disastrous for them. The abandonment of the area meant people were now free to wander at will and pillage the nests, and up to six egg-hunters at once was a frequent sight here in the spring of 1901. Around the middle of the century the Redshank was a common passage migrant and winter visitor along Hull's east and west foreshores and up the River Hull. Redshanks were also resident all year round in the old Hull boundary at this time and breeding certainly occurred, probably on boggy wasteground along the Humber or in wet fields along the River Hull north of Stoneferry.

The Humber estuary holds important numbers of Redshank at various times of the year and counts in the late 1970s revealed a wintering population of up to 1,500 birds along the north bank between December and March. During this time a roost of up to 100 birds had become established on The Growths, reclaimed land between King George Dock and Saltend, with the birds feeding on the upper shore of the Saltend mud. This flock accounted for around 4% of the north bank population in 1978.

Autumn passage can swell numbers at Saltend to 300 or more from September to November as totals on the estuary reach 5,500 on the north bank alone. Spring passage is also well pronounced and large counts can again be made on the Saltend mudflats: 300 counted from Paull on 23rd April 1997 had fallen to 76 a week later, with 300 again in February 1999 and no less than 500 logged on the 23rd April 1998. These figures are significantly higher than those recorded during the mid 1980s when peak passage counts only occasionally topped 200. Fewer than 20 Redshanks are present at Saltend in May and June as birds move away to breed, but numbers build again from mid July and counts of up to 100 are possible by the end of the month. Numbers are somewhat lower on the western mudflats, from St Andrew's Quay to the Humber Bridge, with perhaps 50 being a typical count in autumn. Many of the Redshanks passing through and wintering in the Hull area are probably British birds, though many Icelandic Redshanks undoubtedly occur on passage. These northern birds are often tentatively identified by their larger size and darker colour but hard evidence comes in the form of three birds ringed as chicks in Iceland being recovered at Saltend.

Redshanks are frequent inland in the Hull area and any expanse of wet mud or flash of shallow water will attract them. In the mid 1980s up to 30 could be found on the Priory Road fields and Willerby Carrs between December and February, while up to 10 were attracted to flooded fields at North Bransholme in the late 1980s and early 1990s. Wet fields on the Sutton Fields Industrial Estate were drawing in very large numbers of Redshanks in the late 1990s, with the Oak Road playing fields on the west bank of the River Hull holding 155 on 26th February 1997, 91 on 9th February 1998 and 145 on 20th November. Small numbers feed along the River Hull at low tide and can often be seen anywhere from Victoria Pier to Wawne, with the odd bird moving on to the Bransholme Sewage Works as the tide rises. In February 1998 I found a dead Redshank in the carpark of 'PC World' on Clough Road. It had been killed by a car, probably while it roosted after feeding on the nearby River Hull.

Breeding is now a very rare occurrence in the Hull area. Open marshes or large areas of undisturbed floodwater may tempt the occasional pair if the water lasts until spring. One pair reared a single chick at Saltend Marsh (which developed on The Growths) in 1985 and breeding was proven at North Bransholme during the late 1980s. In 1991 a pair nested in marshy fields to the south-east of North Bransholme, but they were not successful.

Greenshank
(Common Greenshank)
Tringa nebularia

Boylan (1967) lists just three Greenshanks within the old Hull boundary between 1960 and 1966, all on passage on the Humber shore near the eastern docks. Counts from Saltend in the mid 1980s give a better indication of the species' status in the wider Hull area - a light spring passage of up to six birds at any one time occured between April and early June while the autumn passage lasted from the third week of July to the end of September. Despite 14 roosting at Saltend during high tide on 17th August 1984, the autumn counts rarely exceeded two birds at any one time and this state of affairs is still pretty much the case today. Predictably, Saltend appears to be the prime site for Greenshanks in Hull, although occasional birds can stop by at any freshwater pool or marsh.

Green Sandpiper
Tringa ochropus

Annual but by no means common, a Green Sandpiper may be flushed from a ditch, drain bank or beside a boggy pond at almost any time of year, though most birds occur on spring passage in April to May and particularly on autumn passage from July to September.

In contrast to most waders, Green Sandpipers shun the mudflats at Saltend but may still be found in the tidal channels, as well as the ditches behind the embankments. Records from Saltend include singles in late July and August 1985, 8th August 1986, 28th May 1996 and 12th August 1997. Boggy fields and wide drainage channels on the outskirts of Bransholme and between Cottingham and Hull have attracted several birds over the years. These are possibly the best places to look away from the Humber, although one could turn up in literally any wet field or ditch outside of the built up areas. Three were on flooded fields at North Bransholme, on and off, between 23rd July and 7th August 1987, with four on 4th. The occasional bird may also be found beside one of the quieter stretches of open water, such as the Thwaite Hall Lake, while one was in the company of Common Sandpipers at the Bransholme Sewage Works reservoir in September 1991.

Green Sandpipers at North Bransholme on 31st March and 30th November 1988 may have been early and late migrants or perhaps some of the occasional birds that stay to winter in the East Riding, such as the birds present near Cottingham from October 1984 to February 1985 and St Andrew's Quay on Boxing Day 2000.

Wood Sandpiper
Tringa glareola

The Wood Sandpiper is one of the rarer and more irregular waders to occur in the Hull area on passage. Just one was recorded in Hull between 1960 and 1966 but no other details are available. Wader counts on the north shore of the Humber in the late 1970s revealed just one in May and up to three in July and August, though these were not necessarily in the Hull area. One was seen on floodwater pools on a large field south of Carlam Hill Farm, North Bransholme, on 12th and 13th May 1985 and another was at Saltend in late August 1985. One was back on the pools at Carlam Hill Farm on 19th August 1987 but the only other record to have reached me is of one at Saltend again on 8th September 1998.

Common Sandpiper
Actitis hypoleucos

This wader is a regular and fairly common passage migrant throughout the Hull area and occurs in a wide variety of wet habitats from the Humber to the parks. Birds may be seen from mid April to late May and mid July to October, though autumn passage is much stronger than spring with the ratio being in the region of five to one. Peak counts usually occur in late July or early August and the greatest concentrations have been recorded on the Saltend mudflats and adjoining areas of foreshore along King George Dock. A total of 20 were counted on the dock foreshore on 6th July 1978 and again on 16th August the following year, with 13 at Saltend on 25th July 1984 increasing to 23 on 22nd August and

28 on 28th. Peak counts there in 1985 were four in May and 15 in late July, with five in April 1986 and 12 the following August. Counts at Saltend in more recent years include maximums of 11 on 28th July 1998 and 15 on 4th August.

Away from the Humber, sightings are regular along the River Hull at low tide and beside the reservoir at the Bransholme Sewage Works, with up to four together at the latter on several occasions. Birds are also occasionally seen beside the Thwaite Hall Lake in Cottingham, the Holderness Drain and rainwater floods such as those on the Priory Road fields or east of North Bransholme. Common Sandpipers are also seen annually beside the larger park lakes and three were in East Park on 28th May 1997. I have seen and heard birds over the rooftops in the streets around East Park on several occasions as disturbance eventually moves them on.

Wintering in Africa, the earliest recorded spring Common Sandpiper in the Hull area appears to be one on the Holderness Drain at Bransholme on 18th April 1992, though I imagine there have been others a little earlier than this. The last one of autumn was a rather late bird at Saltend on 31st October 1970.

While the sight and sound of a piping Common Sandpiper skimming away over the water is a welcome sight, the birds are also night migrants and can occasionally be located by their call on calm nights as they pass overhead, either singly or in small parties.

Turnstone
(Ruddy Turnstone)
Arenaria interpres

Turnstones are present on the Humber virtually all year round but are most abundant during autumn passage. Surprisingly, Boylan (1967) reported only three records in the old Hull boundary in the first half of the 1960s but they have always been much more frequent along the city waterfront and beyond than this implies.

The rocky Hessle foreshore, where the Humber cuts through the Wolds, is just the type of shoreline that Turnstones like and the building of the Humber Bridge did nothing to put them off, with 20 counted there in January 1981. Similar numbers were occurring on the other side of Hull too, and 16 were at Paull in August 1985 while birds were being seen in virtually every month around Saltend at that time. Peak monthly counts from Saltend between 1984 and 1986 revealed up to 20 being present up to early June before most birds left for their northern breeding grounds, with just a couple of birds being seen on and off in July until the autumn

build up towards the end of that month. Around 30 could be found in August, this being the best month of the year at Saltend in those days, before numbers settled down to 20 or less from September to the end of the year. Counts in the late 1990s revealed a broadly similar pattern. Reports from 1998 and 1999 indicated an increase at Hessle foreshore since the early 1980s with Turnstones being common throughout the year, except June and July, and numbers occasionally reached 200 or more. This is a significant proportion, perhaps a quarter, of the Humber's Turnstones.

There are also important Turnstone roosts around Hull and up to 40 were roosting on Albert Dock on 26th January 1999 before climbing to 220 on 19th February. A total of 280 were counted there the following December, this being the largest gathering of Turnstones ever reported in the Hull area. In April of the same year around 50 were roosting on a buoy in the Humber, numbered 28A, near the Humber Bridge.

Turnstones are very rare away from the Humber, but on 5th February 1994 I saw one feeding on floodwater pools on a ploughed field at Carlam Hill Farm, North Bransholme. The bird was in the company of large numbers of Lapwings, Golden Plovers and Dunlins and had evidently followed them from Saltend as they moved inland to feed while high tide covered the mudflats; the other waders were frequently seen to arrive from and depart in that direction over the following weeks. What may have been the same individual was back on the Carlam Hill field on 6th March but I have received no other records of inland Turnstones. The origin of the Turnstones visiting the Hull area is hinted at by an interesting ringing record from 1974 when a bird ringed as a chick at Vaasa, Finland, on 21st August was recaught at Hull just 53 days later.

Grey Phalarope
Phalaropus fulicarius

The peculiar little Grey Phalarope has been recorded just once in the Hull area, with one at Saltend from 5th to 6th September 1988 being seen by many observers.

Pomarine Skua
Stercorarius pomarinus

The Pomarine Skua, known as the Pomatorhine Skua until the middle of the 20th Century, is a rare autumn passage migrant along the Humber off the Hull area. The first documented occurrence was of an unseasonal bird that hung around off Hessle during early January 1979. The autumn of 1985 was the best of the century for this species in the Hull area, with incredible numbers recorded off Saltend. The first was a lone bird flying upstream on 25th September, followed by another on 6th October, before 15 moved upstream on the morning of 18th November alone. The following day saw an amazing 45 being logged off Saltend, with singles lingering over the next few days until 24th. Three went upstream again on 30th November and were followed by another on 2nd December before the last on 8th. Most of the birds seen that autumn were immatures and they were usually first noticed arriving high from the east, circling over the Humber and, according to S. L. James, looking like Buzzards before dropping down to head upstream. Some also hung around to chase gulls, the parasitic urge being strong in all Skuas.

No more Pomarine Skuas were reported in the Hull area until 1993, however, when one was near the Humber Bridge after easterly gales that had also brought in a couple of Long-tailed Skuas, three Arctic Skuas and around 30 Great Skuas! The autumn of 2000 was better than most and produced a Pomarine Skua at the Humber Bridge on 6th

November and an immature flying east there on 27th, all providing further evidence that a November vigil over the Humber offers the best chance of finding one of these birds around Hull.

Arctic Skua
Stercorarius parasiticus

The most frequently sighted Skua in the Hull area, most Arctic Skuas have occurred on autumn passage and all have been on the Humber. The first documented record was in 1962 when one passed upstream at Hull on the typical date of 9th September. Boylan (1967) gave two more passage records for Hull between 1960 and 1966 but provided no further details. One was at Hessle Haven on the very strange date of 7th January in 1979 with another slightly odd record being one heading inland at Saltend on 23rd May 1985. As with the Pomarine Skua, however, the autumn of 1985 was probably the best ever for Arctic Skuas around Hull and a whopping 33 were logged at Saltend on 14th September, while around 10 were present throughout the month. Most of these birds were feeding on the

Humber and not actively migrating, though 16 were moving upstream on 7th September and five followed them the next day. Six were still at Saltend on 6th October with up to three stragglers being seen on and off until late November. There were more unusual records in 1986, in terms of date rather than numbers, with three heading east at Saltend on 21st June and another couple of birds the same month being decidedly unseasonal. A light autumn passage that year lasted from 26th August until 1st November and usually involved just one or two birds on most dates, though nine flew downstream on 26th August. The following autumn, in 1987, was all but a washout and just one was seen at Paull on the rather early date of 4th July. On 27th August 1988 an observer at Sunk Island, several miles downstream of Hull, counted over a hundred Arctic Skuas flying upstream but only 23 later flew back towards the open sea, suggesting that the other 85 all continued upstream and probably passed Hull.

A decrease in observers looking over the Humber since the mid 1980s led to a subsequent decline in the number and frequency of Arctic Skuas reported off Hull and the adjoining waterfronts. Three seen heading upstream past Hessle on 13th September 1993 showed that Arctic Skuas were still occurring on passage but were probably just not being recorded, though things improved a little towards the end of the decade. In 1997 a juvenile was seen off Victoria Dock on 19th August and two were at Sammy's Point, now home to 'The Deep', at the mouth of the River Hull on 20th September. Records from 2000 were a little later, with three at the Humber Bridge during an easterly blow on 6th November and a late bird at St. Andrew's Quay on 22nd December.

Long-tailed Skua
Stercorarius longicaudus

This member of the Skua tribe breeds in the high Arctic and winters in the Atlantic Ocean, being only a rather scarce and irregular autumn passage migrant on the Yorkshire coast. Large numbers can pass the coastal watchpoints in some years, such as 1988 and 1991, after good breeding seasons in the far north and the vast majority move through between August and late October. There are just two records for the Hull area, however, both on the Humber. The first was of two juveniles at the Humber Bridge after easterly gales on 13th September 1993. The only other record came on 19th September 1997 when a single, unaged, bird flew northwest at Victoria Dock and inland towards the River Hull.

Great Skua
Catharacta skua

The old Shetland Isles name for the Great Skua, 'Bonxie', is in fairly common use among birdwatchers along the Yorkshire coast and is the name I usually call it by, being somewhat less clumsy than the 'standard' one and a little more informal. Not that the Bonxie is a friendly bird, however, as it is a powerful and formidable predator and harasser of all other smaller seabirds, regularly forcing gulls to disgorge their catch of fish. A visit to the breeding colonies in northern Scotland will soon show their vicious streak as they will readily dive bomb you, even striking your head, if you wander too close to their nest. In the Hull area, however, they are merely uncommon and irregular passage migrants on the Humber between late August and early November, sometimes after being blown upstream by strong easterlies.

The first record comes from Boylan (1967) who mentions one passage record between 1960 and 1966 but gives no further details, though this was probably the bird seen off Hull in October 1962 and reported in the Yorkshire Naturalists' Union Ornithological Report for that year. The next were not until 1985 when a dedicated group of birdwatchers, none more so than S. L. James, put in many hours of observation at Saltend and the eastern docks. Single Bonxies were seen on five dates between September and November that year, with three on 11th September. Another was seen flying upstream the following year, on 26th August, this being the earliest Bonxie recorded in the area.

13th September 1993 was something of a red letter day for Skuas at the Humber Bridge, not least for Bonxies, as easterly gales had encouraged all four regular British species well upstream to be seen by a lucky few observers. This bonanza included at least 30 Bonxies, heading a cast of three Arctic Skuas, a couple of Long-tailed Skuas and a Pomarine Skua, with nothing like this number of Bonxies having been reported before or since. The only other reported sighting of Bonxies in the Hull area was a muted echo of 1993, when two were watched at the Humber Bridge after easterly gales on 6th November 2000.

It is highly likely that a small number of Bonxies wander up the Humber in most autumns, being either unseen or unreported, though if a strong easterly blow has been a feature of the previous day or two then expectations may justifiably be raised.

Mediterranean Gull
Larus melanocephalus

The 'Med' Gull used to be an extreme rarity in Britain until a range expansion in Europe fuelled an increase in British sightings from the 1960s onwards. A pair bred in southern England in 1968, creeping up to 31 pairs in 1992 and by 2000 at least 70 pairs were nesting in English gull colonies. This change in status was reflected in sightings in East Yorkshire, these being rare but annual by the 1970s at well-watched sites such as Spurn before increasingly rapidly since then. The first record for Hull did not occur until 1984 when one was spotted at Saltend. The Saltend mudflats were, and still are, the best place to find Med Gulls in the Hull area and have regularly produced birds since the mid 1980s, when people started looking. The build up in records there and elsewhere in the Hull area is worth documenting and is outlined below:

1984: an adult in full summer plumage at Saltend on 7th July.

1985 (all Saltend): an adult with a partial hood on 20th August; a first-winter and a second-winter in the gull roost 22nd October; presumably the same first-winter on 23rd and 26th October; an adult in the gull roost on 1st and 3rd December; probably the same adult at nearby West Wharf on 18th and 28th December.

1986: a first-winter at Saltend on 26th February; an adult at Saltend on 22nd March; maybe the same adult over a Kirk Ella garden on 28th March.

1988: a first-summer at Saltend on 18th May.

1990: one "in Hull" in late August and again on 26th October.

1991: one at Hessle on 24th September.

1993: one at Hedon on 9th February. A definite increase in records during the late 1990s coincided with an upsurge in the British breeding population. Regular watching at Saltend produced at least seven birds in 1996, five in 1997, six in 1998, at least three in 1999 (a bad recording year) and five in 2000 (though, again, not a good recording year):

1996 (all Saltend): a second-summer on 3rd July; an adult from 11th to 17th July and 8th to 13th August; two adults and a second-winter on 17th September; a phenomenal six adults in the roost on 19th September with one again on 25th; a first-winter on 30th September; an adult on 12th December.

1997: an adult at Saltend on 16th July; two adults and two first-summers at Saltend on 23rd July; three still at Saltend on 25th July; an adult at Saltend on 30th July; three adults at Saltend on 8th, 15th and 26th August with one adult from 11th to 13th; one adult at Saltend on 3rd September and 7th November; an adult in East Park on 7th and 17th November, and again on 17th December.

1998 (all Saltend): a first-summer on 24th and 29th June; a second-summer on 28th July; an adult on 5th, 16th and 26th August and 2nd, 14th and 16th September; two second-winters on 8th September; four adults on 2nd October; one adult on 19th October.

1999: an adult at Bransholme Sewage Works on 22nd January; an adult at Saltend on 20th August and another on 21st November.

2000: an adult west past Hessle fore-shore on 4th March; an adult at Hedon foreshore on 10th August; a first-winter at Hessle on 18th November; an adult at St Andrew's Quay on Christmas Eve; a second-winter at St Andrew's Quay on 28th December.

The above records show that the majority of Med Gulls seen in the Hull area are adults, though this may be due to the fact that this is by far the easiest age group to identify. Birds can turn up at almost any time of year although most occur in late summer and autumn, with the ones seen between May and early July often being sub-adults - the mature birds presumably being away at the breeding colonies. While Saltend has provided the bulk of the records, anywhere that attracts gulls in the Hull area is likely to harbour a Med Gull at some point, particularly areas bordering the Humber. With the

British population going from strength to strength it looks as if the very attractive Mediterranean Gull is going to become an increasingly familiar sight in the Hull area.

Laughing Gull
Larus atricilla

Two, possibly three, examples of this North American gull have crossed the Atlantic Ocean to be recorded in Hull, incredibly all in the same year with none before or since. The first was found by P. Coupland on 16th April 1984 when, on a visit to photograph the waterfowl at East Park, he noticed an unusual gull swimming among the Common and Black-headed Gulls on the lake. The bird eventually settled on a log alongside three Black-headed Gulls and Coupland was able to take several pictures, revealing the bird to be a second-year Laughing Gull moulting out of first-winter plumage.

Later that year, on 9th November, A. Wrightson discovered a second-winter Laughing Gull on wet playing fields off Wold Road in West Hull. Probably the same bird as the one seen at East Park that spring, this time it hung around until New Year's Day the following year, attracting many birdwatchers and twitchers throughout its stay. The bird settled into a regular pattern of arriving at Wold Road most mornings at around 7.30 am, often favouring the area around Bristol Road, before moving to the Priory Road fields with the local gulls later in the day. Interestingly, what was possibly the same bird was discovered up the coast at Filey on 23rd July that summer when a second-year Laughing Gull was seen among a flock of the usual gulls sat on the end of the Brigg.

The story was not over yet, however, for on 14th December 1984, while the Wold Road bird was still in residence, a second-winter Laughing Gull that was considered to be a different individual from the other one was found at William Wright Dock by S. L. James.

Little Gull
Larus minutus

Little Gulls are rather scarce birds on the Humber, despite being regular passage migrants along the Yorkshire coast as they move between their breeding grounds in Scandinavia and Eastern Europe and wintering areas off Western Europe and in the Mediterranean. All records in the Hull area have come from the Humber, usually in autumn from September to November.

The years 1960 to 1966 produced two records, sadly undated, while regular watching at Saltend in the mid 1980s revealed that a handful of Little Gulls were annual on the Humber. One or two birds were seen here on at least one day in almost every month from February to October in 1985-6, with a higher frequency in autumn. These birds were often sub-adults, though four adults passed by on 25th July 1986. Irregular coverage since then has resulted in infrequent sightings but easterly gales in September 1993 brought 15 Little Gulls well up the Humber between Hessle and North Ferriby on 13th and a first-summer bird was at Saltend on 8th July 1996. In 1998 a first-summer bird was seen at Saltend on 11th June and three were recorded on 6th October. More recently still, a further three birds were at the Humber Bridge on 6th November 2000 and a late adult was at Paull on 11th December.

An autumn vigil over the Humber therefore appears to be the only way one is likely to encounter the Little Gull in the Hull area, although the precious few appearing each year mean a certain amount of luck is required.

Sabine's Gull
Larus sabini

Sabine's are highly oceanic gulls that breed in the High Arctic of Siberia and North America and winter in the southern Atlantic. Small numbers are regularly reported off British coasts when autumn storms blow them towards shore. The only record for the Hull area occurred after easterly gales blew a juvenile Sabine's Gull well up the Humber on 13th September 1993, where it was seen at the Humber Bridge.

Black-headed Gull
Larus ridibundus

Along with the Common Gull, the Black-headed Gull is one of the most familiar birds to be seen around Hull. The name is something of a

misnomer, however, as the head is not black at all but a deep chocolate-brown and even then only in the spring and summer, being reduced to a dark 'ear-like' mark behind the eye in winter. Further more, this is the real 'common gull' in the area, outnumbering the so-called Common Gull in virtually all situations. This was not always the case, however, as back in the 1960s Boylan called the Black-headed Gull "the second commonest gull in Hull", after the Common Gull. Despite large numbers gathering at the sewage outfall near St. Andrew's Dock in Boylan's time, Black-headed Gulls were only noted visiting places such as Northern Cemetery in wet conditions during the winter months, suggesting that they were fairly infrequent and not too common at all.

Despite 11,000 being counted along the Humber shore between North Ferriby and the mouth of the River Hull in January 1979 the number of Black-headed Gulls around Cottingham and northwest Hull was still being eclipsed by that of Common Gulls during the first half of the 1980s, though flocks of up to 350 could still be found in that area. Numbers roosting at Saltend during the mid 1980s told a different story, however, with Black-headed Gulls outnumbering Common Gulls by more than five to one. In late July 1984 observers counted 2,500 Black-headed Gulls coming to roost on the mudflats. This had risen to 4,000 by mid August, almost 8,000 by late October and 8,700 by mid November. By December numbers had rocketed to 20,000 and remained so well into the following year, dropping to 5,000 by March 1985, 300 in May and just 120 by mid June before returning birds took the numbers up to 500 by early July and the cycle began again. In my youth, during the 1980s, large flocks of Black-headed Gulls, intermingled with Common Gulls, could be seen flying in loose 'V' formations during late afternoons in autumn and winter as they passed south over Hull and made their way to the Saltend roost. A noticeable dwindling of the flocks in recent years suggests that many now prefer to roost elsewhere.

The variation in the numbers at the Saltend roost in the mid 1980s reflects the annual waxing and waning of the number of Black-headed Gulls throughout the Hull area that is still apparent today. The general trend is for a build up from July throughout the autumn towards a midwinter peak, then a decline to the nadir in late spring and early summer. Indeed, Black-headed Gulls are virtually absent around Hull from mid April to June while they are away breeding in large colonies around lakes, sand dunes, marshes and moorlands throughout Britain and Europe. There are no colonies anywhere near Hull, however, and the birds roosting at Saltend between mid April and June in the mid 1980s would have been non-breeding birds that had decided to linger in the area.

The first Black-headed Gulls to return from the breeding colonies appear from mid to late June and they often have juveniles among them. Despite the growing flocks around Saltend at this time, numbers throughout most of the Hull area remain fairly low until the autumn when a big influx of Continental birds occurs in November. The Saltend roost of the 1980s probably pulled in birds from a wide area that had spent their day feeding in surrounding towns and farmland, but local feeding flocks can also be large in midwinter. Around 2,000 were feeding at St. Andrew's Dock in the early months of 1985, around 500 used to gather on the filter beds at the Bransholme Sewage Works (when they were in operation) during mid winter in the early 1990s, 250 were on Priory Road fields in February 1996 and flocks of 50 to several hundred can often be found around many of the parks, playing fields and shopping centres at this time.

Many of the Black-headed Gulls that arrive in the November influx appear to hail from the Baltic, with one ringed as a chick on Lake Engure, Moskwa, in Latvia on 2nd June 1965 being found dead in Hull the following December. Another bird rung in Denmark was spotted on Hessle Foreshore in January 1997 and again the following December. Some birds have moulted into their dark hood as early as Christmas, but most do not assume breeding plumage until March and it is around then that birds start to drift away to the breeding grounds at home and abroad. On sunny spring days one can often see courting Black-headed Gulls wheeling and calling loudly overhead but by mid April most have gone, leaving just the non-breeding birds that linger around the Humber.

Black-headed Gulls often get a bad press, as many successful birds do, but they are undeniably full of character. I used to feed a small flock of Black-headed Gulls by throwing bread over my garden fence first thing in the morning and, regular as clockwork, there would a couple of birds waiting each morning. As soon as they saw me throw the first handful, the 'sentries' would give a few loud calls and within minutes a flock of 30 or more would be scrabbling for food. The mere sound of the back door closing at any time of day was sometimes enough to draw a crowd, even when I had nothing to offer! Many times in East Park, and sometimes Queen's Gardens, I have been enchanted by the antics of entirely wild Black-headed Gulls that have learnt to swoop down and take food from an outstretched hand, sometimes hovering at my fingertips for several seconds while deciding whether or not to be brave enough and take the titbit. To interact so closely with birds as wild and free as this, which may have travelled many hundreds of miles to be here, is a wonderful way to raise the spirits on a cold grey afternoon. The reputation of the Black-headed Gull as an intelligent and resourceful bird nevertheless took a battering, quite literally, after the laying down of Hull's 'Fish Trail' in 1992. For several days after shiny metal anchovies were embedded in the pavement outside the Tourist Information Centre near the City Hall, groups of determined Black-headed Gulls repeatedly swooped down to peck in vain at the tempting fish!

Ring-billed Gull
Larus delawarensis

A frequent transatlantic vagrant to Britain, and a possible breeding bird in the near future, there is nevertheless just one record of Ring-billed Gull for the Hull area. On 23rd November 1985 S. L. James was observing the birds over the Humber from his vantage point on the West Wharfe, near Alexandra Dock, when he began scanning through a large flock of gulls flying upstream. James immediately noticed that the very first bird in the flock looked "decidedly odd". With a few Common and Black-headed Gulls in the field of view for comparison, James was quickly able to determine that the bird was a probable Ring-billed Gull. As the flock drew closer they banked over the water and gave excellent views, enabling James to take the detailed

description of the bird that appears in the 1985 *Saltend and Hull Docks Bird Report*. As the bird flew out into the Humber and landed on a sand bank, James was in no doubt that it was a first-winter Ring-billed Gull. It was watched on the sand bank at some distance through a telescope before moving over to the Lincolnshire side and being disturbed by a low-flying Arctic Skua. Many of the accompanying gulls flew off inland, into Lincolnshire, and the Ring-billed Gull could not be relocated either then or the following day.

This record was apparently never submitted to the British Birds Rarities Committee for adjudication, appearing in neither the accepted nor rejected records in the subsequent reports of rare birds in Britain, though it was included in the Yorkshire Naturalists' Union's *Ornithological Report for 1985*.

Common Gull
(Mew Gull)
Larus canus

Until the 1980s the Common Gull was just that in the Hull area, the most common gull of the region.

Boylan (1967) called them "really common" throughout the city and large flights of many thousands of birds regularly passed over in the late afternoon on their way to roost at Saltend. Common Gulls were familiar almost everywhere at that time, from the city centre, the parks, gardens and the cemeteries, only being absent for a short period in June and July, though a few immature birds could still be found roosting at Saltend even then. The Common Gull remained a very common bird in the Hull area into the 1980s, as it is today, and the change in status from 'commonest gull' to 'second commonest gull' is merely due to an increase in the numbers of Black-headed Gulls visiting us, rather than a decrease in Common Gulls.

Counts at the Saltend roost in the mid 1980s revealed a minimum of less than 10 during early June, though up to 100 were often present from the middle of the month and 500 could be roosting there by the end of July. Numbers slowly built up during the late summer as birds returned from their northern breeding grounds and up to 1,000 could be present by the end of August. An influx in late autumn saw the roost grow to 5,000 by December, with over 2,000 feeding around St. Andrew's Dock during the day. Common Gulls were also described as "very common" around Cottingham and northwest Hull during this period, compared to a comment of merely "common" for the Black-headed Gull, although the latter species was outnumbering Common Gulls at the Saltend roost by then.

Despite being overtaken by the Black-headed Gull in terms of numbers these days, Common Gulls still often outnumber that species in early autumn before the big influx of Black-headed Gulls arrives from the Continent, and also in late spring when the bulk of the Black-headed Gulls have left. In October and March/April large flocks composed solely of Common Gulls are often seen patrolling arable fields, sports fields and any area of short grass for slugs, snails and worms. Over 300 were observed doing just this on the Priory Road fields in October 1995.

Common Gulls showing characteristics of the eastern race, *Larus canus heinei*, have been reported from the Hull area in small numbers for many years, usually in midwinter. Birds were seen at Earles Road (near Alexandra Dock) on 24th November 1985, the Saltend/eastern docks area on 26th February 1986, two were at Saltend on 1st January 1997 and again at Hessle Foreshore on 5th, with three at Hessle Foreshore on 11th January and one at East Park on 10th February the same year. Plumage abnormalities are also reported on occasion, this being more common than in the Black-headed Gull, with an albino bird around the eastern docks on 13th April 1987. In the winter of 1990 I regularly saw a leucistic first-winter Common Gull at North Bransholme, this bird having the normal plumage pattern but the colours being very pale and washed out with pure white wing-tips. It looked somewhat like a small first-winter Iceland Gull. What was undoubtedly the same bird returned towards the end of 1991, by now in second-winter plumage with a dark grey mantle, scapulars, lesser and median coverts on the upperparts but very pale grey greater and primary coverts and pure white flight feathers. It was a very beautiful bird, now looking like a smaller, darker-backed version of an adult Iceland Gull, but I never saw it again. Wintering Common Gulls in Hull do show striking site fidelity, however, with recognisable birds returning to the same place year after year. One very characteristic bird that I often saw in the 1990s at the North Point Shopping centre, in the heart of Bransholme, was immediately recognisable on account of a broken leg that had healed imperfectly and was stuck out at an odd angle. I used to change buses at the North Point centre on my way to college and, from around October to March for at least three winters, this bird would usually be sat on the same lamppost near my bus stop, looking for bits of discarded sandwich or a dropped chip. I last saw the bird in 1995 when I stopped passing through the North Point centre, but it would be intriguing to know for how many years it kept returning.

Lesser Black-backed Gull
Larus fuscus
This is one of the less common gulls around Hull but is still a regular passage migrant, especially in autumn,

and uncommon winter visitor. This was much the case in the 1960s with most records coming from East Park, and occasionally Northern Cemetery, in autumn. Counts between North Ferriby and the mouth of the River Hull in 1977 revealed large numbers of Lesser Black-backs roosting and loafing on the Humber, with 100 in mid January, 52 in mid February but just 10 in mid December. Counts of adults at the Saltend roost in the mid 1980s rarely exceeded 20 or 30 birds in the peak months of September and October, while around five were present in in August and November and just one or two could be found at other times.

The above counts refer to birds of the Western European race, *Larus fuscus graellsii*, as this was the first time that attempts had been made to sort out the racial makeup of Lesser Black-backs in the Hull area. Birds of the southwest Scandinavian race *L. f. intermedius*, and Baltic race *L. f. fuscus*, were also reported from Saltend at that time but most ornithologists are now of the opinion that *L. f. fuscus* has never been reliably recorded in Britain, so references to this race can be discounted or perhaps be assigned to *intermedius*. Birds identified as *intermedius* were fairly frequent at the Saltend roost in the mid 1980s, however, with 29 on 28th October 1984 and one or two between late July and December 1985. Up to 16 were also counted at the eastern docks in the closing months of that year. Counts at Saltend in 1998 provided a useful update and revealed the presence of one to four Lesser Black-backs from February to May, up to nine from June to October and one or two until December. The observer, B. Richards, estimated that roughly a quarter of the birds seen were *intermedius*, with the rest being *graellsii*. Sightings away from the Humber are rather uncommon in autumn and winter. Groups of up to five were occasionally seen flying over North Bransholme in the early 1990s, including three *intermedius* on New Year's Day 1992, and one or two turn occasionally up at the Bransholme Sewage Works and East Park, often in midwinter. Others may be picked out among the more usual gulls on any sports field or other large expanse of short grass throughout the Hull area, but they are always less common than their Herring and Great Black-backed cousins.

Herring Gull
Larus argentatus

It has always been possible to find Herring Gulls around the Hull area, most notably near the Humber, but they are often present in surprisingly small numbers. Boylan (1967) lists the Herring Gull as a scarce resident and fairly common winter visitor, especially at St. Andrew's Dock, and this could be amended a little in the mid 1980s after detailed information from Saltend and the East Hull docks. Just a handful of birds, usually less than five, could be found at the Saltend roost between June and August before a slow increase as autumn turned into winter. The 10 to 15 birds of September and October 1985 had grown to 80 by late November and then very hard weather brought in a record 3,800 in late December. The number of birds feeding at St. Andrew's Dock during the day was a better indication of local numbers, however, and 200 to 300 were often present between December 1984 and February 1985 with a short-lived peak of 650 in mid January. Observers estimated that around 5% of the wintering population were of the Scandinavian race *Larus argentatus argentatus*, this rising to 40% during hard weather peak counts although these birds often moved on quickly. The remainder were of the Western European race *L. a. argenteus*.

Small flocks of Herring Gulls, usually a dozen or less, can be seen passing overhead anywhere in the Hull area at virtually any time but particularly winter. They are probably passing between the Humber and the landfill tips, gravel pits and reservoirs north and east of Beverley. Smaller numbers, perhaps one to five birds, can occasionally be seen among other gulls on playing fields and the East Park and Pickering Park lakes or the Bransholme Sewage Works, with the Herring Gull being the most frequent 'large gull' inland.

Caspian Gull
Larus cachinnans

As with the Yellow-legged Gull, this species was previously considered to be a race of the Herring Gull but is now thought by many to be a species in its own right. Caspian Gulls hail from the eastern Mediterranean and the species has been claimed twice in Hull, possibly involving the same bird. A bird resembling a first-winter Caspian Gull was observed at the Bransholme Sewage Works on 3rd January 2001, with a first- or second-winter bird being seen there again on 8th.

Yellow-legged Gull
Larus michahellis

This is the common large gull of the western Mediterranean and it was only recently recognised as a full species (although some still deny it this status and consider it a race of the Herring Gull). They are increasingly being recorded in Britain and there are two records from Hull. The first was an adult roosting at Victoria Dock's West Wharf on 5th November 1997 and the second was a bird at the Bransholme Sewage Works on 9th November 1998. More will undoubtedly be seen as the species becomes better known and more frequent.

Iceland Gull
Larus glaucoides

Despite the name, Iceland Gulls actually breed in Greenland and northeast Canada and they are scarce winter visitors to Britain. Fewer than 20 have been reported from the Hull area, the vast majority in late December or early January, but the species is probably under-recorded and may occur annually.

The first record was of a second-year bird at Albert Dock on 20th December 1943. Boylan mentions three winter records from Hull in the 1960s, one of which was probably the near-adult at St. Andrew's Dock on New Years Eve 1962 and reported in the Yorkshire Naturalists' Union report for that year. None were reported in the 1970s, probably due to a lack of observation, but hard weather at the end of 1985 brought a rash of reports from St. Andrew's Dock. The first was a first-winter on 28th December, with two first-winters and a third-winter on 29th, a single first-winter again on 30th, a third-winter once more on 31st and an un-aged bird on 1st and 2nd January 1986. A first-winter was there again on 15th March 1987, the latest spring date reported for a Hull area bird. Another comparatively late bird, a first-winter, flew west over North Bransholme on 11th March the following year.

There was little recording from the docks in the 1990s and the next report of an Iceland Gull did not come until 1997, when a first- or second-winter was at Hessle Foreshore. The area around Hessle Foreshore and the Humber Bridge has been the most productive of recent years, since the decline of the fish dock. Two un-aged birds were there on 2nd January 2000 while a third-winter at the Humber Bridge Country Park the following day was probably one of these birds, and a first-winter was near the Humber Bridge again on 11th. There is also an undated record from East Park between 1959 and 1992.

Glaucous Gull
Larus hyperboreus

Glaucous Gulls mostly breed within the Arctic Circle although around 350 winter in Britain in an average year, most of these birds probably coming from Greenland. As with the Iceland Gull, a bird or two probably visits the Hull area each winter but most are likely to go unrecorded.

The first record was of a bird at one of the docks on 6th March 1956 and Boylan noted that singles were regular at St. Andrew's Dock in the 1960s, usually annually, and gave a total of seven birds between 1960 and 1967. The 1970s were a washout due to a lack of recording and the next records were not until the mid 1980s, the first of that period being a first-winter at St. Andrew's Dock between 2nd and 4th February 1985. A large influx occurred at St. Andrew's Dock in the 1985/6 winter beginning with another first-winter from 27th December 1985, with two from 29th, three on 3rd January 1986, four the next day in company with a second-winter and an adult (making a record six birds), with a

lone first-winter lingering until 5th February. That was not all, however, as a second-winter bird was back again on 13th February before the last one, a first-winter again, was seen departing to the east on 1st March.

On 2nd January 1989 an adult was well inland flying over North Bransholme, though no more were reported from around Hull for several years. The next was not until 1994 when an adult brought an echo of the past back to St. Andrew's Dock and another alighted there the following January, but reports from anywhere in the Hull area have been very thin on the ground in more recent years. A first-winter bird on Hessle Foreshore on 8th March 2000 raised hopes that Glaucous Gulls were still there to be found if one looked for them.

Great Black-backed Gull
Larus marinus

These huge, fierce-looking gulls are largely winter visitors to the Hull area, mainly on the Humber, though birds can usually be found somewhere along the waterfront through-out the year. Over 1,800 were logged between Hessle and Hull in late January 1980, although counts at the Saltend roost in the mid 1980s rarely exceeded 200 birds. Larger numbers could be found at St. Andrew's Dock, however, where this species had been referred to as being "common" since at least the 1960s. Up to 350 were present there in January 1985, with 150 by February and fewer than 30 throughout the summer until around 125 were back again from October onwards. Hard weather in December 1985, meanwhile, brought 1,200 into St Andrew's Dock. More recently, the largest count has been just 300 on the sandbanks off Hessle in mid October 1997.

As with the other large gulls, Great Black-backs are often seen passing over Hull and the surrounding area as they commute between the Humber and feeding and roosting sites in the East Riding. I regularly saw groups of up to 15 birds flying over North Bransholme in the early 1990s, usually between November and February and often mixed with Herring or Lesser Black-backed Gulls. A few birds may drop down to rest on quiet areas of short grass, such as playing fields, or areas of water such as East Park Lake and the Bransholme Sewage Works. The flocks of several dozen that hung around the Waste Disposal Plant at the north end of Mount Pleasant are a thing of the past, however, since waste handling methods changed in the mid 1990s.

Kittiwake
(Black-legged Kittiwake)
Rissa tridactyla

The Kittiwake, a proper 'sea gull' that comes to land only to breed, is frequently recorded in the Humber estuary and this is no doubt a product of the enormous colonies just up the coast at Flamborough and Bempton. Most occur off Hull during spring and autumn passage but the occasional bird or two can turn up at any time of year. The Kittiwakes that enter the Humber estuary and penetrate as far as the Hull area are rather unobtrusive, however, and do not usually stray inland at all. To see them requires a dedicated river watch as the paltry three records from the 1960s, when nobody really looked at the birds moving on the Humber, clearly indicates.

Regular watching off Saltend, Paull and the eastern docks in the 1980s revealed the true status of Kittiwakes in the upper Humber. One or two were frequent on the Humber or around the docks from January to April, with an increase from May to June before a midsummer lull and then another increase in numbers and frequency from September to November as autumn passage was played out. The highest count in 1985-6 was 95 passing west on 7th June 1986, with most spring and autumn day counts being less than 10, though 20 were moving downstream off Paull on 17th May 1986 and a total of 30 passed by on 27th March 1987. A total of 50 in two flocks flew west under the Humber Bridge on 26th March 1991 and 8 were west of Hessle on 13th September 1993. Lack of regular coverage in recent years has resulted in a corresponding lack of sightings, with four off Saltend on 19th March and two first-summers at the mouth of the Holderness Drain on 6th June being the only records in 1998. A lone bird was at St Andrew's Quay on Christmas Eve 2000 when most of its brethren were far out to sea, only going to show that a look out over the Humber from any vantage point is worthwhile at any time of year.

An adult Kittiwake was seen at North Bransholme, four miles from the Humber, on 11th March 1988, while on 7th February 1989 I found a freshly dead adult Kittiwake in a field of winter wheat opposite Dalkeith Close on North Bransholme. Although it had been picked at a little it appeared in good condition and was probably killed by a fox or stoat as it rested after being blown inland by strong winds. Another live adult bird was inland in 1999, this time at the Bransholme Sewage Works on 18th March.

Sandwich Tern
Sterna sandvicensis

Sandwich Terns are regular passage migrants along the Humber and are quite frequent and numerous in some years. The only counts come from the mid 1980s off Saltend when up to five birds were seen on many days from mid May to late June, with fewer in July, before autumn passage brought up to 55 per day in September. Most birds had left by mid September but there was a late one on 29th October 1985. Inland Sandwich Terns are virtually unheard of around Hull, but M. Flowers tells me that their raucous call is very occasionally heard over Hedon Road.

Common Tern
Sterna hirundo

Common Terns are primarily passage migrants on the Humber off Hull and large numbers are sometimes seen from the waterfronts. Boylan gave five passage records in the 1960s but, as was often the case, provided no details as to numbers or dates. It was not until the 1980s that any detailed counts were made, these being from around Saltend and the eastern waterfront. Most sightings were between mid April and mid September, with the latest one on 6th October. Spring passage was much lighter than in autumn and generally produced a maximum of five birds on any one day in April and May. Sightings were less frequent in summer as the birds were away breeding on inland lakes and coastal marshes, but birds were regular in autumn from early August. Usual counts involved less than 20 birds at this time, although up to 150 were logged on some days.

Reports have been few and far between in recent years, largely due to a lack of recording and reporting along the Humber, but counts of up nine at Saltend in autumn 1998 show that Common Terns are still present for those willing to look for them.

Arctic Tern
Sterna paradisaea

Arctic Terns are doubtless regular passage migrants on the Humber but occur in far fewer numbers than the very similar Common Tern. Counts off Saltend in the mid 1980s revealed up to 10 per day passing offshore between mid April and late May, with S. L. James watching 82 birds "tumble from the sky" on 12th May 1985 before flying off downstream. Autumn passage lasted from August to mid September and involved up to 25 birds per day. The only recent report is of two birds flying upstream at Saltend on 2nd July 1998, but regular observation anywhere along the Humber shore during passage periods would probably produce small numbers of Arctic Terns sooner or later.

Little Tern
Sterna albifrons
Little Terns breed sparingly around the British coast, including at the mouth of the Humber, but are scarce passage migrants away from the

breeding sites and are very rare inland. Despite the small breeding colonies less than 30 miles away there are very few records of Little Terns in the Hull area, all of them on the Humber during May.

Regular watching at Saltend in the mid 1980s produced a few records, these beginning with one fishing in Saltend Channel on 27th May 1985 and then another on 10th, 14th and 16th May 1986. One at North Ferriby, upstream of Hull, on 7th July 1990 must have passed the Hull area at some point while the most recent record came from Saltend again on 14th May 1996. Under-watching and under-recording are likely to be factors in this scarcity of records, but the main reason is that Little Terns are genuinely rare birds in our area.

Black Tern
Chlidonias niger
Now an uncommon passage migrant over the Humber, the Black Tern may have once bred on the fens and marshes of the Hull area in the dim and distant past, although the only direct evidence of breeding in the Hull valley is a comment regarding

the Driffield area in the early 19th Century or before (Nelson, 1907). Birds were still common about the River Hull up towards Beverley at the beginning of the 20th Century but the first solid record for the Hull area was of three birds "at Hull" on 7th May 1954.

Boylan (1967) mentions two passage records for Hull in the 1960s and large numbers were seen out in the mid Humber off Hessle in August 1979, with 76 on 17th and 14 to 19 until 21st. Observation at Saltend in 1985 and 1986 produced two spring records, both singles, in mid May and late June and eight records of one to six birds between mid August and mid September. The most recent report to reach me was of three birds flying upstream off Hessle Foreshore on 13th September 1993, but many more must have passed by unrecorded.

Guillemot
(Common Guillemot)
Uria aalge
While around 15,000 pairs of Guillemot breed on the cliffs at Bempton, very few birds seem to enter the Humber as far upstream as

the Hull area. Just two birds were reported between 1960 and 1966, probably as tideline strandings, and the next were not until 1985 when regular watching at Saltend and the docks gave an indication of the true status of the species on the Humber in our area.

The 1985 sightings, added to those from continued coverage in 1986, revealed the Guillemot to be a scarce winter visitor and regular autumn passage migrant, albeit in small numbers. After the occasional single birds seen in January and February there were no more sightings until autumn when movements began with odd birds in September before peaking in November. A maximum of 14 birds moved downstream on 4th in 1985 before sightings petered out and just the occasional bird was seen again in December. Daily counts were mostly less than five and usually just one or two, but it was also felt that the same few birds were probably involved in several of the sightings. The only recent reports of Guillemots in the Hull area are of a lightly oiled corpse on the tideline just west of the Humber Bridge on 25th July 1997, though it might well

have been brought up on the tide already dead, while another was in much finer fettle as it flew downstream past St. Andrew's Quay on 15th January 2001.

Despite the general lack of records a handful of birds are seen most years at the head of the estuary, at Blacktoft, between September and December and these must have passed Hull at some point. Small numbers are also seen flying west at sites downstream of Hull, such as Sunk Island, at this time of year and some of these might also carry on to pass the city's waterfront. The lack of recent records from the Hull area, therefore, probably means that nobody is really looking.

Razorbill
Alca torda

The Razorbill is much scarcer than the Guillemot in Yorkshire, though over 3,000 pairs breed at Bempton Cliffs and many thousands pass along that coast during autumn. Even less Razorbills than Guillemots enter the Humber, however, and there are just five specific records from the Hull area. On 19th November 1984 two Razorbills were seen on the Humber off Saltend, with two again on the 24th. A badly oiled Razorbill was found alive at Saltend on 17th January 1985 and an untarnished bird was seen offshore on 15th January 1986, while two flew downstream on 16th February. As with the Guillemot, though, the one or two autumn birds that are seen flying upstream at sites such as Sunk Island may well carry on past Hull and the lack of coverage must be at least partly responsible for the lack of sightings.

Little Auk
Alle alle

Nesting in the high Arctic, most Little Auks also spend the winter in the Arctic Ocean but unknown numbers winter as far south as the North Sea. Autumnal and winter winds with a northerly or easterly element in them bring variable numbers within sight of the coastal seawatchers and Little Auks sometimes pass offshore in their thousands. So-called 'wrecks' of dead and dying birds occur now and again on the coast and also inland after very bad weather. The numbers of Little Auks appearing in the Hull area is usually

an echo of what is happening at the coast, with a scattering of singles and small flocks during large flights and often none reported in more average years. Most Hull area records are from November and all dated occurrences were between October and February, with a significant proportion being of birds that came to grief on land.

The first record was of an unfortunate bird that flew into the side of a shed in a timber yard at Victoria Dock on 15th January 1913, promptly shattering its beak and killing itself. One was found dead at Cottingham in February 1916 and others were recovered in Hull in November 1948, 1st January 1956 and again on 10th November, with one picked up alive on 12th November 1958 and another dead in October 1959. Boylan (1967) gave 10 autumn and winter records for Hull up to 1967 that probably included the 1950s records at least, mentioning that all were after north-easterly gales.

The first specific record of live birds in something like a natural setting came on 10th November 1979 when nine were in the mid-Humber off the western waterfront. On 29th October 1983 huge numbers of Little Auks were seen from the Yorkshire coast and a record total of 36 birds seen the same day at the head of the Humber, well upstream of Hull, undoubtedly passed our waterfronts unseen. Another good autumn on the coast in 1984 produced a grounded Little Auk at the eastern docks on 7th November. It was taken to the RSPCA for treatment but unfortunately died the next day.

The autumn of 1985 was less than memorable on the coast but regular observation at Saltend made it the best autumn for the Hull area so far as recorded individuals go. Little Auks were observed flying up the Humber on four days in the first two weeks of November, with three birds on 2nd, one on 3rd, five on 4th and a total of 47 on 13th. This record day count for the Hull area still stands. The lack of regular observation and recording from around the Humber since then has resulted in a near complete lack of reports, the most recent being of 16 birds flying downstream off Saltend on 9th November 1989 while a typically grounded bird was found in a West Hull garden on 10th November 1999. Like most of the others, this bird was taken into care but died two days later. Enormous movements on the coast in the early 1990s must have surely seen more Little Auks entering the Humber or crash landing throughout the Hull area but, alas, they were not recorded.

Puffin
(Atlantic Puffin)
Fratercula arctica

The Puffin is one of the few birds known to most everyday people and its comical appearance and colourful bill ensures it a special place in the public's affection, though it is surprising how many people comment on how small they are in the flesh! The nearest breeding Puffins to Hull are on the cliffs of Flamborough and Bempton and it is a very scarce bird on the Humber. On 4th February 1887 H. J. Robinson Pease, of Hesslewood Hall, shot a winter-plumaged female Puffin on the Humber near Hessle, bagging yet another on 14th at the same place. There was one sighting during the first half of the 1960s and just one more in the 1970s when a single bird was sat in the middle of the Humber off St Andrew's Dock. An adult flew downstream past Saltend on 23rd June 1986 and four flew upstream at Paull on 13th July. As with the other auks and seabirds, however, many of the handful of autumn Puffins observed heading upstream further down the estuary, and certainly those already upstream of Hull, could have been seen from the Hull area had anyone been watching.

Pallas's Sandgrouse
Syrrhaptes paradoxus

Pallas's Sandgrouse breed on the steppes of central Asia and are extremely rare vagrants to Britain, with just seven records since 1958. The late 19th Century saw a succession of huge invasions into Britain when vast flocks dispersed westwards across Europe as snow and hard frosts forced them from their homeland. The first really big invasion was in 1863 but there were no records from the Hull area, although the next one in May and June 1888 saw flocks of up to 100 birds on all sides of Hull from Hollym to Beverley and Market Weighton. Up to 500 were estimated to have been present in the East Riding, with two pairs even nesting near Beverley, and despite the absence of documented records some must have surely passed through the Hull area. A hand-written note in Thomas Nelson's personal copy of his 1907 *The Birds of Yorkshire*, reported in Ralph Chislett's 1952 *Yorkshire Birds*, mentions a flock of "several" Pallas's Sandgrouse in a field at Dunswell in November 1908. The Hull area can, therefore, confidently add the species to its list.

Feral Pigeon/Rock Dove
(Rock Pigeon)
Columba livia

They may get under the feet of shoppers around Victoria Square, make a mess on the Cenotaph and pester people feeding the ducks in Queen's Gardens but Feral Pigeons are a part of Hull bird life just as much as any other species and there is a lot more to them than meets the eye. Feral Pigeons were semi-domesticated from the wild Rock Dove of the sea cliffs several thousand years ago, traditionally being provided with elaborate dove cotes in which they would nest and the fat youngsters, or squabs, could be harvested for their meat. The pigeons we see around the streets today are the descendents of these birds that have totally reverted to the wild, with the addition of many absconding homing and racing pigeons. All of the varieties of feral pigeon and all of the colour types, from the virtually black birds to the white 'doves' and the red-coloured ones, black-and-grey chequered ones and combinations thereof, are all the same species as the Rock Dove and some still resemble their wild ancestors. These 'wild-type' birds, with their silvery-grey backs, white rumps and double black wingbars, make up around 10% of the Hull population but differ from true Rock Doves with their thicker beaks. Melanistic birds, with sooty or chequered backs, seem to be the dominant colour form around Hull, as even the wild-type birds will produce young of this variety much of the time due to the dominance of the dark genes that they all carry.

Feral Pigeons have always been very common in the city centre, around the docks and in the inner suburbs and industrial areas although they are currently quite uncommon in the outer suburbs of Bransholme, Orchard Park and the like, probably due to the lack of feeding and nesting opportunities and increase in predators. The old housing areas backing onto Spring Bank and the town ends of the Holderness, Beverley and Anlaby Roads, many with derelict attic spaces and gaps in their roofs, are perfect breeding sites for Feral Pigeons. The loft space of one property down Albany Street, off Spring Bank, that I visited in the 1994 held a large colony of pigeons that gained access through a hole in the roof. When the roof was repaired after several years of negligence I was called in to take away young pigeon chicks that were found running about the place; I gathered five chicks but there were around 20 other chicks and eggs that had died after their parents were shut out. I hand-reared the five lucky youngsters and later released them, but the story indicates the source of the many thousands that visit the city centre and surrounding places to feed. In the 1960s at least there was a large feeding flock of several thousand Feral Pigeons that gathered around the grain silo on King George Dock alone, and up to 3,000 could still be found throughout the eastern docks and Saltend area in the 1980s. In recent years I have seen flocks of up to 1,000 birds around Albert Dock and there are always several hundred around Queen's Gardens, Victoria Square and up King Edward Street. Feral Pigeons are also common around parts of Cottingham and northwest Hull, the Avenues and in the Hull parks, though they never occur in any great numbers.

In the city centre it is difficult not to stand on pigeons sometimes, as they are so tame, while in Queen's Gardens they will actually sit on your hand if you offer them grain. Indeed, I have occasionally demonstrated to companions the tolerance that Queen's Gardens pigeons have for people by showing how easy it is to pick them up as they feed at your feet, a useful trick if you spot twine or such like trapped around its leg. Closer observation of these city centre birds, however, will reveal their propensity to gather in a swirling flock, spiral high over the rooftops and head purposefully out of town. These flocks are heading for the outlying fields to feed on grain and shoots, particularly in autumn, and, away from the relative safety of the city centre, they become very different animals. Now shy and wary out in the open, the flocks often join up with Wood Pigeons and Stock Doves and they are then subject to the same dangers, such as shooters, Sparrowhawks, foxes and power lines.

During my days of regular observation at North Bransholme I often saw fairly large flocks of Feral Pigeons heading into and out of Hull between July and March, with many over a hundred-strong. These flocks often dropped down to feed in the fields and it was then possible to confirm that these were Hull pigeons, rather than part of the large population that breeds on the Flamborough cliffs, by the number of 'pure' wild-type birds. As mentioned above, around 10% of Hull birds resemble the ancestral Rock Dove whereas at Flamborough this proportion is more like 60%. A flock of 114 at North Bransholme on 7th November 1993 contained 17 with wild-type colouring while 400 at Saltend and 75 at Alexandra Dock on 14th April 1998 also obeyed the 'roughly 10%' rule. These outlying feeding flocks can be quite large, though nowhere near as large as the estimated population around the eastern docks and Saltend in the 1980s, mentioned above; 600 were feeding at North Bransholme on New Years Day 1993, with 270 there on 20th November 1993 growing to 400 by 27th while 700 at Saltend in December 1997 is the maximum there in recent years. Exactly how far into East Yorkshire the Hull birds penetrate in their quest for food is not known, however. Flocks of up to 200 have been seen as far out as Tophill Low, between Beverley and Driffield, though in the absence of any information on the numbers of wild-types among them it is impossible to say if they were from Hull or Flamborough.

Stock Dove
(Stock Pigeon)
Columba oenas
Boylan (1967) said that this species was resident in Hull but there were few records. The Stock Dove tends to keep a low profile, but it is possible that it was genuinely scarcer in those days. After a lone record from near Kirk Ella in 1975 Stock Doves were noted to be increasing at Hedon Road Cemetery in the early 1980s. This coincided with a dramatic decline in the number of Woodpigeons, but the Stock Doves later decreased as the Woodpigeons recovered. Up to 14 were regularly seen around the nearby eastern docks and Saltend areas in 1984, with at least five pairs breeding in 1985. Large flocks were also noted around Saltend and the docks in 1985, with up to 45 in January, 30 in March, 50 in October, 100 in November and 90 in December.

Small numbers were breeding around Cottingham throughout the 1980s but they were generally absent in winter. In the late 1980s and early 1990s up to 15 could be found at North Bransholme throughout the year, with a peak in winter and a maximum of 21 in January 1994, and one or two pairs regularly bred. A lack of suitable nesting sites, in the form of tree holes or nest boxes, is certainly limiting the species in less wooded districts such as this.

Breeding was reported from unnamed Hull suburbs in 1997 and at least one pair was still nesting at the Hedon Road Cemetery in 2000. In April 2001 a total of around 10 birds could still be found in the fields east of North Bransholme and the pylons along the Foredyke Stream are still a good place to find a pair or two. Around the same time, spring 2001, two pairs seemed quite attached to the mature trees in the grounds of the old Haworth Hall, off Beverley Road.

Stock Doves are clearly thinly distributed residents throughout the Hull area and breed wherever there are suitable nest sites in old trees, even well into the suburbs, as well as in the outlying woods and plantations. They seem to be more abundant and widespread in winter and often associate with foraging flocks of Woodpigeons and Feral Pigeons, and a close look through such flocks will often reveal a few Stock Doves.

Woodpigeon
(Common Wood Pigeon)
Columba palumbus

This is one of the most widespread resident birds in the Hull area,

breeding wherever there are trees and tall shrubs and feeding on any open fields or areas of short grass. Large numbers flood in from the Continent in winter, when big flocks are common around the city outskirts and the villages.

In January 1940 huge flocks of Woodpigeons were hindering the war effort around Cottingham and Skidby by raiding gardens and allotments and damaging the vegetables. An organised cull on 31st saw groups of men shooting at the birds all day long, which they sold for tuppence and threpence each. In the 1960s Boylan described Woodpigeons as widespread breeders in small numbers, once again mentioning their tendency to descend on gardens in large numbers during severe weather, but they were noted as being only occasional visitors to Northern Cemetery. Bonavia (1990) described them as still being abundant around Cottingham and northwest Hull in the 1980s, though S. L. James found them to be quite scarce around Saltend and the eastern docks in the mid 1980s with just three pairs breeding and small flocks of 25 or so in autumn. Large numbers were noted passing over Saltend in hard weather movements, however, with 425 heading north on 14th December 1985 and 310 following them on 28th. The thick hedgerows and copses east of North Bransholme appear to suit them better and up to 20 pairs were breeding in little over a square mile between the housing and the Holderness Drain in the early 1990s. Large midwinter foraging flocks are also a feature there, with 200 in the early months of 1993 and 300 at the back end of that year. Many hundreds roost is the woods at Woody Carr and Long Carr, between Wawne and Swine, but they are heavily shot over for both sport and for damaging crops.

P. Milsom's survey of the birds of the Priory Road fields in 1995/6 revealed Woodpigeons to be a daily sight, building up in autumn to 70 or more before a January peak of 150 and then a rapid decline to around 20 by spring. Further into Hull, H. Crowther's survey of the birds in the Avenues in 1996 found Woodpigeons to be fairly common in parks, gardens and along the railway. Their flimsy nests can frequently be found in trees and bushes along many of the major roads in the city, with nearby lampposts being favourite perches for the adults. The pair of pure white eggs and young squabs are vulnerable to predation, however, and Carrion Crows, Grey Squirrels and Magpies are top of the list. In 1998 I kept a close eye on a relatively open nest site in an apple tree in the grounds of the University of Hull on Cottingham Road, being able to watch the progress of the two fluffy squabs from below. Right at the point of fledging I was saddened to find both chicks lying dead under the nest, having been mauled around the head. A Grey Squirrel appeared to be the most likely culprit.

In 1992 I found a young Woodpigeon squab, too young to be off the nest, wandering on the Highlands School playing field on North Bransholme. Probably a victim of local children who had robbed the nest, I took it upon myself to hand feed the bird to maturity, this being one of the easier species to succeed with. When it was fully grown and feeding itself I released it at the Bransholme Sewage Works where, weeks later, I came across an immature Woodpigeon sat in a tree in the plantation off Thomas Clarkson Way. As all birdwatchers know, Woodpigeons are very nervous and will explode into the air with a clatter of wings before you get anywhere near them, but this bird sat quite calmly on a low branch as I approached within ten feet of it. I like to think it was 'my' bird and it recognised me, but I just hope it was not that confiding with everybody. I had been at great pains not to let the bird get too tame and with good cause, for Woodpigeons are a favourite quarry of the airgunner and are fairly good to eat. The species absorbs the losses well, however, and continues to spread into urban areas in the Hull area, now being a fairly common sight in Queen's Gardens.

Collared Dove
(Eurasian Collared Dove)
Streptopelia decaocto
The history of the Collared Dove in Britain is truly astonishing, and no more so on a local scale than in the Hull area. It is incredible to think that less than fifty years ago this species had never been seen in Britain, yet after the first breeding in Norfolk in 1955 they were nesting in

every English county by 1970 and were being destroyed as pests in some areas soon afterwards.

The first Collared Dove to be recorded in Hull was seen in West Hull in 1959, and the first pair bred in Westbourne Avenue in 1960. There was a big increase in 1962, with birds frequently heard singing around Chanterlands Avenue and Northern Cemetery, and Cottingham and Skidby saw their first birds in 1963. Hedon had its first Collared Doves in 1964. In this year large numbers were making feeding flights from the main breeding areas in the Avenues, Newland Park and Endsleigh to the British Oils and Cake Mills in Stoneferry and up to 25 regularly travelled to a lorry park that handled grain in Humber Dock Street. Incredibly, by 1966 the Collared Dove was described as a common breeding species in Hull, all this just eight years after first being seen in the city and only 11 years after the first pair nested in the UK! The invasion continued unabated over the following years, with a flock of 90 at Hymers College in January 1969 and a roost of no less than 400 birds in East Park on 21st

of that month. The following year saw 200 in the grounds of Hymers College.

The Cottingham Bird Club survey of northwest Hull, Cottingham and the surrounding villages in the 1980s revealed Collared Doves to be widespread residents and breeding abundantly in all habitats. At least three pairs were breeding around Saltend in 1985, with a roost of up to 30 birds, while Paul Milsom's research in the Priory Road area in 1996 discovered breeding at Wood Lane, Wood Farm and in the Pickhill gardens, with flocks of up to 20. Helen Crowther's survey of the Avenues in 1996 found them to be common and there were around 70 in Willerby in late July and mid September 1999. Michael Flowers reported five pairs breeding within the confines of Hedon Road Cemetery alone in 2000 but colonisation of the northern and eastern outer suburbs, such as the newer housing estates of Bransholme and Orchard Park, was less dramatic than in West Hull and the inner suburbs. Despite an exceptional flock of 71 at Bransholme Dairy Farm on 8th October 1989 breeding birds are still rather thin on the ground in these districts though a slow expansion and infilling of vacant sites appears to be underway. From just one to three pairs breeding at North Bransholme in the early 1990s, with my well-stocked bird table not seeing a single bird during those years, there are now noticeably more singing birds in the area, including a pair in 2000 nesting in the very garden where my bird table once stood. There is plenty of good habitat and feeding opportunities for them in the outer suburbs and it is likely that it is human predation in the form of airgunners that is holding them back. Certainly in the North Bransholme of my youth, during the late 1980s and early 1990s, most of the pioneering pairs in the neighbourhood were shot for sport sooner or later.

The East Park roost, though fluctuating in size from year to year, has lasted up to the present time and hundreds of birds can still be seen arriving to settle in the trees in and around the animal enclosure and the eastern islands in the lake from late afternoon onwards, particularly in winter. Sample counts over the years have been 187 on 11th August 1970, 117 on 27th March 1984, 620 on 20th January 1989, 277 on 8th December 1998, 120 in January 1999 and around 150 in the animal enclosure alone on 29th December 2000. The East Park roost is the largest regular concentration to be found in the Hull area, and perhaps East Yorkshire.

Collared Doves are now so familiar, so common and so widespread that it is difficult to grasp the suddenness and scale of their arrival in Britain and around Hull. They owe their success to being opportunistic feeders, taking seed from bird tables, farmyards and waste ground alike, while nesting in all local habitats where a suitable bush or tree exists, from Queen's Gardens to Wawne gardens and all areas inbetween. Able to breed throughout the year (the pair nesting in my former Bransholme garden in 2000 were doing so at Christmas), the soft cooing song can be heard anywhere anytime and has led more than one Hull resident to think they've heard a winter Cuckoo!

Turtle Dove
(European Turtle Dove)
Streptopelia turtur

While the number of Turtle Doves in Britain has plummeted in recent decades, it seems that the species was never very common in the Hull area anyway. Despite recording such species as Cuckoo, Yellowhammer and Pied Flycatcher in and around his Hull garden in the first few years of the 20th Century, John Nicholson makes no mention of the Turtle Dove. By 1910, however, the species was reported to be increasing in the East Riding and spreading ever closer to Hull as a breeding bird.

Spring migrants were being seen in the 1940s and no doubt before, with the first East Riding bird of the year in 1944 reported from Hull on 3rd May. During the 1960s members of the Hull Scientific and Field Naturalists' Club recorded the species only twice in the old city boundary, although spring migrants were regular in May at Kirk Ella's Kerry Woods throughout the 1970s and 80s and may still occur. Spring passage migrants are regularly seen passing up the Humber from mid May to mid June, but few seem to stop off in the Hull area in recent years compared to previous decades. Five new arrivals were at Saltend on 6th May 1985, with up to three on several dates until five again on 8th June. One pair probably bred there that year and five were seen yet again on many dates until the last bird on 26th September. In *The New Atlas of Breeding Birds* for 1988 - 1991 breeding is clearly recorded in the Hull area, very likely around Saltend and/or the western villages, and a handful of pairs bred throughout the 1980s just outside the Hull area to the south of Beverley.

A pair of passage Turtle Doves were at the now demolished High Bransholme Farm on 6th June 1992 and a singleton was at the Bransholme Sewage Works on 2nd June 1997. Passage birds have also been recorded from the Priory Road fields, Priory Sidings and no doubt elsewhere, but they rarely linger for more than a day. On 17th June 1993 a farm worker saw an unusual bird land in a tree just north of Wawne. Not recognising the species, he mindlessly shot it with his airgun. I was shown the body and it proved to be a male Turtle Dove, the crop being full of poppy seeds.

Autumn passage is usually much lighter than the spring movement, and an immature feeding on stubble at Bransholme in mid September 1995 was the only record for that season in five years of observation. Despite the possibility of the odd breeding pair on bushy ground to the north or west of the Hull area, the Turtle Dove is now generally no more than a scarce passage migrant. The peak time for seeing them around Hull is from May to mid June, the earliest record for the area being one on 25th April at Kirk Ella.

Ring-necked Parakeet
(Rose-ringed Parakeet)
Psittacula krameri

Ring-necked Parakeets have been living and breeding in the wild in southeast England for several decades now, with winter roosts of over a thousand birds occurring in Surrey during the 1990s. The origins of this feral population stem from escapes and deliberate releases from cages and aviaries all over Britain throughout much of the 20th Century. It is thought that all of the birds recorded in Yorkshire so far have been recent escapes and not members of the wild group. The only documented Hull records are one at Kerry Woods, west of Kirk Ella, on 11th March 1978 and another at Bransholme Sewage Works on 4th May 1992, with both birds sharing the dubious origin although it is impossible to know for sure.

Cockatiel
Leptolophus hollandicus

As with the Budgerigar, the Cockatiel is a common cagebird from Australia that has long been domesticated and regularly escapes from captivity. Less colour varieties exist than for the Budgerigar and many birds show the natural colours of grey body, white wing panel and yellow crest with an orange cheek-spot. Yellow and white varieties are also common and such birds are encountered not uncommonly each summer in the Hull area after escaping through open windows and the like. Often attracting attention with their characteristic whistle, imitating the call can often draw them closer and hopefully enable them to be recaptured; although Cockatiels can survive for some time by feeding on buds and blossom during summer they are highly likely to attract the attention of predators before too

long. Escaped Cockatiels, along with Budgerigars, Zebra Finches and other cagebirds, can turn up anywhere in the Hull area and usually do so in hot weather when doors and windows are left open.

Budgerigar
Melopsittacus undulates

This small Australian parrot, known to everyone, is hugely popular as a cage and aviary bird in Britain and large numbers are bred each year. Wild birds stopped being imported many decades ago, so the long history of captive breeding means that the domesticated birds available today come in a huge variety of colours as well as the original bright green with black and yellow trim. The large number of Budgies kept in Hull, and the tendency of many owners to allow their birds occasional freedom of a room or to place their cage in the garden on a sunny day, means that they regularly escape during the summer months. These escapees are often completely bewildered by their new surroundings and may sit calling forlornly on a roof or tree, though they can maybe find enough food during summer to keep them going for a while. The biggest risk they face is not bullying by Sparrows or Starlings, as many people believe, but being eaten by a passing Carrion Crow, Sparrowhawk, cat or other predator. In March 1993 I found an owl pellet under a Tawny Owl roost on North Bransholme that contained the turquoise feathers and distinctive skull of a Budgerigar, and later that summer a characteristic pile of green and yellow feathers nearby was all that was left of another bid for freedom that was cut short, probably by a Sparrowhawk. Several Budgerigars are probably at large in the Hull area at any one time during summer, and the best thing to do if coming across one is to try and catch it if it allows close approach. Of those that defy capture most probably only survive for a matter of days.

Cuckoo
(Common Cuckoo)
Cuculus canorus

The Cuckoo is another of those birds that is well known among the general public despite few having seen one or even knowing what they look like. It is, of course, the song that is famous and the "cuc-coo" of the male Cuckoo is a regular spring and early summer sound throughout the Hull area. The song is predominantly heard in the outlying fields and hedgerows but also in the suburbs of Hull and the satellite towns and villages along railway lines, drain banks or wherever there are lots of trees and bushes. Along with the Swallow, the Cuckoo is a classical harbinger of spring, but as it arrives later than the Swallow and often sings only in good weather then it is perhaps more justified in being so.

Cuckoos generally arrive in the Hull area from their African wintering grounds around the last week of April or first few days of May and John Nicholson reported them among the visitors to his garden near Pearson Park, when this was one of the outer suburbs, as long ago as the beginning of the last century. In the 1960s they were regular yet uncommon breeding birds within the old Hull boundary, with Northern Cemetery often being visited. One or more Cuckoos could be heard singing in Hedon Road Cemetery and along the nearby Hull to Withernsea railway line every spring throughout the 1970s, while up to three together could be found at Kirk Ella's Kerry Woods in the same period. A few pairs bred around Cottingham and northwest Hull during the early 1980s, with one usually in fields north of the Recreation Ground, and one was reported from a Cottingham garden on 19th May 1982. Breeding was occurring around Saltend in the mid 1980s, with up to five birds present in May and June, while four young were reared in 1985. The last adult seen that year was on 30th June although the juveniles stayed on until 21st August.

Birds were still being heard at the Kerry Woods throughout the 1980s, if a little less frequently than in the 1970s, while sightings at Hedon Road Cemetery were becoming few and far between until they petered out completely by the 1990s. Birds can still be heard along the old Hull to Withernsea railway line as it passes behind Hull Prison and makes its way through Marfleet, but they are now much scarcer here too. Cuckoos were regular but thinly distributed around North Bransholme throughout the 1990s, though one or two juveniles were occasionally seen in July and August between the housing and the Holderness Drain. An impressive six were counted around the Priory Road fields on 1st June 1996, favouring the Pickhills area between Priory Road, Hull Road and Wood Lane to the south of Cottingham. All were gone by the end of the month, however, and none were heard from the regular haunts in the Avenues area of Hull that year.

Dunnocks were reputed to be the favourite host species for the Cuckoo around Cottingham in the 1980s but, while there is a wide range of known host species available throughout the Hull area, there are no reports of eggs or young being found in the nests of other species. Reports of the rufous form of the female Cuckoo are also very rare but I was lucky enough to see one at North Bransholme in the spring of 1988.

Barn Owl
Tyto alba

Formerly common over much of Britain in the first half of the 20th Century, Barn Owls became a cause for serious concern during the 1980s when numbers plummeted to around 5,000 pairs as a result of agricultural intensification and the resultant pesticides and habitat loss. There are now less than 4,000 pairs in Britain. The East Riding remains something of a stronghold for this beautiful and enigmatic species, however, and there are several places in the Hull area where they are a regular sight.

The first mention of the Barn Owl around Hull comes from the carnage wrought after a severe frost in early 1947 when G. H. Ainsworth, the East Riding recorder for the Yorkshire Naturalists' Union, had no less than five dead Barn Owls brought to him, along with a Little Owl and four Tawny Owls. Boylan (1967) regarded the Barn Owl as a regular but uncommon breeding bird in the suburbs of Hull during the 1960s, while a pair bred in the chimney of a house in Thwaite Street, Cottingham, in 1968 and could often be seen hunting on the Priory Road fields. Others were seen in Thwaite Street and also at The Lawns during spring in 1984 and 1985. Hunting birds were seen around Kirk Ella and Anlaby in midwinter during the late 1970s and early 1980s but sightings were rare around Saltend, with just a single record during the well-watched mid 1980s of one hunting over Saltend Marsh in late November.

Barn Owls were regularly observed around North Bransholme from the late 1980s onwards, though they were no doubt present before this. A pair was hunting along Foredyke Stream, between North Bransholme and the Holderness Drain, in October 1989 and a bird hunting there in broad daylight in early June 1992 probably had chicks to feed nearby. From late May 1993 Barn Owls were seen almost daily as they hunted along the eastern margin of North Bransholme, but especially on the marshy grassland between Foredyke Stream and Bransholme Road. In early June I watched two birds hunting there in broad daylight and was delighted when both carried off prey in different directions, one towards Carlam Hill Farm (near Wawne) and the other towards Thirty Acre Farm (near Swine), where both surely had chicks in the nest. Shortly afterwards a third bird was seen carrying food towards Fairholme Farm, between Wawne

and Swine. Throughout June all three birds were regularly followed through binoculars, often just minutes apart, as they flew in a direct path to their respective nests with voles in their talons before returning to the grassland at North Bransholme. The fact that three pairs were travelling to hunt on this piece of land, the Fairholme birds flying over a mile each way to do so, just goes to show the conservation value of this unbroken area of rough grassland. Through a telescope I was able to locate and observe the Thirty Acre Farm nest from my back garden and watched the six youngsters fledge in the first week of July. Interestingly, the other adult from this nest always flew off to hunt in the opposite direction to Bransholme. Birds were seen on the Bransholme hunting grounds throughout the winter and into 1994, with at least one of the nest sites used annually since then. In addition, there were at least three active pairs in the Wawne area in June 2001.

A pair of Barn Owls were hunting at Bilton in January 1993 and there were three sightings in the Avenues area of Hull in 1996. Another pair nested in the derelict Haworth Hall, upstream of Sutton Road Bridge on the River Hull, before it was restored and in 1998 a pair bred near Sutton Golf Course while another was present at Hedon during the breeding season. Winter records in the late 1990s came from Hedon by-pass, Clive Sullivan Way, Stoneferry Road, Sutton Fields Industrial Estate,

Saltend and Bransholme, so one may reasonably expect to see a Barn Owl over any suitable area of rough grassland anywhere in the Hull area if they watch regularly enough.

Little Owl
Athene noctua

The British population of Little Owls largely stems from deliberate introductions in the Midlands in the late 19th Century. The first birds in the Hull area probably arrived during the 1920s, by which time E. W. Wade stated that they seemed to have spread across the whole of the East Riding. Breeding was confirmed just east of Hedon in 1938 and a nest was found at Willerby in 1942, with a bird picked up dead in Hull after heavy frosts in early 1947. By the 1960s Boylan described the Little Owl as an irregular breeder within the suburbs of the old Hull boundary and two were near the Springhead Golf Course, between Hull and Willerby, in July 1975 and April 1976. One was at Preston in April 1979 and another spent a week in Hedon Road Cemetery that summer. Singles were seen between North Bransholme and the

Holderness Drain throughout the late 1980s and nesting was reported from fields north of Wawne around that time, with birds still present during the breeding season in 2001. Nesting has also been confirmed around Meaux Abbey, just north of the Hull area, since at least the 1970s. There were curious reports of Little Owls being heard and seen at Holderness House, at the corner of Holderness Road and Laburnum Avenue in Hull, in the early to mid 1990s, this being very unusual so far into the suburbs. More recent records involve a dead bird found just north of the Humber Bridge in February 1997 and another, very much alive, at Dunswell in January 1999.

Tawny Owl
Strix aluco

Although less visible about the Hull area than the Barn Owl, the highly nocturnal Tawny Owl is nevertheless likely to be the most common owl in the region, with hooting being a familiar sound even well into the built up areas of Hull and the surrounding villages. Tawny Owls occur wherever there are suitable mature trees to nest in and enough wild ground to hunt on, with roosting birds not uncommonly discovered high in the branches of some tree or deep in a hawthorn bush.

Boylan (1967) reported that the Tawny Owl was a fairly widespread breeding species within 1960s Hull and roosting birds were sometimes spotted in the elm trees down Barrington Avenue, near Northern Cemetery. Hedon Road Cemetery, on the other side of town, has also had a complement of Tawny Owls for many years. The Cemetery was not always without hazards for unwary Tawny Owls, however, and birds occasionally drowned in the public water tanks although up to three pairs still manage to make a living in that part of the city.

A Tawny Owl or two was occasionally heard or seen in woods around Kirk Ella in the mid to late 1970s and Bonavia (1990) described them as common around Cottingham and northwest Hull in the early 1980s, with fluffy young seen in Cottingham in May and June. There were just three sightings around Saltend and the eastern docks in 1985 and only one the following year, but breeding has been occurring in East Park and Pearson Park for many years. Hooting is often heard along the Old Main Drain hedgerow at North Bransholme, as well as from the mature trees down Wawne Road and around Sutton. Between 1991 and 1993 a pair roosted daily between November and April in a Scots Pine off Cumbrian Way, the conifer offering some cover once all the other trees had lost their leaves. I often used to check on them and occasionally analysed their pellets to see what they had been preying upon. I was very surprised one day to find a pellet composed entirely of turquoise feathers that, on closer inspection, also contained the characteristic skull, feet and long tail feathers of a Budgerigar! The remains of House Sparrows were often found in the pellets, alongside the more usual small rodents, and Tawny Owls are clearly not averse to picking off any suitable roosting birds they come across, even if they are an exotic colour.

There is some evidence of a slight decline in the population of Tawny Owls around the Hull area in recent years, with 1996 sightings around the Avenues being less frequent than formerly and there was just one record from the Priory Road fields in the same year.

Eagle Owl
(Eurasian Eagle Owl)
Bubo bubo

To come across one of these huge owls in Hull must be a bit of a shock, but one was nevertheless discovered down Shaftesbury Avenue, just off Holderness Road near East Park, on 13th February 2001 by startled passers-by. Obviously an escapee from a local aviary, the bird was later believed to have been caught and returned to captivity. There are many of these impressive birds in British aviaries, several of them in the Hull area, but escaped birds have actually managed to pair up and breed elsewhere in Yorkshire in recent years. Their huge size and voracious appetite, with animals as large as young Roe Deer being on the menu, means that they can wreak havoc if left in the wild. An escapee at Wath Ings, South Yorkshire, in March 1995 was feeding on Coots for two weeks until it was recaught. Even worse, it also managed to pick off a Barn Owl and Little Owl during its bid for freedom. Another escaped Eagle Owl in a Sheffield cemetery around the same time was reputed to be dining on the local cat population!

Long-eared Owl
Asio otus

Long-eared Owls are mainly passage migrants and winter visitors in the Hull area, being unpredictable in occurrence and nowhere common. Long-eared Owls are renowned for their habit of communal winter roosting and the sighting of one bird sat tight in the depths of a hawthorn bush often leads the eye to another bird or two nearby.

There was just one passage record from Hull between 1960 and 1966, with another in Hedon Road Cemetery in early spring sometime during the early 1970s. One was found roosting in a willow tree in Appleton Road, behind Bricknell Avenue in West Hull, on 7th November 1979 and two were roosting in hawthorns near Saltend in early December 1985. Another was along the Hedon Road stretch of the Holderness Drain at the end of March the following year and again in mid April, when two were also roosting on Saltend Marsh. Two more were in the Saltend area again in mid November 1986. There were six sightings of roosting Long-eared Owls in the Avenues area of Hull in the mid 1990s, between September and May, and a well-watched bird was sharing the limelight with a Great Grey Shrike southeast of North Bransholme in late March and early April 1996. More were seen at Saltend in 1998, with singles on and off in April, June and November. The June records are a little unusual, as most Long-eared Owl sightings are between November and April and there is no evidence of breeding anywhere in the Hull area. Even more tantalising was the sight of a Long-eared Owl leaving a roost in a copse just east of North Bransholme on the late afternoon of 17th July 1993. The tree the bird flew from, a Scots Pine, had an old Carrion Crow nest in the upper branches, just the sort of nesting site Long-eared Owls like, but that was the first and last time it was seen and no calling was ever heard. It was probably just passing through. On 5th December 2000, just a few hundred yards away at the Old Main Drain hedgerow, my dog got a little excited at something among the hawthorns and eventually flushed a large brown bird that revealed itself to be a Long-eared Owl as it flew past me. Still not satisfied, the dog promptly flushed at least another two from roughly the same spot. This trio constituted the largest roost reported from the Hull area.

Short-eared Owl
Asio flammeus

Primarily a passage migrant in the Hull area, the Short-eared Owl is also a winter visitor in small and decreasing numbers. On 30th August 1946 two birds were seen quartering fields at Sutton, these being the earliest autumn migrants recorded in the Hull area, while breeding was recorded 'near Hull' in 1948. Just two passage migrants were seen within the old city boundary during the first half of the 1960s, though sightings were more frequent in the Hull area up to the early 1990s.

An impressive four birds were seen along Carr Lane, near Willerby, in January and February 1979. Saltend is traditionally one of the key sites for Short-eared Owls in the area and a few birds can be found there in most winters, with up to three in early 1985 while a late bird was seen from 5th to 8th May 1986. The marshy grassland southeast of North Bransholme also accounted for many records between the mid 1980s and early 1990s and one or two birds were seen on numerous occasions from December to April. A bird quartering the rough grassland there on 22nd October 1988 may have been the same one seen throughout the winter and into the following spring. In March 1989, however, I saw a pair of Short-eared Owls displaying over a field of long grass at North Bransholme, just 300 yards from the housing estate. The birds were talon-grappling before one began wing-clapping and giving the booming display call. Conscious that this was breeding behaviour, I began to move away from the area only for one owl to follow and begin mobbing me and my accompanying dog. Short-eared Owls begin nesting in early April, so this may well have indicated the start of a breeding attempt. A week or so later, in April, a visit to the same area produced three owls. Two birds flushed from a tussock flew off together and were clearly a pair. The third bird, disturbed a short distance away, was probably a passage migrant and it left in the opposite direction. A few days later a Short-eared Owl was seen carrying prey in the same vicinity. Whether this food was for its own consumption, though owls usually swallow prey on catching it, or for feeding to an incubating female or even chicks in the nest can only be guessed at. Whatever the case, soon after these events much of the immediate area was buried under tons of rubble as the site was prepared for a development that never happened. Unsurprisingly the owls disappeared.

Passage birds continued to visit North Bransholme, however, with one on 31st October 1989, while a bird seen arriving at great height on 3rd October 1993 dropped down to hunt and were seen regularly over the following week. Sightings at North Bransholme have been rather rare since then, although one was present in January 1999. West of the River Hull has always attracted far fewer Short-eared Owls than areas to the east, with only very occasionalreports from Priory Road fields or the outskirts of Cottingham. One at Eppleworth, to the west of Cottingham, on 3rd June 1986 was an unusual summer record while one hunting around the gas works and River Hull on Clough Road in 1990 was actually shot and wounded by an airgunner, ending up at the RSPCA for rehabilitation.

Most Short-eared Owls have occurred in the Hull area between early October and mid April, the majority on low-lying rough grassland in the east of the area. With the decrease in records everywhere since the early 1990s it has become increasing difficult to see a Short-eared Owl around Hull, with Saltend now being the most likely place to find one.

Nightjar
(European Nightjar)
Caprimulgus europaeus

The mysterious Nightjar probably still breeds in a few places in the west of the East Riding, mainly in the district of Market Weighton, as mentioned by Nelson (1907), Chislett (1952) and Mather (1986), but it has never bred in the Hull area. Nelson mentions that migrants were regularly encountered in gardens around Beverley at the turn of the last century and comments by John Nicholson, writing in *The Naturalist* in 1902, prove that this partly applied to Hull also, but Nicholson could only say that they were "few and far between" in his town house garden.

The only modern record of a Nightjar in the Hull area concerns one reported in the Yorkshire Naturalists' Union's *Bird Report for 1990*, this being "in the centre of Hull on 1st September". Unfortunately, a large cloud of doubt hangs over this record, as around the same time an article appeared in the *Hull Daily Mail* that featured a 'Nightjar' found in a central Hull garden by a man and his dog. The finder did not know what kind of bird he had found so he telephoned the Royal Society for the Protection of Birds (RSPB) for advice. From his description the RSPB identified it as a Nightjar and advised the man to feed it moths until dusk, when he should then release it by gently throwing it into the darkening sky. Informing the *Hull Daily Mail* of his rare find, a reporter visited that afternoon and an article documenting the event appeared in the paper the next night, accompanied by a photograph of the bird sitting on the man's shoulder. Sadly, however, the photograph clearly shows that the bird was a Swift.

Swift

(Common Swift)

Apus apus

The Swift is an amazing creature. Throughout the course of its life, which can last more than 10 years, a Swift may never touch the ground. Nesting in the roofs of buildings, they feed, mate and even sleep on the wing. Young birds are independent of their parents as soon as they leave the nest and may not breed until their second summer after fledging. During this time, having no nest to attend to, these young birds may not land at all and remain in constant flight for a full two years! If a Swift ever does touch solid ground, after crash-landing, its short legs mean it is usually unable to take off again and it must be 'launched' into the air by a kind passer-by or face death. The sight or sound of the first Swift over the rooftops is the true harbinger of summer more than any Swallow, as Swifts are wholly dependent on good weather to enable them to catch enough airborne insects to be able to breed. The first birds to arrive back from their winter quarters in southern Africa are seen over the Hull area in early May, occasionally not arriving until after the 10th of the month if bad weather holds them back.

In the early 1900s Swifts were breeding in roofs around Southcoates and were commonly seen over the city. By the 1960s the main breeding area was the pan tile roofing of the North Hull Estate, where they were common, although regular breeding was apparently uncommon elsewhere. Breeding was noted in Cottingham during the 1980s and birds have probably always nested here, in the churches and old houses, as they still do today. A wildlife survey conducted by Helen Crowther in the Avenues area of Hull found good numbers of Swifts in 1996, though whether they were breeding here is unclear. Michael Flowers noted an increase in the number of Swifts seen over Hedon Road between the 1970s and 1990s and breeding is suspected in the roof of Hull Prison and old dock buildings. Any church tower, such as those in Sutton or Wawne, or traditional tiled roofing with plenty of gaps to allow the Swifts access is likely to hold breeding birds, but numbers are very difficult to judge. It is clear that the modern housing estates built in the 1970s, such as Bransholme and Orchard Park, are unsuitable for breeding Swifts as they cannot get under the eaves to nest in the loft spaces. Re-roofing of the North Hull Estate during the 1990s led to a decline in breeding numbers as the birds were shut out and known breeding sites are now few and far between, though it is likely that many are overlooked.

Feeding Swifts can be seen anywhere in the Hull area from May to August, with water or stands of trees apparently attracting the most insects and hence the birds. Up to 50 can regularly be seen over the Bransholme Sewage Works, with 100 or so over the Saltend area, while areas such as Northern Cemetery, East Park and Woody Carr near Wawne also have local concentrations. The Priory Road fields regularly attract small numbers. Early August concentrations are often the highest of the year, with up to 200 milling around High Bransholme on occasion in the early 1990s.

Most British Swifts leave the country as soon as their young have fledged and they become quite scarce by late August, though passage birds move through the area well into September. Passage can sometimes be heavy, especially ahead of bad weather, and 222 Swifts streamed south past Swine in just 20 minutes on 13th July 1993. A sample count of an enormous passage down the eastern edge of Hull on 7th August that same year gave 300 birds in just five minutes. The last birds are typically seen around the middle of September, with maybe a handful of stragglers over the next couple of weeks. October Swifts are rare, and the latest bird recorded in the Hull area passed over Bransholme Sewage Works on 9th October 1997.

Kingfisher

(Common Kingfisher)

Alcedo atthis

The Kingfisher is another one of those birds that is widely known among the general public though

few people have ever actually seen one. Even many birdwatchers only ever see them as a flash of electric blue streaking past, accompanied by a strident piping whistle. Despite their dazzling plumage, Kingfishers are incredibly well camouflaged against waterside foliage when at rest and can be very difficult to see. A good way of getting a respectable view of a Kingfisher is to place some kind of perch, perhaps a stout stick, along the edge of a drain or pond that they are frequenting. As the birds rely on suitable perches from which to launch their dives, this approach may also encourage a passing Kingfisher to stick around if the fishing is good. Kingfishers are not common in the Hull area, but they occur more frequently than one might assume and probably breed within the city boundary in most years.

During the 1840s a pair of Kingfishers bred alongside the pond at Hull Bank House on the bank of the River Hull, this being the residence of the Lord of the Manor, Colonel Haworth Booth, and today known as Haworth Hall. The Hall now sits behind the built-up Beverley Road, opposite the Bransholme Sewage Works over the River Hull, but in Haworth Booth's day it was several miles out into the countryside. Despite having recently stocked his pond with yearling trout and being an ardent sportsman, Haworth-Booth hadn't the heart to kill Kingfishers and allowed them to feed on his fish as they nested in a hole in the bank. One year, however,

Haworth Booth was surprised to find a live Kingfisher flapping around his grand house, apparently brought in by his son's cat. By 1895, however, Haworth Booth reported that Kingfishers were becoming rarer each year at Hull Bank House. In the winter of 1906/7 a furore erupted in Hull when the locals of Newland killed as many as 10 Kingfishers in just a few weeks, presumably for their feathers or stuffed trophies. Many people were upset that such beautiful birds, which back then brightened up an otherwise grim area, were allowed to be killed so readily by ignorant residents. Hull kept some of its Kingfishers, however, and on 19th November 1943 no fewer than three were seen over East Park Lake. Another bird wintering in the park in December 1952 was found in a nearby garden just before Christmas after being caught by a cat. Kingfishers bred on the King George Dock until the 1960s, though there were only four more sightings in the city up until 1966. In 1984 at least one bird was present at Thwaite Hall Lake, Cottingham, throughout the breeding season and may have tried to nest. Others were seen around the eastern docks from January to March 1985, becoming regular on the Holderness Drain in that area from August to the year end, with others on Oldfleet Channel (west of Saltend) in December. One was seen on Oldfleet Channel again in April 1986, with singles at Saltend Marsh throughout September and on the nearby stretch of the Holderness Drain in November and December.

The majority of sightings since the mid eighties have come from the two main drains that pass through the Hull area, namely the aforementioned Holderness Drain in East Hull and the Barmston Drain in West Hull. The water in these drains is usually very clear, particularly in the upper reaches, and this enables the Kingfishers to see the tadpoles, Sticklebacks and Roach fry that they feed on in a way that they are unable to do in the muddy waters of the River Hull. Most of the Barmston Drain sightings, from Dunswell to Clough Road, are in autumn as young birds are dispersing from their natal waters, and breeding does not seem to occur on this drain. In contrast, the Holderness Drain appears to be the stronghold for the species in the Hull area and birds have been breeding along the Bransholme stretch since at least the 1980s. A pair has usually returned to this area in March or April since 1989 and this is probably the best place to see Kingfishers in Hull as they fish along the drain or the adjoining Foredyke Stream throughout the summer. Breeding was thought to occur on this stretch in 1989 and in April 1992 a female was disturbed from a nest but high water levels flooded them out soon afterwards. Around 1990 a nest of six young was actually dug out of the bank of the Holderness Drain at Bransholme by vandals, with the chicks being simply left on the bank to die. Luckily, they were later rescued and hand-reared. In 1997 breeding was proven again on the Bransholme stretch when a pair of birds were seen repeatedly carrying fish into a hole in the bank but, again, no fledged young were seen and the nest may well have been flooded again before they had chance to leave.

Kingfishers can be seen on the Holderness Drain up to late autumn, with David Turner seeing two in November 1996 at the Carr Lane Nurseries near Longhill, although they seem to abandon it between December and early March. Wintering birds are more widespread and may turn up on any large pond, lake or substantial ditch. Lone Kingfishers have been recorded several times during recent autumns and winters at East Park and the Bransholme Sewage Works. Wintering has also occurred at Saltend, Thwaite Hall Lake and Willerby Carrs, with a bird seen at Carr Lane near the Springhead Park Golf Course in February 1981. Kingfishers are rarely seen on the River Hull itself, though they sometimes occur along the Wawne stretch, and Richard Middleton of the Hull Natural History Society saw them regularly on the nearby Engine Drain during 2000.

Bee-eater
(European Bee-eater)
Merops apiaster
On 27th May 1997 Brian Fendley saw a Bee-eater flying southwest over his garden in Kirk Ella, calling as it went. This is the only record of

a Bee-eater in the Hull area but, although Fendley was sure of the identification, the sighting was not reported due to the single-observer status and improbability of the bird being re-found and verified.

Hoopoe
Upupa epops

The striking and peculiar Hoopoe is an uncommon vagrant to Britain on migration, particularly in spring when birds migrating from Africa to their European breeding grounds overshoot their destination in fine weather and find themselves on our shores. While most quickly move on, a pair very occasionally remains to breed somewhere in southern Britain. Although most Yorkshire Hoopoes occur on the coast there are a surprising number of records for the Hull area.

On the exceptionally late date of 9th December 1943 a Mr Turpin was watching the Starlings on his lawn in Victoria Avenue, Hull, when a Hoopoe landed on his rosebush not ten feet away. Calling his daughter, they both watched the bird for several minutes as it nervously watched the feeding Starlings, looking as if it wanted to come down to join them. The Starlings eventually turned on it, however, and drove it off. A few years later a spring bird was seen in a garden in Kirk Ella on 17th April 1948, while in 1949 another was seen and callously shot from a flock of Starlings near Hull, though no specific date or location was recorded. A Hoopoe reported from Hull on 15th April 1953 was not sufficiently documented to totally convince Ralph Chislett, editor of the Ornithological Report for Yorkshire at the time, and he expressed some doubt over the sighting. One in September 1953 in the grounds of a Hull factory was less controversial, staying for a full three days. There is a suggestion in Boylan's 1967 *Birds in Hull* of another seen in the city in the early 1960s, though it perhaps refers to one of the previous birds.

S. L. James and B. Richards found a Hoopoe along the Holderness Drain near King George Dock on 23rd September 1985, yet again demonstrating the ornithological calibre of that corner of the city. The bird was watched bounding towards them before alighting on a hawthorn bush, raising its crest, and then disappearing into the thicket, never to be seen again. Another autumn Hoopoe was found in the grounds of Ainsthorpe School, off Willerby Road in Hull, on 6th October 1987. The bird stayed until the 10th, allowing observers from all over Hull to see it. There is another record of a Hoopoe from East Park for which I am unable to provide a date, though I believe it was sometime in the 1980s or 1990s.

That other Hoopoes have occurred in the Hull area over the years is highly likely. Any relatively open woodland, parkland or bushy field may play host to a passing bird, but such a find is very rare and something to shout about as they really are one of the most remarkable-looking species that Europe has to offer.

Wryneck
(Eurasian Wryneck)
Jynx torquilla

The Wryneck has always been a rare bird in the Hull area, even when it was a common summer migrant to southern Britain in the 19th Century. A bird killed on the Holderness coast in 1899 was the first that Colonel Haworth Booth, of Hullbank Hall (now Haworth Hall), had heard of in Holderness. It was

sent to Mr Darley, a Hull taxidermist, and he declared that it was the first specimen he had received for 37 years. This rarity has remained the case throughout the past century and there are just three modern records for the Hull area. One at Paull on 9th September 1969 was a typical location for a Scandinavian passage migrant, these being scarce but regular on Britain's east coast during spring and autumn. Slightly more unusual was another migrant well inland at Willerby Carrs, seen early one morning in the autumn of 1984, this being followed by another "on scrub land in West Hull" on 9th September 1999. This "scrub land" was possibly the Priory Sidings off Clive Sullivan Way.

Green Woodpecker
Picus viridis

The Green Woodpecker, or 'Yaffle' to give it its country name, is a scarce wanderer to the Hull area that has been recorded on only a handful of occasions, chiefly in winter or early spring. Members of the Hull Scientific and Field Naturalists' Club saw just one in the city between 1960 and 1966. The next documented record was not for another 20 years when one was along the Holderness Drain at North Bransholme, intermittently, from 12th November 1983 to 16th February 1984. Another at the Holderness Drain near Alexandra Dock on 19th April 1986 was the first for the Saltend/docks area. Crowther's 1996 survey of the Avenues in Hull uncovered an alleged sighting in 1992 and a reported yaffle, or call, heard in 1995. One was seen on Hessle Foreshore on 5th January 1997, two were in the nearby Humber Bridge Country Park in January and February 1998 and one near Sutton Golf Course in 1999 was seen on the unusual summer date of 18th June.

Peter Bonavia's compilation of the 1981-6 survey of the birds of the Cottingham area found no sign of Green Woodpeckers despite the pasture and good stands of timber in that area. Why our corner of the world should be shunned so much by this loud and assertive woodpecker is a mystery, but it is clear that anyone coming across one should consider themself rather blessed.

Great Spotted Woodpecker
Dendrocopos major
This, the most regular woodpecker in the Hull area, is nevertheless a fairly uncommon bird in our part of the world. West Hull and the villages thereabouts have always had more to offer the Great Spotted Woodpecker in terms of mature trees and woods, with the isolated pockets of woodland in East Hull and beyond being less frequently tenanted. Great Spotted Woodpeckers certainly breed in the Hull area, though most records are of wandering birds in autumn and winter.

Boylan's *Birds in Hull* (1967) mentions just five winter occurrences of the Great Spotted Woodpecker in 1960s Hull but goes on to suggest that breeding may have occurred, indicating that they were being under recorded. Birds were certainly present year-round in Cottingham in the late 1960s and were still regular near the Cottingham Recreation Ground in winter and spring in the mid 1980s, with others seen in the Thwaite Hall grounds around that time. Still in the west of the Hull area, Great Spotted Woodpeckers have been seen on and off around Kirk Ella since the late 1970s at least. Most of the Kirk Ella records were outside of the breeding season, though birds were seen in Kerry Woods during the spring and summer months in 1982, 1987 and 1993. A pair was in Chanterlands Avenue Cemetery in January 1986 and, more recently, others have been seen on the Priory Sidings, off Clive Sullivan Way, during autumn and winter in the late 1990s. Recent breeding has been noted in Western Cemetery. The 1996 wildlife survey in the Avenues area of Hull (Crowther, 1996) revealed Great Spotted Woodpeckers to be occasional visitors to that part of town despite the perception of a decrease since the 1960s.

Over the river in East Hull, Hedon Road Cemetery had its first Great Spotted Woodpecker in September 1977 but birds have occurred most years since then. Breeding has occurred several times at that site, including in the summer of 2000, though M. Flowers was saddened to find a female shot dead by a heartless airgunner along the nearby Hull to Withernsea railway line in November 1998. A Great Spotted Woodpecker was calling from the Paradise Wood at Woody Carr, near Wawne, in April 1989 and it is highly likely that breeding is occurring there but access restrictions make this difficult to confirm. Two juveniles along the Old Main Drain hedgerow near Carlam Hill Farm, just a quarter of a mile from Woody Carr, in August 1990 were a strong hint that breeding had indeed occurred locally that year. Great Spotted Woodpeckers also visit the small copses and scrub to the east of Bransholme, just a little further south of Woody Carr, in most years between autumn and spring.

Great Spotted Woodpeckers have been seen elsewhere along the eastern margin of the city, such as the Carr Lane Nurseries near Sutton. There were just three records from Saltend during the well watched years of 1985 and 1986, all between September and April and all involving lone birds on brief visits. Further into town, birds were present in East Park throughout 1997 and I saw one calling from the top of a tree on James Reckitt Avenue, just outside the park, in November 2000. Breeding has been suspected in East Park for several years and another pair has nested in the grounds of nearby Holderness House, on the corner of Laburnum Avenue and Holderness Road. The loud, metallic call of a Great Spotted Woodpecker was heard coming from the tiny Trinity graveyard behind the Castle Street/Ferensway roundabout in the city centre on 24th February 1998. That just goes to show that one should not be too surprised to come across a wandering bird in virtually any mature trees anywhere in the Hull area, particularly in the autumn and winter months. To see or hear a Great Spotted Woodpecker in the Hull area, however, particularly in East Hull, is not an everyday occurrence and a good view of one of these strikingly patterned birds is certainly something to be appreciated.

Lesser Spotted Woodpecker
Dendrocopos minor

The first record of Lesser-spotted Woodpeckers in the Hull area came in 1944 when a pair were first seen in Anlaby on 27th April and stayed to breed. The species was seen again in 1945 at nearby West Ella and once more on 9th August 1946 in a Willerby garden. It seems likely that this collection of records involves the same individuals or their progeny.

This tiny woodpecker is a very rare bird in the East Riding with sporadic breeding at Hornsea being their only isolated outpost anywhere near Hull since the 1940s. There is a very remote chance of finding a wandering Lesser Spotted Woodpecker in the Hull area these days, most likely outside of the breeding season, but there is tantalising evidence that occasional birds still visit every now and then. In the extreme northwest of the area covered by this book, in Fishpond Wood north of Skidby, there were several unconfirmed reports in January 1986. Helen Crowther's 1996 survey of urban wildlife in the Avenues area of Hull, meanwhile, revealed yet more unconfirmed reports. Clarification of this issue would indeed be useful, not to mention interesting, in light of the species' scarcity in the East Riding. The most reliable record of recent years, however, came on 12th July 2000 when a Lesser Spotted Woodpecker was heard calling loudly from the southeast corner of the Humber Bridge Country Park.

Skylark
(Sky Lark)
Alauda arvensis

This famous songster is a regular breeding bird in the Hull area. They can be heard delivering their complex and melodious song from way up high in many outlying areas of the city and beyond. The Skylark is also a relatively common passage migrant in the area and may be seen or heard overhead right up to the city centre, although they are generally quite scarce in winter.

The *Wildfowl at Hull* decree of 1560, which listed game prices in the town, set the price of a dozen "Larkes" at fourpence. Migrant Skylarks and other songbirds, loaded with sweet fat to fuel their journey, are still popular delicacies in many parts of the Mediterranean but today in Britain we only appreciate them for their song. At the beginning of the 20th Century the Skylark was still a common passage migrant over Hull but there were no specific breeding records from that time. This was more than likely due to the simple fact that Skylarks were breeding in most open spaces and were therefore so common as not to warrant a mention. By the 1960s the Skylark was described as a resident bird that bred in fairly open, rough grassy areas. The abundance on passage was remarked upon once more and migrants were regular over the city centre in October and November. Even after the autumn passage had peaked, and the flocks had moved on ahead of the oncoming winter, large numbers of Skylarks could still be driven over the Hull area in front of severe weather. On 21st January 1970 a total of 1,000 were counted passing over East Park, with 2,000 heading south over Kirk Ella during snowy weather on 31st January 1972.

In the early 1980s the Skylark was found to be a widespread and common breeding bird in farmland around Cottingham and northwest Hull. Around a dozen pairs were also breeding around Saltend and the eastern docks in the mid 1980s. Intensive observation in this southeast corner at that time gave a detailed picture of the autumn passage and hard-weather movements of Skylarks in winter. In November and December 1984 up to 30 birds could to be counted passing over on each visit. A similar number were moving south each day in September and early October 1985 and up to 40 were grounded on most days. There were big movements ahead of bad weather: 395 headed southwest on 13th January 1985, with 66 on 17th and 55 on 18th. A further 218 moved west-southwest on 28th December 1985 and 240 went south on 6th February 1986. Notable flocks could

occasionally be grounded inland, with 36 on Willerby Low Road on 7th January 1984 and 40 at Bransholme on 19th December 1989.

A pair of Skylarks bred in Hedon Road Cemetery in 1979 and a lone bird has sung overhead most years since, albeit less regularly since the 1990s. Between 10 and 20 pairs were breeding in the rough grassland and weedy arable fields between North Bransholme and the Holderness Drain during the 1980s and early 1990s. Regular observation at this site over several years gave a good impression of the movements of Skylarks through the seasons, with birds often being absent in January and February before the breeding birds arrived and started singing in early March. The number of singing birds peaked in May but Skylarks were usually scarce from late July to late September as local birds headed south for the winter. Autumn migrants from the Continent arrived from late September onwards, usually in flocks of between 20 and 30, but occurrences were irregular and most had moved out again by late December.

It was clear by the mid 1990s that all was not well with Britain's Skylarks. National surveys around that time revealed that the breeding population had more than halved in the last quarter of the 20th Century. The decline was blamed on the intensification of agriculture that had rid the arable fields of the weeds and insects that Skylarks depend on. Recent breeding records include three pairs off Priory Road in 1996, several on the Priory Sidings in 1998, one singing over Anlaby Common in 1999 and another over Victoria Dock in 2000, but the pesticides on the farmland, the development and 'tidying-up' of many rough areas throughout the Hull area has hit our local Skylarks fairly hard and they are nowhere near as common as they were just a generation ago. There are still around a dozen pairs breeding at North Bransholme, with a good winter flock of 65 there in December 1999, but this is probably the largest breeding concentration in the Hull boundary now, with increasingly fewer around the outlying towns and villages.

Shorelark
(Horned Lark)
Eremophila alpestris

On 5th January 1997 R. Baines watched a lone Shorelark for 2 hours near the West Wharf at Victoria Dock. This is the only record of this Scandinavian species in the Hull area, which is very rare away from its irregular wintering areas on the coast of eastern England.

Sand Martin
Riparia riparia

The first Sand Martins to reach the Hull area typically arrive around the second week of April. They are rather scarce passage migrants inland, however, as there are no major bodies of water to attract them in any numbers or for any length of time. The nearest nesting site to Hull is at Redcliff, North Ferriby, where around 15 pairs were breeding in the late 1990s.

The larger lakes, namely East Park Lake, Pickering Park Lake and the Bransholme Sewage Works reservoir, are the most regular sites for Sand Martins in Hull. Six were over East Park Lake on 5th April 1943, with the first ones of 1944 there again on the same date. This is the earliest recorded arrival date for the Hull area. Boylan (1967) reported Sand Martins as being scarce spring passage migrants in Hull during the 1960s and this pretty much holds true for today, except that they are just as likely to occur in autumn. Bonavia (1990) stated that they were regular on passage in small numbers during the 1980s, mainly along the River Hull. Between 1992 and 1993 I found them to be scarce but regular on passage at the Bransholme Sewage Works.

Spring passage often peaks in May, though nowhere sees more than a handful of birds and usually only on a very few days. Autumn passage begins around early July and lasts until late September, involving a similar number of birds. The latest autumn date I have come across involved four birds passing quickly through the Bransholme Sewage Works on 1st October 2000. Most records involve birds doing just this, passing straight through and barely stopping to snatch a fly or two.

Swallow
(Barn Swallow)
Hirundo rustica

Everyone knows the Swallow in popular folklore as the harbinger of spring, although the average 'man-in-the-street' would probably struggle to identify one. Country people know them well, however, as the Swallow relies almost exclusively on man-made constructions for its nesting sites. Much superstition grew up around the Swallow in years gone by that is now largely forgotten. Nelson (1907) tells us that rural Victorians in the East Riding considered it very bad luck to rob or destroy a Swallow's nest, going on to recount the tale of the sons of a Hull banker who cleared out such a nest from a farm their father owned on the outskirts of Hull. The farmer's wife told how "the bank broke soon after, and, poor things, the family have had nought but trouble since". It is stories such as this that led to tolerance of the nesting habits of the Swallow. In June 1887, when a pair decided to build their nest on a curtain pole inside the open window of a country house near Cottingham, they were left alone and reared their brood in peace. Perhaps the householder was a banker?

Swallows generally arrive in the Hull area around the third or fourth week of April, after marathon flights from winter quarters as far south as South Africa. The earliest was one in Hull on 18th March 1945. Birds were breeding around Park Grove at the beginning of the 20th Century while nesting occurred as close to the city centre as the old botanic gardens in West Park during the 1960s. Other regular breeding sites around that time were an old shed at Northern Cemetery and a garage on Park Lane, Cottingham. A pair bred in an outbuilding at Hedon Road Cemetery between 1969 and 1973 but only once since, in 1985, although the nest still remains intact.

Bonavia (1990) described Swallows as common breeders and passage migrants around Cottingham in the 1980s. A pair bred in an old railway carriage near Saltend in 1984 and 1985 and three or four pairs have bred around the farms and pumping station between North Bransholme and the Holderness Drain since the late 1980s. Over 20 pairs were nesting around farms off Priory Road in 1996 and three broods were reared in a shed at Bamforth Farm in Wawne the same year, but the regular nest site in the Avenues was deserted that year. A pair regularly nests in the derelict buildings at the Bransholme Sewage Works and there can be few farms, barns or outbuildings on the outskirts of Hull and into the East Riding that do not have Swallows each summer.

Spring passage in the Hull area is significant but much less pronounced than in autumn. Swallows were noted to be very numerous at Saltend as far back as 23rd May 1901. Up to 40 could still be found flitting around there in May during the mid 1980s, though numbers rarely exceeded 10 in June and July 1985. A similar number of spring passage birds could be found at North Bransholme in the early 1990s. Between five and 15 were seen at the Bransholme Sewage Works is spring and early summer during the same period.

Birds begin to move through again in August, invariably heading south, and numbers build to a peak in September. Flocks of up to 50 birds are commonly seen over the Bransholme Sewage Works reservoir at this time. Similar numbers coccur over the rough grassland at North Bransholme and up to 60 were around Swine Bank, off Priory Road, in 1996. Some flocks linger for a few days while others pass straight through. They may gather anywhere that offers shelter from the wind and plenty of insects, with water and the scattered trees of the parks and cemeteries being favourite places. Large, loose flocks of up to 100 birds were gathered around Sutton and Saltshouse Road in late September and early October 1993, no doubt finding food and shelter among the old parkland trees. Temporary roosts can attract large numbers of passage birds for a few weeks during autumn. A total of 200 were dropping down to roost at Saltend Marsh on 29th August 1984. This built up to 1,200 by 1st September, with 300 in September the following year.

Most Swallows have left the Hull area by the beginning of October. Late flocks can occasionally be found until the end of the first week of that month and stragglers until the third week. The latest sightings were at Saltshouse Road on 21st October 1993 and the Humber Bridge on 6th November 2000.

House Martin
Delichon urbica

A thinly distributed breeding bird throughout the Hull area, the House Martin is nevertheless a common passage migrant and familiar summer visitor. Often associating with Swallows on passage and when feeding, House Martins tend to arrive around Hull a little later than that species, usually in the last week of April. The earliest date I have is 18th April 1993.

House Martins have been breeding around Hull for many years. Nesting was noted around Pearson Park at the beginning of the 20th Century and small colonies persist on the Chanterlands and Newland Avenues to this day. Birds were breeding on the Malet Lambert School, near East Park, in the 1940s. Two pairs still had young in the nest there on the extremely late date of 15th November in 1942 and a full grown bird was found freshly dead eight days later. There was a breeding colony on the North Hull Estate in the early 1960s at least and Bonavia (1990) reported that breeding was common around Cottingham in the 1980s. Several pairs were nesting on houses off Cottingham's South Street in 1996 and others were at Wood Farm, at the top of Priory Road.

In May 1991 I discovered a small colony of around 10 to 15 pairs of House Martins at the Dulverton Close end of Bude Road, Bransholme. The remains of old nests indicated that House Martins had been breeding here for a few years and some residents had attached tassels under their eaves to deter the birds from building. Just a handful of birds nested there in 1992 and by 1993 there were none, although around five pairs had relocated a short distance away to the Holwell Road area.

A colony has existed on the Southcoates Junior School, off Southcoates Lane in East Hull, since at least the 1970s although the number of nests has decreased since then. House Martins will readily take to the eaves of new housing if conditions are right, however, and several pairs have recently begun to nest in the new Victoria Dock Village. A few pairs have also nested down Durham Street, between Garden Village and Holderness Road, during the 1990s. Other small colonies are scattered throughout the towns and villages surrounding Hull but most correspondents indicate that the number of breeding House Martins in the Hull area has declined markedly since the 1980s. Each colony, therefore, becomes more precious each year and House Martins should be encouraged wherever possible. Indeed, the erection of artificial nests on suitable buildings may help establish new colonies.

As a passage migrant the House Martin is a widespread and occasionally abundant bird. Spring passage peaks in May and this species, along with the Swallow, was reported to be "very numerous" at Saltend on 23rd May 1901. Numbers rarely exceeded a dozen at Saltend in the spring of 1985 but around 20 could be found over the Bransholme Sewage Works reservoir on many May days in the early 1990s. House Martins typically become scarcer during June and July, reflecting the relatively small breeding population, but numbers build in August as young birds fledge and autumn passage begins. A flock of around 80 birds, many of them juveniles, were milling around over the Loatleys Fields, off Priory Road, in August 1996. August 1998 saw over 200 gathering at Howdale Road in East Hull. I noted large flocks of House Martins and Swallows gathering around nearby Saltshouse Road in September 1993; over 100 could be found there on many days in the last week of the month and several dozen were still present on 5th October. Numerous parties of up to 20 birds were also observed heading south over North Bransholme, in the company of Swallows and a few late Swifts, during the third week of September that year.

The influx of passage birds results in counts of 50 birds or more over the Bransholme Sewage Works reservoir in August and September. Up to 25 have been seen at Saltend in September although the majority will have left the Hull area by the end of that month. Stragglers often pass through during the first or second week of October, however, but November records are rare. Aside from the Malet Lambert birds in 1942, mentioned above, the only other November record is of a single bird over the city on 10th November 1949.

Richard's Pipit
Anthus novaeseelandiae

On 5th October 1986 S. M. Lister watched a Richard's Pipit on the shore at Paull Holme Sands and followed it upriver as it made its way towards Paull. The Paull Holme Sands are just outside the area covered by this book, but this record is included here on the grounds that the bird eventually made its way close enough to Paull to be considered valid. Richard's Pipits breed from western Siberia to Mongolia, wintering from India through to southeast Asia. Very small numbers regularly turn up on the Yorkshire coast from mid September to mid November. In addition to the above record, two other Richard's Pipits have been found at Paull Holme Sands in the past quarter of a century. Others have made it to Pulfin Bog and Tophill Low (near Beverley) and as far inland as South Yorkshire, so the Hull area is well within range for another visit.

Tawny Pipit
Anthus campestris
On the early morning of 21st September 1985 S. L. James flushed

a large pipit at the edge of Saltend Marsh. The calls and flash of the tail pattern as the bird flew off immediately encouraged James to search for it and he relocated it just after midday in the area of the sluice gate. The bird was then flushed again and called with a harsh "splezz", followed by a "chirrup", as it went, prompting James to confidently identify it as a Tawny Pipit as it flew overhead. The bird was followed but was very secretive, often hiding in long grass, but James finally saw it well on the ground and took a detailed description. This appeared in the 1985 *Saltend and Hull Docks Bird Report*. The bird was still present the next day, being seen by around 60 other birdwatchers, but flew off north in the late afternoon. The record was accepted by the Yorkshire Naturalists' Union and published as a juvenile Tawny Pipit in the 1985 *Ornithological Report*.

At least one birdwatcher has since questioned the identification, however, and there are several bones of contention. Firstly, doubts are raised by the fact that the calls described could equally apply to the rather similar Richards' Pipit.

Additionally, one of the most pertinent distinguishing features between Richard's and Tawny Pipits, the presence or absence of a dark loral line, was not mentioned. There is also confusion between the malar and moustachial stripe in James' description. All this is compounded by the possibility that, besides James, just one other observer actually saw the bird on the ground. Indeed, it was felt by some that certain aspects of the written description actually suggested Richards' Pipit over Tawny Pipit. This is all a bit academic, though, as the record was passed by the YNU rarities panel so officially stands.

Tree Pipit
Anthus trivialis

The Tree Pipit is, at best, an uncommon passage migrant in the Hull area. The earliest documented occurrence comes from 1947 when the first Yorkshire bird of the spring was seen at Hull on 13th April. Boylan (1967) gives only two passage records between 1960 and 1966, though Brian Fendley saw two at Kerry Woods, Kirk Ella, on 18th August 1979. The intensive coverage of the Saltend area in 1985 and 1986 revealed a very light passage of Tree Pipits in both spring and autumn. Two birds were logged there in the first half of May and a further eight between mid August and mid September, the majority in the last week of August. The most recent record was of two birds at Saltend on 6th October 1998, though it is likely that the majority of Tree Pipits pass through unseen or unrecorded.

Meadow Pipit
Anthus pratensis

Meadow Pipits occur in the Hull area wherever there is sufficient rough grassland to support them. Things do not seem to have changed much since 1967, when Boylan stated that Meadow Pipits bred sparingly within the old Hull boundary. They were also fairly common on passage when birds could frequently be seen and heard passing over the city centre. I've not heard of Meadow Pipits coming to suburban gardens in winter these days, as they did in Boylan's time, although the smaller gardens of the new suburbs are probably less enticing.

Suburban breeding occurred during the 1960s in an area of weedy ground known as the 'Woolsheds', which lay to the west of Chanterlands Avenue abutting Northern Cemetery, but this ground has long since been tidied up. Up to 18 pairs were breeding on Saltend Marsh in the mid 1980s and another pair was on St. Andrew's Dock. Small numbers were also breeding around Cottingham in the 1980s and at least one pair still rears young on the Priory Road fields. Up to 10 pairs have bred on the rough grassland between Foredyke Stream and Bransholme Road, east of the Bransholme housing estate, since at least the 1980s. Many more do so on nearby North Carr. A pair bred on the strip of rough grassland between Old Main Drain and Cumbrian Way on North Bransholme until the City Council began mowing it, though up to two pairs still breed on the Priory Sidings (off Clive Sullivan Way). Others possibly do so on what is left of the Rockford Fields (behind Chamberlain Road) and doubtless many other places.

Meadow Pipits largely desert their nesting grounds between late November and March. Spring and autumn passage often leads to a noticeable increase in the number of birds on the ground, however, as well producing a constant stream of birds overhead. Peak numbers on the ground at North Bransholme usually occur from August to late October, when 20 or more may be flushed from the fields. Around 100 were grounded at Saltend on 23rd September 1985 while 180 passed south overhead. In the same period almost 400 birds flew south there on just one September day and up to 60 were grounded in October. More recently 80 were grounded at Saltend on 6th October 1998. There are typically less than 10 birds in this area after November, but just after Christmas 2000 I counted more than 20 scratching a living on the Humber embankment at Paull, the only snow-free patch of grass around. Spring passage can be just as impressive as the autumn period; 220 flew northwest over Kirk Ella on 17th April 1970, with 110 going north on 13th April 1972.

Development and general tidying up of the pockets of rough grassland throughout the Hull area have deprived many Meadow Pipits of their nesting sites. It is still possible to see their parachuting display flight in many places around the outskirts and beyond, however, usually from late March until June or July. Passage birds, meanwhile, can be heard giving their 'seep' call note overhead almost anywhere.

Rock Pipit
Anthus petrosus

The nearest breeding Rock Pipits to the Hull area are on the cliffs at Flamborough but the species is a regular, if scarce, winter visitor and passage migrant on the Humber waterfront. This is more or less how Boylan (1967) described their status in Hull during the 1960s - a scarce winter visitor that could turn up anywhere on the waterfront - but he also mentioned that they had occurred on the River Hull in the north of the city.

There were no more reports of Rock Pipits around Hull until the mid 1980s, when small numbers were again found to be visiting the Humber waterfront. Close scrutiny of birds around Saltend and Paull seemed to reveal the presence of both the British race (*Anthus petrosus petrosus*) and the Scandinavian race (*Anthus petrosus littoralis*) of Rock Pipit. This raised intriguing questions regarding the species movements in the Hull area. Birds of the Scandinavian race began appearing on the Humber embankment or around the docks in late September, with up to a dozen at any one time. They had apparently left by mid October, only to be replaced by a similar number of British birds. These remained throughout the winter, on and off, until around mid March. Scandinavian birds, easily recognisable in full or part summer plumage, then appeared again for a couple of weeks.

This situation continues up to the present day. Peak day counts at places such as Paull and Saltend may reach half a dozen, but mystery still surrounds the movement of the individual races. It could be that the Scandinavian race is purely a passage migrant, moving through the Hull area in September/October and again in late March/early April. This would make the British birds winter visitors between late October and mid March. The alternative theory is that the vast majority of birds seen in the Hull area are Scandinavian. These birds are recognisable in autumn as they arrive in the remnants of their characteristic summer plumage. Once they moult into winter plumage, however, they are very similar to British birds and only reveal themselves as Scandinavian when they moult back into summer plumage the following spring. Recent opinion leans towards the latter scenario, but close examination of birds in the hand or the results of genetic analysis would be interesting and useful in clearing this up.

Whatever the origin and racial identity of the Rock Pipits, a handful of birds can be found anywhere from the Humber Bridge to Paull between late September and early April, such as the two birds at Albert Dock on 15th January 2000 and another at St Andrew's Quay in December. Sightings away from the Humber are very rare, with the only recent record being of a single bird at the Bransholme Sewage Works on 14th March 2000. It is likely that many go unnoticed and close scrutiny of pipits beside any watery habitats may well reveal a few more.

Water Pipit
Anthus spinoletta

Water Pipits are scarce winter visitors and passage migrants in East Yorkshire, being treated as a race of our Rock Pipit until 1986. Two birds, reported as the *spinoletta* race of Rock Pipit, at Saltend on 28th October 1985 would now be classified as Water Pipits, as would the one seen there again the next day. The only other record for the Hull area is of a single seen at Saltend by B. Richards on 7th April 1998. Others must surely have occurred over the years and gone unrecorded, the similarity to Rock Pipit perhaps masking appearances during autumn or winter when the two species are similar in plumage. Areas with a strong freshwater element are, as the name suggests, the most likely places to find a Water Pipit at any time from autumn through to spring, with Saltend being the clear favourite.

Yellow Wagtail
Motacilla flava

The British race of the Yellow Wagtail, *M. f. flavissima*, starts to reach the Hull area from its African wintering grounds between mid

April and the first week of May. The earliest arrival was a bird at Cottingham on 11th April 1910. Peak spring passage occurs in the first two weeks of May. Birds are nowhere numerous these days and a handful per year is the most that individual locations can expect to see. Few, if any, stay to nest in the area now, with suspected breeding at Hull's east and west waterfronts in the early 1960s and two pairs seen carrying food into wheat fields north of Wawne in July 1994 being the only indications over the last 40 years.

Yellow Wagtails were more numerous at the turn of the last century than today, with John Nicholson noting them as occasional visitors to his Hull garden in 1901. Reports were contradictory during the middle of the century, with the species being described as "very plentiful" around Hull in 1942 but "sparsely distributed in the East Riding" the following year. Yellow Wagtails have certainly been a little scarce in the Hull area since at least the 1960s, in line with the national decline in numbers during the latter half of the 20th Century. Back then records

averaged a little over one per year within the old city boundary. During the 1980s Bonavia (1990) described them as only "occasional" around Cottingham and they were just about annual at Bransholme in the 1990s.

Farms and wet, preferably grazed, grassy areas are the preferred stopover sites in spring, though one was seen in Queen's Gardens in the early 1960s. Migrants may also be located passing overhead, giving their characteristic whistle as they bound towards the horizon, and some years this is all one may see of them. Autumn passage is not usually as heavy as during the spring, lasting from August to mid September, although larger parties may be involved. Fourteen roosting at Saltend on 10th September 1998 is by far the largest number recorded in the area. A male of the nominate Blue-headed race, *M. f. flava*, from Central Europe, was at Paull lighthouse on 16th May 1997.

Grey Wagtail
Motacilla cinerea

A scarce but regular winter visitor from fast-flowing upland streams, Grey Wagtails can occasionally be found near any stretch of water in the Hull area from September to April. The majority of sightings occur between October and December.

Bransholme Sewage Works is a favourite site for this species and a couple are seen each year around the filter beds or next to the reservoir. Two together is not infrequent there and no fewer than nine were roosting at nearby Sutton Road Bridge on 29th September 2000. Saltend and the docks have produced many sightings over the years, although birds can turn up literally anywhere. One trying to land on the fountain in Queen's Gardens in December 1988 emphasised the attraction of running water for the species, while another wintered at nearby Prince's Quay in 1998. Indeed, wintering birds were regular in the city centre and around the River Hull in the 1960s and probably still are. The parks are also a good place to look out for Grey Wagtails, with no less than three in East Park on 24th September 1997. Two were present in East Park from October to December as far back as 1943 and again as recently as October 1998. Singles were also seen in the Pearson Park Wildlife Garden in February and December 1996. Other places to host a bird or two in recent years include the Humber Bridge Country Park, the Foredyke Stream at North Bransholme, Oak Road Playing Fields, Hedon Road Cemetery, Ryde Avenue in Newland, Hull Marina and the Victoria Dock development. Such a spread clearly indicates that not all urban or suburban wagtails should immediately be dismissed as Pied.

On 9th June 2001 I was surprised to see an unseasonal Grey Wagtail at the Bransholme Sewage Works. I was even more shocked when it was joined by a second. The birds appeared to be an adult female and an immature, the latter seemingly independent and complete with a full-length tail. Their presence at the height of the breeding season indicates that breeding may have occurred locally that year.

Pied Wagtail
Motacilla alba yarrellii

The cheery Pied Wagtail, still known among some Hull folk as the 'Willy Wagtail' or 'Paddy Wagtail', is a widespread and not uncommon bird throughout the area. The species is familiar to many due to its close association with urban and suburban habitats, earning its name with a constant bobbing of the tail. Advertising itself with a breezy "chissik!", a Pied Wagtail can often be seen running across car parks or school playgrounds, especially after rain, in farmyards or beside one of the park lakes or other stretches of water. They can be found all year round in the Hull area, being quite thinly distributed as a breeding bird but often forming flocks to feed and roost at favoured areas during winter.

Boylan (1967) regarded the Pied Wagtail as a resident bird that bred sparingly throughout Hull during the 1960s. It was also a frequent visitor to the city centre and Northern Cemetery in autumn and winter. A pair nested under the ornamental bridge over East Park Lake in 1967, and no doubt many times since, and an albino bird was seen there in September 1953. Bonavia (1990) listed the Pied Wagtail as an uncommon and localised bird around Cottingham and northwest Hull in the 1980s. The species was nevertheless present all year round and was often seen at the University of Hull campus, Cottingham Road, and on the Priory Road fields in winter.

A large winter roost was established at the Saltend chemical plant until 1981. A total of 221 birds arrived from the north/northwest in the half an hour before dusk on 14th February 1980 to spend the night on a warm 'drumming shed' roof. This roost had decreased to just 30 or so birds in 1985/1986, between October and February, with a couple of pairs remaining to breed each summer.

One or two pairs of Pied Wagtails were regularly seen at North Bransholme during the early 1990s, usually around the farms. In 1989 a pair nested on a classroom shelf at the newly opened Perronet

Thompson School (now called Kingswood High) on Wawne Road, gaining access to the building via an air vent. I found Pied Wagtails to be common at the Bransholme Sewage Works in the early 1990s, with at least one breeding pair in summer and a wintering flock of 70 or more between late October and early April. The wintering flock at the Sewage Works appeared to grow throughout the 1990s, with 114 in January 1998 and 200 in February 2000. The filter beds that the birds found so attractive are now abandoned, however, and I struggled to find a mere handful in late 2000. Good numbers can sometimes be found in East Park though, and 28 were counted in March 1998. A further 200 were seen going to roost in Queen's Gardens in March 2000.

Other recent nesting sites round and about Hull have included Willerby Carr Farm in the west, Wawne's Bamforth Farm in the north (where a pair built their nest on top of an old blackbird nest in a shed) and Hedon Road Cemetery in the east.

'White Wagtail'
Motacilla alba alba

The silvery-backed White Wagtail, the Continental race of our Pied

Wagtail, is a scarce spring passage migrant in the Hull area. Boylan (1967) mentions one in Queen's Gardens sometime between 1960 and 1966 but the next recorded instance was not until 1997, when one was seen in East Park on 10th and 14th March. One at Bransholme on 7th May the following year is the most recent record but they are almost certainly under recorded.

Waxwing
(Bohemian Waxwing)
Bombycilla garrulus

Waxwings are strikingly beautiful birds that nest in the remote taiga zone of Scandinavia across to Siberia. In winter they feed almost exclusively on red berries, particularly rowan, and very small numbers visit Britain each year. In years when the berries become exhausted in their usual winter quarters, however, large numbers of Waxwings can invade Britain from the east. During such invasions Waxwings are often found in built-up areas where ornamental trees and shrubs still bear fruit. Coming from the far north, the birds can often be extremely tame.

The recorded occurrences of Waxwings in the Hull area are as follows:

1921: Four at Sutton on 21st November.

1946/7: A big invasion winter. The first to arrive was a large flock on Holderness Road in late November, growing to 100 birds by 15th December when another 30 were in Tweendykes gardens. The Holderness Road flock decreased to 56 by New Years Eve, but 30 were in nearby James Reckitt Avenue the same day. The last was on Holderness Road on 15th March.

1951: One fell down the chimney of G. H. Ainsworth's house in Gillshill Road, near East Park, on 5th February. It was released unharmed after Ainsworth had ringed it.

1957: Single figures in Hull in February, a poor showing for a national invasion winter.

1958: Three near Sutton on 13th December, another invasion winter.

1965/6: Another big invasion winter, and one of the best ever in the Hull area. 50 were "near Hull" and 300 were near Kirk Ella on 14th November, with birds being "common" well into the New Year.

1966: One was on Holderness Road on Boxing Day.

1970: Another invasion year, with 45 in Hull in November.

1971: 16 were at Kirk Ella on 21st December.

1977: One was in Kerry Drive, Kirk Ella on 9th January.

1979: Five were down National Avenue, West Hull, between 25th January and 11th February.

1982: One in Hull from 2nd to 3rd March.

1985: One at Stoneferry on 18th January.

1985/6: Another irruption winter, starting with one on Carr Lane in Willerby from 8th to 27th November and three west past King George Dock on 19th November. Singles made brief appearances in Chanterlands Avenue and Spring Bank in January.

1987: One on Staveley Road, East Hull, on 7th March.

1988: Three in the Old Main Drain hedgerow, North Bransholme, on 26th November, with one to two again in mid December.

1989: Four on the Old Main Drain hedgerow, North Bransholme, in November.

1990: 30 at Hessle on 27th January.

1990/1: Another good winter around Hull, with 18 in Bricknell Avenue on 19th November and six the following day. Up to 30 in Anlaby at the end of January and into February, when 13 were also in First Lane in Hessle.

1991/2: An even better winter than the last, starting with 25 in West Hull on 27th December before 10 on Bricknell Avenue in January. Eighty were near the Kingston General Hospital, Beverley Road, from January to March.

1994: A group of 11 in Park Avenue, near Pearson Park, on 21st April were the latest spring Waxwings recorded in the Hull area.

1996: A record invasion in the UK during the early months of the year and Hull saw its fair share of birds.

The first were six in Kerry Drive (Kirk Ella) on 7th January, with two off Priory Road on 10th and three on 13th. A flock of 50 was in the Avenues area of Hull throughout much of January and into February. Another 35 were on the Pickhills hawthorns, at the north end of Priory Road, in February.

1997: One in East Park on 3rd January was the first of a good late winter period. Three were at the Holderness Drain on Holderness Road a few days later and up to four were in Bricknell Avenue, West Hull, the same week. 20 were back on Holderness Road on 14th March with the last of the winter being four on Sutton Fields Industrial Estate on 25th.

1997/8: A well-watched bird was feeding in a tree outside the Brazil Street Post Office, at the town-end of Holderness Road, in December. Two were on berries near the Park Avenue Adult Education centre on 2nd February.

1999/2000: Another good winter and probably the best documented irruption in the Hull area, with small flocks being widespread. The first were three in Willerby on 11th November, followed by 10 at the junction of Staveley Road and Diadem Grove (at the far end of Holderness Road) three days later. Two appeared on Sutton Road on 21st November and 18 spent the following week down First Lane, Anlaby. Birds then disappeared for a while until 14 arrived on Brindley Street, Holderness Road, in mid December. Ten on Diadem Grove on

21st coincided with two near Ennerdale Sports centre and one at Bransholme Police Station. Another was on Sutton Road the next day. Two were on the shrubs outside Britannia House on the Beverley Road/Spring Bank junction in the city centre on 3rd January. Nine turned up at Victoria Dock two days later and 10 were in the Vane Street playground, at the town-end on Spring Bank, a week later. The Vane Street flock remained until at least 8th March, ranging from five to 11 in number.

2000/01: A single bird at Hedon on Christmas Day 2000 heralded what was to become another great irruption winter in the Hull area and across Britain. Eight were in the Safeway car park in Willerby on 29th December. Twelve were present the next day and a further 28 arrived on Chamberlain Road, East Hull. Another three were on Beverley Road the same day. The Willerby flock grew to 15 on New Years Eve and several flocks totalling around 50 birds were present in the Hull area, on and off, from January until late March. Peak counts in any one place were 46 in the Avenues, 35 on Hedon Road, 19 in Anlaby, 53 in Kirk Ella, 14 at Victoria Dock, 16 off Holderness Road, 21 in Vane Street, six in Willerby, 30 on Boothferry Road, three on the County, Salthouse and Beverley Roads and eight over Leads Road.

Waxwings can therefore turn up almost anywhere in the Hull area, wherever berries are available. Birds are much more likely during invasion years, usually arriving between mid November and January and maybe staying until late March, though numbers are very variable.

Wren
(Winter Wren)
Troglodytes troglodytes

The Wren is one of Britain's smallest birds and is often the most common, except when harsh winters severely reduce their numbers. Such a winter drastically cut numbers in Hull in 1941, and Wrens were scarce throughout the area for some time afterwards. Boylan (1967) only regarded the Wren as a regular, occasionally uncommon, breeding bird in the old Hull boundary during the first half of the 1960s. This apparent underestimate of the population of one of our most common birds may have been due to the impact of the severe 1962 winter.

By the mid 1980s the Wren was described as a common breeder around Cottingham and northwest Hull. At least 10 pairs were also nesting around Saltend. From the late 1980s onwards I found the Wren to be a common bird along the hedgerows and copses east of North

Bransholme. I regularly counted between five and 10 birds there on my regular circuit between Old Main Drain and the Holderness Drain. A small peak was apparent in spring as the males become more noticeable while belting out their rapid, powerful songs. Birds often became unobtrusive in midsummer, though I found many nests in the old hawthorns, while the greatest numbers were noted between October and December when the population was at a high. I recorded no less than 20 Wrens at North Bransholme on 19th December 1989, but counts always reached a minimum around February as winter took its toll.

A study of the birds on the Priory Road fields, between Willerby and Cottingham, in 1996 revealed a similar pattern to that observed at North Bransholme, although maximum counts only involved six birds. A survey of wildlife in the Avenues area of Hull in the same year found Wrens to be present in most gardens and areas of scrub and brambles. Several pairs breed at the Hedon Road Cemetery, where the species is described as being very common, and the city centre also has a few birds. There can be virtually no modest area of scrub, tangled vegetation, ivy or shrubbery that is not regularly visited by a Wren in its endless quest for spiders and insects.

Dunnock
(Hedge Accentor)
Prunella modularis
Still known to many as the Hedge Sparrow, the Dunnock is one of our most common and successful birds. They can be found in urban, suburban and rural areas alike, setting up home among any scrap of shrubbery or patch of bushes. Dunnocks penetrate right into the city centre, although their unobtrusive nature means that they are often overlooked. Regarded by many as a rather boring grey-brown bird that shuffles about below bird tables and under shrubs, the low profile belies an extraordinary sex life. Monogamous pairs are something of a rarity amongst Dunnocks and each bird, of either sex, may have several breeding partners at any one time.

Dunnocks have always been common in Hull, being noted as a frequent visitor and breeding bird in gardens around Pearson Park as early as 1901. In 1967 Boylan described the Dunnock as a "very common garden bird" in Hull but they were no doubt just as common in all other bushy habitats in the city. Five pairs were nesting in Northern Cemetery alone at that time. Regarded as an abundant breeding and resident species in the Cottingham area in the 1980s, up to 45 males were singing around Saltend and the docks around the same time. Another 10 or so males were present to the east of North Bransholme during the 1990s. Common throughout the Avenues area in the mid 1990s, around a dozen territories were found between Wood Lane and Hull Road to the south of Cottingham in 1996 and several pairs were breeding at Hedon Road Cemetery in recent years. Recent comments regarding status from all parts of the Hull area equate to "very common".

As well as being an abundant resident and breeding species, the Dunnock is also an autumn passage migrant. Peak numbers are often observed between September and November when large numbers of Continental immigrants arrive and the population of our local birds is at a maximum. Dunnocks seem to become more prominent again from late March and into May as the males emerge from the undergrowth to trickle out their song, which is often compared to the sound of a squeaky wheel on a shopping trolley. In 1908 and 1909 a pair of Dunnocks reared a single white youngster each summer at Kirk Ella but Dunnocks seldom draw such attention to themselves at that time of year. Once the twiggy nests of moss and coarse grass, with their clutch of clear blue eggs, is established low in some thicket the birds largely melt away once more until the autumn.

Dunnocks will readily come to food provided by people, but in November 2000 I spotted five of them in one of the larger aviaries in East Park. The birds seemed fine, with plenty of food, water and shrubs to hide in, but there was no obvious escape route for them and I was left wondering if they had become trapped after finding their way in through some hole that had since been repaired. For five to get trapped at once seemed a little strange, too, so perhaps it started off as two and the rest were bred in there?

Robin
(European Robin)
Erithacus rubecula

The Robin is instantly recognisable to most people and is well loved by many, being a common resident, passage migrant and winter visitor throughout the Hull area. Many people think of the Robin as only a 'winter bird' and friends still occasionally tell me of their surprise at seeing one in their garden during the summer. Robins are certainly more noticeable in winter, when large numbers of Continental birds arrive to join the local population and both are more likely to visit gardens for food. We are never without a large complement, however, and one can confidently expect to find a Robin in any bushy or wooded habitat throughout the year.

Robins have always been common birds in the Hull area, being in frequent attendance of gardeners in the Pearson Park area at the beginning of the last century. Boylan (1967) described them as "breeding fairly widely, mainly in suburbs, parks, cemeteries and docks". Two pairs regularly bred in Northern Cemetery in the early 1960s and the species was noted to be an abundant breeding bird around Cottingham in the 1980s. Up to five pairs bred around Saltend in the mid 1980s. Another five or so pairs bred in hedgerows and copses between North Bransholme and the Holderness Drain throughout the 1990s. In 1996 a study at the Priory Road fields, between Wood Lane and Snuff Mill Lane, found up to 22 breeding territories in hedges, scrub, gardens and around farms. In the same year the Robin was found to be common in the Avenues area of Hull, being present in most gardens. Comments from Hedon Road Cemetery suggest that Robins are very common there, too, with several pairs breeding. Robins can similarly be found in virtually all of the municipal spaces, such as the parks, cemeteries, school grounds and public gardens, wherever there is enough bushy cover for them. A couple of Robins in the High Street in April 2001 just goes to show how widespread they are, occurring right into the city centre.

Like those other common residents, the Dunnock and the Wren, Robins tend to keep a very low profile during the summer months. They emerge from the undergrowth and begin to sing again in the autumn, to establish their winter territories, being joined by passage migrants and winter visitors from September onwards. Most of the 100 Robins counted in East Park on 19th September 1969 were certain to have been recent immigrants and up to 27 were counted at Saltend in late October 1985. On 7th October 1992 a newly arrived first-winter Robin was trapped and ringed at Spurn before being released and subsequently making its way inland to Bilton, where it was found dead on 1st November.

Many Robins come to bird tables in winter, which is why they seem to be more common at that time of year, but the resident territorial birds can be very aggressive and will attack or even kill intruders. My local Robin spent half an hour pecking chunks out of a dead bird in my garden one November. It may well have killed the intruder itself but, in the eyes of the resident bird, the dead rival was now refusing to leave its territory! This particular Robin was soon taken down a peg or two, however, and a few weeks later I opened my back door to be greeted by the bird flying past my head and into the house, with a female Sparrowhawk in full pursuit a few feet behind. The Sparrowhawk performed a rapid about-turn and disappeared over the fence, but the Robin was now fluttering up against the inside of the window. After catching the bird I attached a colour-ring to its leg and freed it, but it was soon back in the garden and throwing its weight around with the sparrows. It remained for the rest of the winter but was not seen subsequently.

As spring approaches Robins begin singing in earnest, frequently at night if a nearby lamppost is lighting up their territory. The nest is often placed in an artificial site, and a pair built theirs in a potted fern in a Hull conservatory in May 1884. Shelves in open sheds or garages are often used these days. My local pair usually built low down in the forks of old hawthorns, rearing up to three broods of speckled youngsters throughout the summer.

Nightingale
(Common Nightingale)
Luscinia megarhynchos

The Nightingale, famed and admired in natural history, literature and popular culture alike, is actually a rather rare bird in Yorkshire. The British population has been contracting in range and numbers for many years and is now largely confined to southeast England. While it was never a common summer visitor to the Hull area it was certainly singing and probably nesting in the region until around a century ago. Nelson (1907) mentions that Nightingales were breeding at Brough and Patrington, either side of Hull, in the late 1870s, with no less than seven heard within a mile of Patrington alone on one evening. Songsters were also reported from Beverley around that time. While numbers appear to have fluctuated from year to year it seems likely that sporadic breeding was occurring in woods and copses throughout Humberside and south Holderness, from the Wolds to the coast. There were certainly many suitable places around Wawne, Cottingham, Skidby and Sutton. Unfortunately, the singing males were rarely left unmolested by the professional bird-catchers that proliferated in those days. Many East Yorkshire Nightingales ended up in a Victorian gentleman's cage or specimen cabinet. Collectors also prized the eggs of any that managed to live long enough to breed and these were actively sought if birds had been heard singing in the neighbourhood. Chislett (1952) states that singing Nightingales were reported from "Sutton...Wagden...and Elloughton" in the spring of 1907. While there are several Suttons in Yorkshire, I think it is likely that he is referring to 'our' Sutton, Sutton-on-Hull, as Elloughton is just a few miles from Hull and Wagden seems to be a misspelling of Waghen, now called Wawne. Assuming these records are from the Hull area then they represent some of the last, for Nightingales were decidedly rare in the East Riding by then. The last record for the Hull area is of a male in full song at Cottingham on 16th May 1938. He was no doubt a spring overshoot trying his luck in vain, as any potential mate would have been well out of earshot by that time. While a singing Nightingale was reported from a Hedon churchyard in the spring of 1998, and a recording allegedly made, there is no confirmation and others doubt the claim.

In May 2000 I had the pleasure of listening to around a dozen Nightingales almost daily at a Cambridgeshire lakeside. The birds were delivering their beautifully powerful song throughout the day but it was at night when it really had the power to entrance. One very mild, still night a companion and I stood for half an hour listening to a pair of disputing males as they battled to outdo each other with the volume, complexity and variety of their song. It was a mesmerising experience, with the moon so bright that it cast a shadow. While the demise of our Nightingales is only partly down to them, I wonder if those early bird-catchers knew what a void they were leaving behind when they set their traps and stole such a delight from the people of Hull and East Yorkshire.

Black Redstart
Phoenicurus ochruros

A bird of cliffs and boulder-strewn mountain slopes, the Black Redstart also occurs in built-up urban areas, docklands and industrial installations, where concrete and steel seem to suit it just as well as rock and scree. The species has always been quite a scarce bird in Britain but the blitzing of Hull during World War Two created ideal habitat for Black Redstarts. Overgrown bombsites replicated rocky slopes down to a tee, and the decade or so after the war produced a clutch of records. The first was a male singing among blitzed buildings from 21st June to 9th July 1949. On 10th July a pair were seen flying from a crevice high up on the High Street. Nesting was not confirmed that year, although two males were singing in the High Street on 25th September. Singing males were then recorded annually in the Old Town until 1952, when birds were seen around the Market Place and Paragon Station, but breeding was never proven. As the bombsites were cleared sightings gravitated towards the industrial areas. It was not until 1973 that a nest was found, however, when a pair was discovered breeding in the vent pipe of tugboat in dry dock. The six chicks left the nest on 22nd and 23rd June and this constituted only the second confirmed breeding record for East Yorkshire up to that point (the other being a pair that bred in the Flamborough cliffs in 1972). None were reported in Hull for the next decade until one was seen at the King George Dock in 1983.

Regular watching around Saltend and the eastern docks in 1985 revealed Black Redstarts to be rather frequent passage migrants with a tentative presence throughout the summer. The first of 1985 was one in King George Dock on 9th April. Another was on the railway line behind Saltend Marsh on 13th, with two on 15th. There were eight sightings around Saltend in May, including two birds on 7th. Singles were seen on 5th and 26th June, 1st July and 19th August. The last of the year was in Alexandra Dock on 22nd October. None of these birds were adult males.

Further Saltend coverage in 1986 revealed the presence of a female on 6th April before successful breeding was confirmed at Saltend Marsh when this or another female was seen feeding two fledged young on 21st June. These birds were present until the end of August and, while two males were singing around the eastern docks and in the city centre from May to late June, no male was ever seen in the near vicinity. Was the docks male the father of the Saltend young?

Autumn passage was strong that year, with four birds on 9th September, two on 13th October and one on 20th. A male was back singing in the city centre in 1987, and in 1988 another was singing again at the docks. Sightings then petered out, with a single at King George Dock on 28th August 1991 being the only one seen at that site throughout the entire decade. Another single, on autumn passage, was in East Park on 23rd November 1998, but the final years of the century were characterised by the scarcity of sightings. As the above records show, however, Black Redstarts seem to inhabit the Hull area in fits and starts with long periods of absence inbetween. The 1985-6 Saltend coverage, meanwhile, suggests that they may be regular passage migrants at this currently underwatched site.

Redstart
(Common Redstart)
Phoenicurus phoenicurus

The Redstart is an uncommon passage migrant in the Hull area, though it breeds in open woodland in many parts of the north and west

175

of Britain and sparingly in the south and east. Breeding occurs throughout much of Yorkshire but is rare and sporadic at best in the East Riding, usually on the Wolds. Redstarts have summered in the Hull area on at least one occasion, however, with a pair being seen in gardens off Boothferry Road throughout June and July in 1948 but there was no hint of breeding. One seen in Kirk Ella on 5th July 1972 was also unseasonal; too late for a spring migrant and a little too early for an autumn bird, it may have spent the summer in the area.

Boylan (1967) gave nine records of Redstarts in Hull prior to 1967, with all but the summering Boothferry Road birds being on passage. Despite considering the Redstart to be a rare migrant in Hull, Boylan mentioned that they had been seen right into the city centre in Queen's Gardens. Most passage records since have been in autumn, between 26th August and 12th October. The only spring records are of a male next to Hedon Road at Saltend on 26th April and a female in nearby Jubilee Copse, along Paull Road, the next day. Most of the autumn records have also been from the Saltend area and a handful of birds stop off there each year, with a maximum of four together on 6th October 1998 and seven in total that year. There have been two records from North Bransholme, with a female on 12th October 1988 and two birds on 20th September 1992. A female was in a Kirk Ella garden on 12th September 1981 and another was at Victoria Dock on 26th September 1997. There is also an undated record from the Priory Road fields.

Whinchat
Saxicola rubetra

A summer visitor from Africa, the Whinchat is a very rare breeding bird in East Yorkshire and occurs only as a scarce passage migrant in the Hull area. A Whinchat was at Sutton on 18th April 1943 and one or two were seen each spring or autumn during the 1960s, usually around the eastern waterfront. Slightly more are recorded today, despite a national decline, probably as a result of better coverage.

Autumn records tend to outnumber those in spring, both in terms of the number of sightings and the number of birds. Three at Haltemprice Farm near Willerby on 24th August 1982 was a typical encounter; autumn birds move through from late August to early October and are often in small groups. Seven were at Saltend on 22nd September 1984, with five on 8th October and four on 17th August 1986. Six were on weedy ground at North Bransholme on 22nd September 1989 and four were there again on 20th September 1992. Spring passage usually lasts from mid April to mid May, usually consisting of a fleeting visit by a lone bird. A pair were at what is now the Bransholme Fishing Pond on 23rd April 1994 and a male spent two days at Saltend in early May 1986. On 23rd May 1991 a male was singing along the Foredyke Stream where it meets the Holderness Drain at North Bransholme, though he was not seen again. Whinchats on passage seem to prefer moist areas with patches of bare ground and plenty of tall herbage to perch on, as characterised by much of the so-called 'wasteland' around the Hull area, and they often turn up alongside Wheatears.

Stonechat
(Common Stonechat)
Saxicola torquata rubicola

The Stonechat is a scarce breeding bird on the moors and heaths of Yorkshire, and elsewhere in upland Britain, with most departing in the autumn. Some British Stonechats retreat to the coastal lowlands for the winter, with others possibly joining them from the Continent, and it is these birds that appear in the Hull area in very small numbers. One near Hessle in December 1970 was followed by up to six, an extraordinary number, at the Bransholme Sewage Works from October to December 1973. The next was not until 1985 when one was at Keldgate, Cottingham, on 27th March. The following year saw a single bird settle at the eastern docks for six days from 5th November. Another long gap followed until the next record, when a female was found among a tumbledown hawthorn hedge on scrubland at North Bransholme on 1st March 1992, with a pair in the exact same spot on 3rd October the following year. A further lengthy spell followed before another was found, this time a male near the Paull Lighthouse on 18th October 1997. One more was near the River Hull on the Sutton Fields Industrial Estate on 10th January 1998. Stonechats can therefore appear almost anywhere in the area from early October through to late March, with weedy or scrubby areas near water being the clear preference.

'Siberian Stonechat'
Saxicola torquata maura

A female or immature bird showing characteristics of this or another of the eastern races, such as *S. t. stejnegeri*, was seen at Paull Fort on 5th October 1986 by S. M. Lister. These eastern races, which breed in Kazakhstan and across Russia, are distinctly paler than our European birds and have a characteristically unstreaked rump. Studies of mitochondrial DNA, genetic material from within the birds' cells, suggests that the European and eastern races have been keeping to themselves as far as breeding is concerned for around 150,000 years. They are possibly distinct enough to be split into separate species. Whatever the species status, the bird at Paull Fort had flown a very long way!

Wheatear
(Northern Wheatear)
Oenanthe oenanthe

The Wheatear is one of the earliest passage migrants to reach the Hull area, arriving from Africa as early as late March. The spring passage is often much stronger than the autumn movement, with many more birds seen. Two Wheatears were noted at Saltend on 5th April 1901 and they were fairly common on passage during the 1960s, with the occasional bird even dropping in to feed on the turf in Queen's Gardens in the city centre. Areas of short grass,

such as playing fields, or stony wasteland and ploughed fields are the preferred feeding sites for migrant Wheatears, especially those near water. Favourite sites in the Hull area include Saltend, Paull and the carrs and playing fields east of Bransholme. Birds have also been seen at Sutton Fields and around Cottingham in recent years, with several around Kirk Ella, Willerby and the Hedon Road Cemetery in the 1970s. Stopovers are therefore possible almost anywhere.

The earliest date for a spring migrant in the area was a male at North Bransholme on 22nd March 1989, though the main influx occurs in mid to late April. These birds usually arrive singly, though small 'falls' can occur along the Humber with four at Saltend on 29th April 1997 and 12 on 13th May 1998.

Birds passing through in late April or May can sometimes be assigned to one of the northern races. One found dead at Paull on 4th May 1959 was of the race *Oenanthe oenanthe schioleri*, which breeds in Iceland and the Faeroes. A large bright bird on the playing field of the now Kingswood School on Wawne Road was considered to be of the race *Oenanthe oenanthe leucorrhoa*, which breeds in Greenland. It is sobering to think that as this small bird rested in Hull after flying from Africa, it still had to cross the North Atlantic to reach its breeding grounds. This is the longest migration of any land bird. Another in Hull on 9th September 1950 was also assigned to the Greenland race.

Autumn passage in the Hull area usually begins in late August, though far fewer birds are seen than in spring. Again, short turf and bare or weedy ground are the preferred sites. Singles or a handful of birds regularly appear at Saltend, with four on disturbed ground at North Bransholme on 1st October 2000. Most birds have departed by October, with the latest recorded in the area being one at Bransholme on 4th October 1992. Wheatears that appear in the Hull area are sometimes accompanied by Whinchats, fellow migrants from Africa. It is always a good idea to look out for either bird when finding the 'companion'.

Ring Ouzel
Turdus torquatus

Known to many rural people as the Mountain Blackbird, the Ring Ouzel is an uncommon and declining summer migrant to Britain that arrives from Africa to breed in upland valleys and crags. The nearest breeding birds to Hull are on the North Yorkshire Moors, though they are becoming very scarce there, and in the Pennines.

Ring Ouzels are uncommon passage migrants in the Hull area, with most sightings occurring in autumn. There were just three records during the first half of the 1960s, with a very late female in East Park on 11th November 1969. Incredibly, a male was also seen in East Park on 3rd December and these two birds must have been migrants from the continent rather than British birds on the way out. A spring bird was at the Holderness Drain near Wawne from 19th to 20th April 1989, with two very early autumn migrants there on 14th July. A Ring Ouzel was at the Kerry Woods near Kirk Ella on 24th October 1987 and females were at North Bransholme on 28th April 1987 and 20th April 1988. In October 1991 a group of five Ring Ouzels were in a thin hedgerow along Bransholme Road, between Bransholme and the Holderness Drain, but, typically, the birds were very shy and flew some distance when disturbed, giving the hard alarm call as they went. A stunning male was seen in a hawthorn hedge nearby on 23rd April 1994, accompanied by a female. What was probably a different pair were seen at the same place on 14th May the same year. A very unusual midwinter record concerns a bird at Saltend on 28th January 1996. A more typical autumn bird was there on 23rd September, with two on 25th and one again on 5th October 1998.

Ring Ouzels are, therefore, a rather good find anywhere in the Hull area. Saltend or a hedgerow on the outskirts of the city in September or October probably offers the best chance of reward, with mid to late April being the peak time for the weaker spring passage.

Blackbird
(Common Blackbird)
Turdus merula

The Blackbird is one of the most common, widespread and familiar birds in the Hull area. As well as an abundant resident and breeding bird, the Blackbird is also a very common passage migrant and winter visitor with large numbers flooding in from Scandinavia and the Continent each autumn.

Blackbirds breed everywhere in the Hull area, including the city centre, and can be found wherever there are a few bushes or a patch of grass where they can forage for berries in winter and worms in summer. The nest may be built in a bush, among a creeper or in some artificial site; examples of the more bizarre nesting locations from around Hull include under the bonnet of a lorry and on the shelf of a garden shed, with stories of unusual nests appearing in the local press each spring. They will readily breed in gardens and the beautiful fluting song of the male drifting over the rooftops is one of the joys of warm summer evenings.

A great many of our suburban Blackbirds die on the roads and the almost flightless newly-fledged chicks are easy prey for cats and small boys. The persistent chirruping begging call of the young bird, which lets the parents know where it is, leads some people to think the chick is 'lost' but they should never be picked up unless they are in danger of being harmed. If this is the case they can be put among nearby vegetation and then left well alone. Despite the depredations, comments regarding the breeding status of the Blackbird throughout the Hull area are invariably along the lines of "common", "very common" or "abundant".

A noticeable influx of Blackbirds occurs between mid October and late November. Large numbers arrive on the east coast along with the Redwings, Fieldfares and Song Thrushes, and all soon penetrate inland. These Continental Blackbirds are often more highly strung than our local birds and will fly off high and far when flushed. Visible migration of high flying Blackbirds is occasionally noticeable overhead; 100 passed west over Kirk Ella on 14th October 1971 and again the next day. Over 30 in nearby Kerry Woods on 15th October 1980 were part of a big arrival of winter thrushes that day. A total of 25 at Saltend on 15th September was a relatively good count there and probably part of an early arrival. The average day count of around 20 Blackbirds in the Old Main Drain hedgerow, east of North Bransholme, was inflated to 50 on 28th November 1992 and again on

16th October 1993. Both of these days saw a large arrival of other thrushes. An October peak of 30 at the Priory Road fields in 1995 contrasted with a usual count of around a dozen, while 65 passed through East Park on 17th November 1998 during a period of very visible migration.

Blackbirds often roost communally in winter and their noisy clucking is a familiar sound around dense thickets at dusk. A long-standing roost in the Pickhills, off Hull Road near Cottingham, held many hundreds of Blackbirds during the early 1960s. Over 200 were counted heading towards the roost over Cottingham Road alone in February 1963. As spring approaches the migrants leave and the local birds begin singing, often starting well before dawn in urban areas where street lights illuminate the neighbourhood. Plumage abnormalities are fairly common in Blackbirds, with birds of both sexes sometimes sporting irregular white feathers. A female in East Hull in November 1944 had a completely white head, though total albinos are rare.

Fieldfare
Turdus pilaris

Somewhere in the region of a million Fieldfares come to Britain each autumn to feast on our hedgerow berries and escape the winter of their Scandinavian homeland. A handful of pairs also breed in the Yorkshire uplands. Located as it is on the England's east coast, the Hull area has always been witness to some of the first arrivals of Fieldfares in the country as they make landfall in Holderness and move inland. Arrival dates vary from mid October to early November, with the earliest at my North Bransholme patch being 9th October 1993.

After their initial arrival the Fieldfares quickly strip the local hawthorns of their fruits, often in the company of migrant Blackbirds, Song Thrushes and, especially, Redwings. Very large numbers of Fieldfares have been recorded in the Hull area at this time as flocks stop off to feed or pass over on their way inland. A flock of 315 were feeding in hedgerows at North Bransholme on 16th October 1993, with 573 moving north on 24th. Around 170 were feeding again on 26th and more than 400 passed through on 1st November. At least 1,150 passed over Holderness Road in just one hour on 1st November 1998. Feeding flocks are usually much smaller than this, however, with between 20 and 40 being the average size once the new arrivals settle in and disperse. These feeding flocks are much more mobile and irregular than those of the Redwings, with which they often associate, and they never seem to hang around a particular area for very long.

Being a little more wary and alert than Redwings, Fieldfares do not usually enter the more built-up areas of Hull so readily. Harsh weather may drive them into more urban or suburban areas, however, and during the 1960s small numbers were occasionally seen in the parks and cemeteries, as they are today. The severe winter of 1969 saw Fieldfares entering Hull gardens for berries and fruit. This was also recorded in Cottingham in the 1980s. Helen Crowther's 1996 survey revealed that Fieldfares could sometimes be seen in tall trees in the Avenues area of Hull each winter.

By December or January, once the bushes are bare, the Fieldfare flocks often move on to work their way across the countryside, consuming the berries as they go. They can then be quite scarce in the Hull area until their return migration brings them back again the following March. By now there is nothing for them in the hedges and the birds turn to open fields for seeds and invertebrates, usually preferring pasture such as that off Priory Road and around Wawne, or even playing fields. The lack of an obvious bounty of food, such as the burgeoning hawthorns that they found on their autumn arrival, means that these late winter and early spring flocks pass through fairly quickly.

Small numbers of Fieldfares can linger into early May, when it is possible to be in the strange position of hearing the 'chacking' of a Fieldfare coming from the same tree as the song of a Cuckoo. Such late birds have included singles at the Bransholme Sewage Works on 4th May 1992 and Castle Hill Farm (between Bransholme and Swine) on 25th April 2000, a pair at North Bransholme on 5th May 1991 and 13th May 2001 with a flock of nine there on 1st May 1989. A most intriguing report from Hessle in 1995 concerned an adult Fieldfare seen carrying food on 21st June, this being tantalising evidence of possible breeding close by.

One can reasonably expect to encounter Fieldfares in the Hull area anytime from mid October to early May. The best chance and highest numbers are likely to be in October and November. The hedgerows and fields away from built-up areas are most attractive to the feeding flocks, though hard weather may drive them further into the city and visible migration can be witnessed overhead anywhere.

Song Thrush
Turdus philomelos

Despite the massive decline suffered by the once abundant Song Thrush in recent decades, they are still fairly common birds in Hull area. Much of the reduction in numbers has been attributed to habitat loss and pesticides in farmland. The use of slug pellets on both arable land and in suburban gardens is also a problem, rendering the Song Thrushes' favourite prey poisonous. Pure arable farmland, the sort which predominates in the East Riding, is now a rather inhospitable place for Song Thrushes. Most are now found in suburban habitats and at the interface of town and country. Here the birds have the benefit of the farmland hedgerows for nesting and the pesticide-free verges, wasteland and shrubberies for finding food.

John Nicholson included the Song Thrush among the birds nesting around his Hull town house, near Pearson Park, in the early 1900s. In 1967 Patrick Boylan described it as a common breeding bird in the parks, gardens and cemeteries of Hull, with four pairs nesting in Northern Cemetery alone. Several pairs were breeding around Saltend in the mid 1980s and Bonavia (1990) considered it to be a widespread and common breeding bird around Cottingham and northwest Hull at that time. Up to five pairs were breeding between North Bransholme and the Holderness Drain throughout the 1990s, as they still do, and a pair or two were nesting along Snuff Mill and Wood Lanes, between Cottingham and Hull, in 1996. Recent breeding has been noted in the Trinity graveyard, right in the heart of Hull at the top of Ferensway, and three or four males were singing along the old Hull to Withernsea railway line between Hedon Road Cemetery and the city centre in 1999 and 2000.

Most of the larger gardens, parks and cemeteries will have a pair or two of Song Thrushes but many areas have reported serious declines over the past 10 years. Once common in the Avenues area of Hull, Song Thrushes were rare by 1996 and seemed to be hanging on by a toehold. Just one nest in Hedon Road Cemetery in 2000 contrasts with a comment of "very common" there in the 1980s. They are holding their own in other areas, however, with several pairs in the Sutton Fields Industrial Estate and Humber Bridge Country Park.

The Song Thrush is most common in the Hull area as a passage migrant in autumn, when substantial numbers fly in from Scandinavia with the Redwings, Fieldfares and Blackbirds. The curt "sip" call is often heard overhead on still autumn nights as migrants pour in and relatively large numbers can be grounded in October and November. Up to 50 passage Song Thrushes occasionally dropped into Northern Cemetery in the early 1960s and there was a heavy passage overhead on the night of 1st October 1965. A peak of around 10 birds was noted at Saltend in October 1984, with a similar autumn peak at North Bransholme during the 1990s. Occasionally larger numbers were recorded at the latter site, however, with 23 grounded on 29th October 1993 and 19 on 13th November. The usual count of two or three birds at the Priory Road fields was inflated to 11 on 2nd October 1995. A whopping 40 in East Park on 2nd October 1998 was to be eclipsed by 60 at Saltend on 5th. A dead bird at Paull on 12th September 1995 had been ringed at Spurn as a first-winter bird on 8th March 1993, but whether it was a local bird or a returning migrant is not clear.

Song Thrushes are often seen smashing snail shells against favourite stones, or 'anvils', to get at the meat but Rob Atkinson saw an interesting twist on this technique at Wawne in March 1996. Watching a Song Thrush struggling with a large piece of stale toast, Atkinson was impressed to see the bird break it apart against a stone and then eat the pieces, a clear sign of adaptive behaviour.

Redwing
Turdus iliacus

A common winter visitor to the hedgerows on the outskirts of Hull and in the surrounding villages, the Redwing is the harbinger of winter. Our wintering Redwings breed in Scandinavia and arrive on the east coast in October, quickly moving inland and feasting on the haws as they make their way westwards. They are often scarce in midwinter, once the berries have gone, but pass through again in spring on their way back to the coast. They can often be found feeding on the fields at this time. As a mainly nocturnal migrant, the high, thin 'seeep' of passing Redwings is a familiar sound on starry nights in late autumn and winter anywhere in the Hull area.

Redwings usually arrive during the second or third week of October, the earliest arrival date being 18th September 1993. Boylan (1967) described them as fairly common winter visitors and passage migrants, being much more abundant than the Fieldfare and occurring in large numbers in the parks and cemeteries of Hull. Small parties were seen on the verges of Boothferry Road in the spring of 1964 and several birds were heard to sing. A Redwing that was ringed as a chick in Finland was found dead in Hessle in January 1968, showing just how far they come to feed in our hedges.

Huge numbers of Redwings pass through the Hull area during mid October and observation of visible daytime migration during the early 1970s produced impressive counts. A total of 15,000 passed northwest over Kirk Ella on 13th October 1971, with 3,000 the next day, 5,000 the day after that, 1,000 on 25th and 2,000 on 26th. This was over just one house, so the total passing through along the whole front must have been enormous. The largest flocks of the year can be found in the berry-filled hedgerows during this initial arrival. Up to 200 were occasionally in the Old Main Drain hedgerow (east of North Bransholme) during mid October in the early 1990s. Over 100 were counted off Priory Road in the early 1980s and 315 at Saltend on 26th October 1985 were superseded by 370 on 28th. A later influx at Saltend the year before produced 450 on 11th November and 300 on 28th. The flocks tend to decrease in size as the autumn progresses. Around 50 was the norm at North Bransholme in November and December during the 1990s while up to 80 were counted off Priory Road in 1995. Redwings are often scarce by January, once the berries have gone, but they start to trickle back during late February and March when they take to open fields in search of food. The numbers passing through on spring passage are nothing like those of the autumn, however, with 100 being a relatively large flock.

Redwings will readily visit the urban and, especially, suburban green spaces throughout the Hull area. They are annual in Hull's Avenues area and all of the parks and cemeteries, as they were in Boylan's day. Redwings will occasionally come to gardens for berries in very cold weather but will not touch any artificial food and have been known to starve to death rather than eat the usual bird table fare.

Mistle Thrush
Turdus viscivorus
The Mistle Thrush has been through its ups and downs in the Hull area over the past century but it is pleasing to note that they are currently increasing and spreading in the region. Very harsh winters in the mid 1890s virtually wiped out East Yorkshire's Mistle Thrushes, but they soon recovered and were breeding in gardens near Pearson Park by 1901. In 1951 G. H. Ainsworth described the Mistle Thrush as "numerous as ever" around Hull and in 1953 considered it to be the commonest thrush in Sutton, ahead of Blackbird and Song Thrush! A Mistle Thrush ringed in Sutton in May 1958 was found dead in the same place a year later, illustrating the highly resident nature of our local birds. Two pairs were nesting in Northern Cemetery in 1965 and Boylan (1967) mentioned another one or two pairs near the city centre around the same time, but noted that the species was "more a bird of parks and cemeteries". Two were reported from East Park in 1967 and another pair were in Cottingham the next year, but the fact that these were deemed noteworthy suggests that the very harsh 1962/3 winter hit them hard again.

Several pairs were nesting around Cottingham by the 1980s, with small numbers present all year round, but they were very scarce in East Hull around that time. Despite a few sightings in the Wawne area in the early 1990s, and possible breeding, the first birds I ever saw at adjoining North Bransholme were not until May 1993. One was singing there a few weeks later. A definite increase in numbers and range was beginning to get under way by then, with birds spreading from the strongholds of Cottingham and the western fringes down Cottingham Road and into East Hull as well as into the city centre. Mistle Thrushes have been heard singing at the University of Hull campus, down Salmon Grove, since 1997. The following spring I spotted a pair at the convent on the corner of Beverley Road and Cottingham Road. A pair nested near the Marina in 1996, often perching on the rigging of the old *Manxman* ferry, but the single fledged youngster was found dead in Queen Street in late April after having been hit by a car. An adult at Minerva Pier in January 1999 indicates that they have not forsaken that part of town, however, and others have been heard singing in Queen's Gardens since 1998. On 9th June 2001 I saw a fledgling Mistle Thrush in the Mason Street car park, off Freetown Way near the Old English Gentleman pub, proving that breeding had occurred in the city centre once more. Up to four were in East Park during the autumn and winter in 1998, although breed-

ing did not occur. Nesting has occurred in Hedon Road Cemetery since 1997 and by 2000 they were frequent around Wawne. They were also being recorded from the Bransholme Sewage Works for the first time in 2000.

As well as a resident breeding bird, the Mistle Thrush is also a passage migrant in the Hull area. These or wandering local birds may occur in rarely visited parts of the region at this time of year. Singles at Saltend in October and November 1985 and May 1986 were possibly migrants, as were the 14 at the Priory Road fields on 18th September 1995.

Grasshopper Warbler
(Common Grasshopper Warbler)
Locustella naevia

Nelson's *The Birds of Yorkshire* (1907) mentions that the Grasshopper Warbler had been reported from near Hull. This was probably based on a bird near Sproatley, outside of the area covered by this book, in May 1897. Grasshopper Warblers were certainly rare in these parts back then; the Sproatley bird was the first that the observer, who was from Hedon, had ever heard in

Holderness. Boylan's 1967 *Birds in Hull* makes no mention of the species.

A bird singing in Saltend Marsh from 2nd to 10th May 1986 was the first modern record of the species in the Hull area. The second Hull record, and my first, came on the evening of 27th April 1989 when B. Richards and I were birdwatching along the Foredyke Stream opposite Ladyside Close, North Bransholme. Richards alerted me to a monotonous buzzing sound, almost electrical in quality, that I had dismissed as being the result of mist cloaking the conductors of nearby telegraph poles. Richards immediately recognised it as the song of the Grasshopper Warbler and patient stalking revealed the bird to be singing from the dense stands of cow parsley, burdock, hogweed and rough grasses that fringed the channel. It or another was heard singing there again on 13th May, with two on 14th July.

The following year at least five individual Grasshopper Warblers were singing from brambles and herbage along the Foredyke Stream and opposite the Highlands School at North Bransholme. The first bird of 1991 was heard singing at the now regular Foredyke Stream site on 28th April and again on 25th May, but that was all that year. None were singing beside Foredyke Stream in 1992 but one was heard from the scrubby fields off Thomas Clarkson Way, east of the Bransholme Sewage Works, on 4th May. One was back at Foredyke Stream on 24th June 1993.

Another single there on 13th May 1994 was followed by two singing throughout July 1995, despite poor coverage in those years.

The years 1996 and 1997 saw a return to 1990 numbers at North Bransholme, though by now the dominance of grasses along Foredyke Stream meant the singing birds had relocated to stands of herbage in the nearby scrub. Up to two singing birds were also reported from near the Carr Lane Nurseries along the Holderness Drain, east of Sutton, at that time. Singing birds are now annual in the Hull area, with numbers at North Bransholme varying between one and four individuals per year. It is probable that other singing Grasshopper Warblers have gone unrecorded around the outskirts of Hull, although regular watching of sites such as the Priory Road fields in the mid 1990s failed to find any.

A singing Grasshopper Warbler does not necessarily indicate breeding, as passage migrants commonly sing in suitable habitat but may only be present for a day or two before moving on. This was probably the case at North Bransholme in several years during the 1990s. In other years, however, birds have been heard singing from the same site for several weeks at a time throughout the summer, so breeding is highly likely. Breeding nevertheless remains very difficult to prove in light of the incredibly skulking habits of this bird.

The best place to find Grasshopper Warblers in the Hull area, therefore, appears to be the scrubby fields south of Foredyke Stream, southeast of North Bransholme, between the Kingswood High School on Wawne Road and the Great Culvert Pumping Station on the Holderness Drain. At least one bird should be singing sometime from late April to July, being most vociferous in the early mornings, evenings and after dark on warm still nights. The song is audible over more than half a mile and has been compared to the sound of a fisherman's reel winding in the line. It is monotonous in tone though not irritating, changing in volume as the bird turns its head from side to side every so often, with occasional pauses between 'reels'. I have a special regard for the Grasshopper Warbler, for on many a balmy evening during the 1990s I have stood at the bottom of my then Bransholme garden to hear the reeling song drift across the fields. To me, it really is the sound of summer.

Sedge Warbler
Acrocephalus schoenobaenus

Boylan (1967) regarded the Sedge Warbler as a regular yet uncommon summer visitor to Hull in the 1960s, with passage migrants cropping up as far into the city as Queen's Gardens. It was still regarded as an uncommon breeder in Cottingham and northwest Hull into the 1980s. Just a single male was singing down Snuff Mill Lane in 1985, with unspecified numbers along the River Hull, while seven pairs were breeding at Saltend in the same year. A notable increase took place during the 1990s, however, with six singing males along Snuff Mill Lane and nearby Swine Bank in 1996. Seventeen songsters were at Saltend in 1998, while 11 singing males between North Bransholme and the Holderness Drain in 1989 had grown to 18 in 1993 and 21 in 2001. Two males were singing on the Priory Sidings, off Clive Sullivan Way, in June 1998 with another at Livingstone Road, behind Hessle Foreshore, in June 1999. A pair was also thought to have bred at Queen Elizabeth Dock the same year.

It hasn't all been good news, however. A marked decline has been noticed in recent years along the Holderness Drain near Hedon Road and in the scrub of the old Hull to Withernsea railway line. Sedge Warblers were formerly common there but are now rather scarce. Other damp bushy areas or dense herbage beside water, such as the banks of the Barmston Drain and along stretches of the River Hull (e.g. parts of Bankside and near the Bransholme Sewage Works), may also have a few pairs.

The first Sedge Warblers of the summer have consistently arrived in the

Hull area between 23rd and 26th April during the 1990s. The earliest bird outside of this period was on 18th April in 1985. Most locally breeding birds have left by mid August but lingerers and passage migrants can occasionally be found until the end of September.

Reed Warbler
(Eurasian Reed Warbler)
Acrocephalus scirpaceus

The Reed Warbler is quite close to the edge of its British range at Hull, with only a few isolated colonies and sporadic breeders further north of a line drawn from Yorkshire to Lancashire. A summer visitor from Africa, Reed Warblers usually arrive in the Hull area towards the end of April or early May. In some years the first birds are not heard singing until the middle of May. The species is very closely associated with *Phragmites* reeds, the tall, feathery-topped reeds that flank the River Hull in places and also occur in pockets along the Humber and other wet areas. The limited range of *Phragmites* in the Hull area is the major factor determining the distribution of the Reed Warbler. The main reedbeds can be found on the Humber side of Clive Sullivan Way (between St Andrew's Quay and Priory Way), the tidal channels flanking Saltend and along the River Hull upstream of the Sutton Fields Industrial Estate. It is difficult to estimate the number of pairs breeding in these locations, but an idea can be gained from sample counts along the River Hull made between the bridge on Thomas Clarkson Way and Sutton Road Bridge. In May and June during the early 1990s there was, on average, one singing male for every 100 metres of reed-fringed river along this stretch. The reedy lagoons on Saltend Marsh, meanwhile, held around 15 pairs in the mid 1980s.

Conditions must have been excellent for the species when Hull was surrounded by marshy fields and the untamed River Hull was flanked by broad stands of reeds. Drainage in the 18th and 19th Centuries would have seriously reduced their numbers. In 1907 Nelson wrote that Reed Warblers were "formerly common" around Hull, implying that they were now scarce, but went on to say that they could still be found where conditions were suitable. They were certainly still breeding along the River Hull at that time, as Colonel Haworth Booth reported finding an unusual nest in a blackcurrant bush at Haworth Hall in 1896.

Intriguingly, a search for breeding Reed Warblers along the Humber and River Hull by J. Lord and G. H. Ainsworth between 1938 and 1945 found many pairs outside the Hull area, at places like Patrington, Burstwick and Melton, but none on the River Hull below Beverley.

Despite finding a nest near Hedon in 1945, Ainsworth and Lord make no mention of any birds elsewhere around Hull. Ainsworth lived on Gillshill Road and knew Hull's birds well, so one would have thought that if Reed Warblers were breeding along the River Hull just over a mile from his house then he'd have known about it. It seems they had totally forsaken the Hull area sometime between 1907 the 1940s. An apparently new colony was discovered at Hessle in 1947 and Reed Warblers seemed to be genuinely increasing their range in East Yorkshire during the forties and fifties.

During the 1960s the species occurred in very small numbers within the old Hull boundary and bred only at King George Dock and one other location. When T. P. Milsom looked for breeding Reed Warblers in the two hectares of reedbeds west of St Andrew's Quay in June 1978 he found just one singing male. This was despite there being many dozens in the reeds between nearby Brough and the mouth of the Ouse. When the Cottingham Bird Club surveyed the birds of Cottingham and northwest Hull between 1981 and 1986, incorporating the full length of the River Hull between Beverley and Sculcoates, the only Reed Warblers were found way outside the Hull area at Beverley Beck. This suggests another decline had taken place. Breeding on Hull's stretch of the River Hull may, therefore, wax and wane to some extent, although I have

a feeling that they were simply overlooked most of the time. Indeed, the 14 pairs breeding at Saltend Marsh in 1985 were within the Hull boundary, if only just.

A very few pairs of Reed Warblers also breed among tiny reedbeds in the marshy fields southeast of North Bransholme these days. Two singing males in 1994 was a typical number, and I suspect a few more may lurk in the upper reaches of the Holderness Drain near Carlam Hill Farm. Other small stands of *Phragmites* in the Hull area may also hold a pair or two. Unlike most warblers, Reed Warblers may sing well into August and an adult was feeding a newly fledged chick at North Bransholme as late as 28th August 1992. The reedbeds are usually deserted by mid September as the birds begin their return migration. Passage birds may be encountered in other habitats in the Hull area at this time, such as along ditch hedgerows or willowherb stands. The latest bird seen in the Hull area was one at Saltend on 19th October 1985 and this was undoubtedly a passage migrant, as the last local bird had departed some three weeks before.

Icterine Warbler
Hippolais icterina

The Icterine Warbler breeds in woods and even urban parkland just across the Channel in northeast France and up to Scandinavia. It is no more than an uncommon, if regular, passage migrant on Britain's east coast and an extremely rare passage migrant in the Hull area. There is just one recorded instance of the Icterine Warbler in Hull, with one being found by S. L. James and a companion along the Holderness Drain near Hedon Road on 22nd August 1986.

Lesser Whitethroat
Sylvia curruca

The Lesser Whitethroat is a widespread summer visitor to the Hull area but is thinly distributed and can nowhere be described as common. Generally arriving between the last week of April and first week of May, there has been a notable increase during the latter half of the last century.

One down Haltemprice Lane, between Cottingham and Willerby, in 1951 was considered unusual and Boylan (1967) reported just one passage record for Hull during the 1960s. Another passage bird was in East Park on 5th October 1969. The increase was being noted towards the end of the 1970s and early 1980s. Probable breeding was noted near Kirk Ella (Kerry Woods) and Cottingham (Wood Lane and elsewhere) at that time, with five pairs around Saltend in 1985. Three birds were reported from Saltend in June 1998, with another three at Cottingham in July 1999. Three pairs was the usual quota at North Bransholme throughout the 1990s, mainly in the thick Old Main Drain and Foredyke Stream hedgerows off Cumbrian Way. I was surprised to hear a bird singing from rose bushes flanking an underpass on Bellfield Avenue, East Hull, in May 1993 but Lesser Whitethroats are rather widespread throughout urban and suburban Hull. Recent breeding has been recorded along the old railway line between Goddard Avenue and Chanterlands Avenue, the Priory Sidings off Clive Sullivan Way, west of Calvert Lane near East Ella, along the old Hull to Withernsea railway line near Hull Prison and on the Holderness Drain behind the Maternity Hospital. The Humber Bridge Country Park also holds several pairs each summer. Indeed, many thick hedgerows and patches of scrub on the margins of Hull and the villages are likely to echo to the rattling song of Lesser Whitethroats at some point.

The Lesser Whitethroat is a little more numerous on autumn passage and roaming birds may be spotted in the parks and cemeteries. Inflated numbers also occur at the more usual sites, such as Saltend, North Bransholme and the Humber Bridge Country Park, but most have left by late September. A Lesser Whitethroat showing characteristics of the Siberian race, *Sylvia curruca blythi*, was seen briefly at Paull by S. M. Lister on 27th September 1986.

Whitethroat
(Common Whitethroat)
Sylvia communis

The Whitethroat was a regular summer visitor and fairly common passage migrant in Hull during the early 1960s. Breeding was recorded along the banks of the Holderness and Barmston Drain, around the docks and in other scrubby places such as neglected allotments off Kenilworth Avenue in West Hull. In 1968 drought struck in their wintering quarters in the Sahel zone of Africa, south of the Sahara Desert. This led to a massive crash in the British population of Whitethroats and three quarters of them failed to return in the spring of 1969. Further knocks led to the low point in the population being reached in 1974. The Whitethroat was notably scarce in the Hull area at that time, with birds at Kirk Ella's Kerry Woods being the only ones reported, though there were no doubt others here and there.

By the early 1980s the Whitethroat was slowly recovering to the point of being an uncommon breeding bird on Snuff Mill Lane and Wood Lane, off Priory Road. Disaster struck again, however, and the famous African droughts of the mid 1980s knocked numbers right back almost to the 1974 level. Around five pairs were breeding at Saltend in 1985 with a similar number east of North Bransholme in 1989, but the 1990s saw a welcome increase throughout the Hull area. By 1992 the number of singing males between North Bransholme and the Holderness Drain had climbed to 12, with a record 25 the following year and 20 in 1994. There were up to 10 pairs off Priory Road by 1996 and 11 males were singing at Saltend in 1998, more than double that of 1985. Whitethroats are now fairly common in scrubby areas and hedgerows around the outskirts of Hull and the surrounding villages, but they seem to be less widespread in the more urban areas than the Lesser Whitethroat. Recent breeding sites and numbers in Hull have included the fields between Thomas Clarkson Way and Bude Road (at least two pairs), King George Dock (one pair), Priory Sidings (unspecified numbers), the Holderness Drain near Hedon Road (several pairs), Victoria Dock (at least one pair), Bransholme Sewage Works (several pairs) and the railway lines between Hedon Road and the city centre (at least three pairs). Scattered pairs are also likely to breed along the banks of the Holderness and Barmston Drains, along parts of the River Hull and along the railway lines as they pass through the city. There can be few hedgerows in the adjoining parts of the East Riding that do not have Whitethroats in them.

The scratchy song and jerky display flight of the Whitethroat is first heard in the Hull area in the last week of April, occasionally the first week of May. The earliest arrival date was 17th April 1981 and the latest 10th May 1991. The males sing frenziedly throughout May, when the peak counts occur, before breeding gets into full swing later in the month. Most of the locally breeding birds appear to leave by mid August but passage migrants from Scandinavia ensure a presence until the end of September or early October. A bird found dead at Cottingham on 10th October 1982 was ringed in Sweden just three weeks before, indicating the origin of these late birds.

Garden Warbler
Sylvia borin

The Garden Warbler is one of the rarest of the regular summer migrants in the Hull area and is very local in its distribution. Boylan (1967) described the species as a very rare summer visitor and passage migrant in 1960s Hull. A failed nesting attempt towards the north of the old city boundary in 1959 was apparently the only breeding record, though migrating birds were seen as far into town as Queen's Gardens.

The region around the villages to the immediate west of Hull is the nearest thing to a stronghold that the species has in the Hull area. Breeding occurred at Little Switzerland (near Hessle) in 1967 and one or two have been seen or heard in Kirk Ella's Kerry Woods most Mays since the mid 1970s. Others were seen on Carr Lane, near Willerby, in June 1975 and in Cottingham's Snuff Mill Lane and University Botanic Gardens in the early 1980s. A pair bred at nearby Wood Lane in 1985. A single pair bred in the Humber Bridge Country Park between 1993 and 1997, increasing to three pairs in 1998, and this site seems to offer the best chance of finding the species in the Hull area.

Over in East Hull, birds were singing in Hedon Road Cemetery in May and June 1983. Passage migrants were noted at Saltend in the mid 1980s, with singles or couples on a handful of dates between August and mid October each year and occasional birds in May. The earliest arrival date in the Hull area is 4th May and the latest autumn migrant was seen on 12th October, though most spring birds are seen in May and most autumn birds in September.

Blackcap
Sylvia atricapilla

This unobtrusive warbler is mainly a thinly distributed summer visitor to the Hull area but increasing numbers are wintering in the region. The breeding and wintering birds come from two distinct populations, with those in summer spending the winter in Africa and the winter visitors coming from breeding grounds in northern and eastern Europe. Preferring a more wooded habitat than the other regular *Sylvia* warblers, the Whitethroat and Lesser Whitethroat, Blackcaps can be found wherever there are tall bushes and trees with a thick understorey. They also venture into the suburbs.

Boylan (1967) tells us that the Blackcap was a rare summer visitor and passage migrant in the old Hull boundary of the 1960s. Breeding was also recorded at Little Switzerland, near Hessle. Bonavia (1990) considered it to a be an uncommon breeding bird around Cottingham and northwest Hull in the mid 1980s. I found it to be much the same at North Bransholme and the Bransholme Sewage Works in the late 1980s and early 1990s, with two or three singing males at both the Old Main Drain hedgerow and the Sewage Works plantation.

A marked increase was noted in many parts of the Hull area in the mid 1990s. The number of singing males at North Bransholme doubled by 1998, three pairs were found around Priory Road (Wood Lane and the Pickhills) in 1996 and more were occurring in the Hedon Road area than formerly. These latter birds included three singing males along the old Hull to Withernsea railway line (behind Hedon Road Cemetery) and another two along the Holderness Drain, near the Maternity Hospital. Breeding is also thought to occur in the larger gardens of Cottingham and Hull's Avenues. Other sites include the Kerry Woods near Kirk Ella (four males in 2000), the old railway sidings west of Calvert Lane and in East Park, where I heard a male singing near the aviaries in early summer 1999. One was also singing in the Trinity graveyard, near Hull Marina, in April 2000. Others are now no doubt breeding in many other localities with a strong element of trees and tall bushes, such as the golf courses, cemeteries, small woods and copses scattered throughout the area. There is little information from what must be one of the best sites for the species in the area, the Humber Bridge Country Park, but breeding numbers must easily exceed a dozen pairs in this prime habitat.

The first birds of spring are generally heard any time between mid April and early May, with the last week of April being the most usual arrival time. Timing the arrival of migrants is a little difficult, however, as the presence of wintering birds singing on sunny days in early spring clouds the situation. Wintering has been noted in the Hull area for almost half a century. A male observed in a Kirk Ella garden for much of March in 1956 is the first on record. Up to three have been seen between November and March in most years since the early 1970s, particularly around Kirk Ella/West Ella, Cottingham and the Avenues area of Hull. This western bias is almost certainly related to the higher proportion of trees and wooded habitats in those areas compared to East Hull. Peak months for seeing winter birds are January and February, when hard weather and exhaustion of natural food forces them into the suburbs and onto bird tables, and in March, when sunny days tempt the males to sing and advertise their presence. Brian Fendley's garden on the western margin of Kirk Ella attracts a Blackcap in most winters, with two on 21st February 1997 and in January 1994. Locally breeding birds probably leave for Africa in late August or September, with passage migrants occurring until October. The handful of wintering birds probably join us around November.

Yellow-browed Warbler
Phylloscopus inornatus

A scarce but regular autumn vagrant to Britain's east coast from the taiga forests of Siberia, the Yellow-browed Warbler has occurred only twice in the Hull area. On 2nd November 1986 D. and J. Wilkinson saw a Yellow-browed Warbler on 'Shrike Hill'. This is a long bush-covered mound on the north side of Saltend Marsh (immediately south of the railway lines) that is now largely gone due to development. The bird stayed for another two days. The second Yellow-browed Warbler was found on the afternoon of 4th November 2000 in trees near the aviaries in East Park, but was gone by the following morning. It is interesting that both of these records share a common date, 4th November, this being towards the end of the typical period during which the species is found in this country.

Wood Warbler
Phylloscopus sibilatrix

Chiffchaff
(Common Chiffchaff)
Phylloscopus collybita

Nelson (1907) mentions that the Wood Warbler was common in a few places in the East Riding at the beginning of the 20th Century but nowhere in the Hull area was specifically mentioned. None now breed anywhere in the East Riding, with the nearest being in woods on the North Yorkshire Moors and Pennine foothills, but Wood Warblers may still occur in the Hull area as very rare passage migrants. There are just six records, however, the first being either one or three birds (depending on your source) in East Park on the late date of 21st September 1969. One was at Kerry Woods, Kirk Ella, between the 9th and 10th August 1979. Two were there on 10th August 1981 with one more on 4th August 1987. One heard singing in Hedon Road Cemetery in early May 1986 is one of just two spring records, this being the only time the metallic, trilling song had reportedly been heard in the Hull area. The other spring bird was a brief visitor to a West Hull garden on 14th April 2000.

Chiffchaffs are regular, if rather uncommon, passage migrants and very thinly distributed breeding birds in the Hull area. They arrive from their African wintering grounds between the last week of March and the second week of April, sometimes later. Many birds quickly move on and much of the area does not see another Chiffchaff until returning birds pass through again from late July through to September. Boylan (1967) described the Chiffchaff as a rare passage migrant in Hull during the 1960s, giving only seven records between 1960 and 1967 and naming Northern Cemetery as one of the sites visited. This scarcity seems overplayed now, but it appears that Chiffchaffs were genuinely scarcer in the Hull area in those days. The slow increase in frequency and numbers seems to have occurred during the 1980s. Trees along the railway line behind Hull Prison did not see their first Chiffchaff until 1980, but up to two singing males are now annual in that area. A few more can be found in nearby Hedon Road Cemetery, where the first record did not occur until 1981.

During the 1980s Chiffchaffs were uncommon passage migrants and possibly scarce breeding birds around Cottingham and northwest Hull. Only a few birds were seen each year, including one singing in Pearson Park in April 1982 and another at Cottingham in May 1988. The Chiffchaff was also described as a scarce passage migrant at Saltend around this time, with other spring birds seen at Kerry Woods (Kirk Ella). A gradual increase has been noted at North Bransholme since the late 1980s, from one or two spring birds quickly passing through to a tendency to remain all summer and probably breed. Up to two pairs are now believed to do so along the Old Main Drain hedgerow. Breeding is also annual at the Bransholme Sewage Works plantation, along Thomas Clarkson Way, with at least two pairs there too. Breeding is also believed to occur in the Priory Sidings off Clive Sullivan Way, near Gipsyville, and doubtless in several other scattered locations where there are trees with a suitable bushy understorey. They are, nevertheless, common nowhere.

Chiffchaffs have been recorded wintering in the Hull area on several occasions. Two did so in December 1987, at Bransholme and elsewhere in Hull. Singles were in a West Hull garden on 25th January 1998 and at the Bransholme Sewage Works on 22nd January 2000. Others at the Sewage Works on 12th March and in East Park on 7th in 2000 were also likely to be winterers rather than early migrants. These winter Chiffchaffs sometimes show characteristics of the eastern races, either birds from Scandinavia or eastern Europe (*Phylloscopus collybita abietinus*) or further east from the Urals to Siberia and Mongolia (*Phylloscopus collybita tristis*). These races may also occur on passage. Birds identified as *abietinus* were reported from Saltend on 26th and 27th January 1988, 12th September 1997 and at the Bransholme Sewage Works on 5th April 2000. One showing characteristics of the much rarer *tristis*, described by its finder (B. Richards) as 'sub-*tristis*', was at the latter site on 3rd January 2000. These races may one day be considered as separate species.

In the spring of 1998 I found a male Chiffchaff that had taken up territory at the southern end of the Old Main Drain hedgerow at North Bransholme, just opposite Ladyside Close, that had a very unusual song. It started familiarly enough, with around eight of the 'chiff' and 'chaff' notes, but then carried on the second half with a descending trill identical to that of Willow Warbler. The song was virtually half of one and half of the other, and I can only assume that it was a hybrid. B. Fendley informs me that he heard an identical song at the Kerry Woods near Kirk Ella on 29th April the following year. B. Richards has noted other peculiar songs from potential Chiffchaff x Willow Warbler hybrids at the Bransholme Sewage Works.

One heard on 15th April 1999 began a little like a Willow Warbler before continuing as a typical Chiffchaff, another on 29th June 2000 mostly sang like a normal Chiffchaff but every so often gave a near perfect Willow Warbler song, while another in the spring of 2001 once sang like a Willow Warbler but usually preferred to sing just the 'chiff' notes of the Chiffchaff song.

Willow Warbler
Phylloscopus trochilus

One of the more common summer migrants in the Hull area, the sweet tumbling verse of a Willow Warbler song may be heard in most outlying parts of the Hull area. The first birds of the spring are most often heard around the middle of April, the 13th being a commonly recurring date. First arrivals vary quite a lot from year to year, however, and have been known to be as early as 31st March or as late as 20th April.

Willow Warblers were reputed to be thinly distributed breeding birds in 1960s Hull (Boylan, 1967), with a key site being the railway embankment near King George Dock. Possible breeding was reported from Northern Cemetery, while young birds were frequently seen in gardens during autumn passage. One such youngster visited a Kirk Ella garden in August 1978, with several more in July 1987, and nesting was occurring in nearby Kerry Woods throughout the 1970s and early 1980s at least. Breeding was common in large gardens and woodland around Cottingham and northwest Hull in the 1980s (Bonavia, 1990). Meanwhile, around a dozen pairs were recorded at Saltend in 1985, with up to 22 on passage in August and September. Between three and six pairs were breeding in hedges between North Bransholme and the Holderness Drain in the late 1980s and early 1990s. This had increased to around eight pairs by 1998. Four pairs were found around the Priory Road fields in 1996 and breeding was also reported from the Priory Sidings, off Clive Sullivan Way, in the late 1990s.

"Dozens" of Willow Warblers could be heard singing along the old Hull to Withernsea railway line throughout the 1990s, especially in the trees and bushes around Hedon Road Cemetery, Hull Prison and the Maternity Hospital. Small numbers are scattered throughout the more built up areas of the city where bushes and scrub has been allowed to develop, such as the old railway sidings west of Calvert Lane and along the Holderness and Barmston Drains. There were several sightings in the Avenues area of Hull in 1996, with breeding possible, and one was singing from the old boundary hawthorns on Bellfield Avenue, in East Hull, in April 1994.

Other regular breeding sites in the Hull area include the Bransholme Sewage Works plantation and hedgerows off Thomas Clarkson Way (at least half a dozen pairs in the early 1990s), the Hull to Hornsea Rail Trail as it passes through Sutton and East Hull out towards Swine, the Risholme Carr area off Saltshouse Road (around the Princess Royal Hospital) and the Humber Bridge Country Park. Breeding is not thought to occur in any of the main Hull parks, although passage birds have been seen in East Park in recent years and they probably visit the others too. Most of the locally breeding Willow Warblers appear to have left by late August and the handful that are seen until early October are likely to be Continental in origin.

Goldcrest
Regulus regulus

The Goldcrest, Britain's smallest bird and one of the World's tiniest songbirds, is a very rare breeding bird in the Hull area. It becomes widespread in autumn and winter, however, after Scandinavian migrants pour in during September and October. Late autumn is the best time to find a small party of Goldcrests flitting among the branches of some wood, hedgerow or other patch of trees and bushes in the Hull area. They are often in the company of tits and warblers and they show a distinct preference for conifer trees. They are very pretty and fragile looking birds but are clearly tough enough to fly across the North Sea non-stop. Their constant calling, a very high pitched, repeated "tsee", gives them away despite the fact that they rarely sit still for long enough to allow a decent view.

Boylan (1967) considered the Goldcrest to be a rare winter visitor to Hull during the 1960s, quoting just five records and going on to describe it as a scarce passage migrant. Summering, and therefore possible breeding, was very rare in the city back then but Northern Cemetery was one of the sites where this had occurred. Goldcrests were relatively common around Cottingham in winter during the 1980s according to Bonavia (1990), although the only suspected breeding was out towards Bentley and Beverley. Rather small numbers were reported from Saltend during the mid 1980s, with a maximum of just four from September onwards in 1985. Goldcrests were unheard of in Hedon Road Cemetery before 1980 but have since increased to be present all year round and have even bred, making this the only confirmed breeding site in the Hull area. As with virtually all places, Goldcrests are always more numerous there once the migrants arrive in September.

I always found Goldcrests to be a little erratic and unpredictable in occurrence at North Bransholme during the 1990s. The best months were October and November but numbers rarely exceeded four or five at a time. Up to 12 were in the hedges and woods off Priory Road in autumn 1995 and a few were seen on and off until March. The best count in recent years was an impressive 30 among Great, Blue and Long-tailed Tits in the Bransholme Sewage Works plantation on 21st November 2000. Autumn or winter Goldcrests may turn up in any trees or bushes right into the city, however. There were three sightings near conifers in the Avenues in 1996 while up to six birds were in East Park during passage in late October and early November 1998.

All the cemeteries, parks, drain banks and railway sides throughout Hull will see a few Goldcrests at some point, as well as the woods and hedges in the outlying areas. I have even heard them in Queen's Gardens in recent autumns.

Firecrest
Regulus ignicapillus

The Firecrest, a rare winter visitor and passage migrant in East Yorkshire, has only been recorded in the Hull area on three, possibly four, occasions. The first record is the only potentially unreliable one and concerns a reported sighting in a Cottingham garden on 6th November 1983. This coincided with an influx of Goldcrests and Firecrests on the coast, but the record remains unconfirmed and there is now no way of knowing for sure. The other records are more straightforward. One was at Paull on 7th May 1987 with another, conceivably the same, found singing near Saltend on 27th. The singing bird was in Jubilee Copse, which lies alongside Paull Road between Hedon Road and Hedon Haven. The final record concerns a bird reported "in Hull" on 30th March 1993. As always with unobtrusive small birds, it is likely that several more have gone unrecorded.

Spotted Flycatcher
Muscicapa striata

The Spotted Flycatcher was once a fairly common summer visitor to our leafy suburbs, open wooded areas and tall hedgerows alike. Things have changed, however, and the decrease in the British population of this species since the 1960s has been greater than for most other small birds that have declined over the same period. The number of

Spotted Flycatchers arriving in Britain each May is now less than a fifth of what it was thirty years ago. The Hull area has not been immune form this crash, although Spotted Flycatchers still breed in several areas. They are also more widespread as passage migrants.

The Spotted Flycatcher was a familiar breeding bird in gardens around Pearson Park in the early 1900s. Boylan (1967) mentions that they bred in a variety of places, mainly cemeteries, in 1960s Hull. Spring birds were seen at Kirk Ella and Hessle during the 1960s and 1970s and breeding was confirmed at nearby Little Switzerland in 1967. Up to three pairs nested at Hedon Road Cemetery until the early 1980s, since which time they have become virtually unknown there. Regular breeding birds at Snuff Mill Lane, Cottingham, disappeared in 1983, although breeding was still fairly common in gardens and woods around the village in the mid 1980s. The decline continued, however, and more long-established nesting sites were becoming abandoned each year. These included a Cottingham pair that bred annually in a South Street

garden throughout the whole of the 1980s but failed to appear in 1991. Helen Crowther's 1996 survey of the wildlife in Hull's Avenues revealed just occasional sightings of Spotted Flycatchers, but breeding could not be ruled out. In the same year there was just one record (in late May) of a pair at the Priory Road fields. A family party along the Old Main Drain hedgerow, North Bransholme, in July 1994 pointed to breeding somewhere close by that year but Spotted Flycatchers are generally no more than a scarce passage migrant in this part of the city. Recent breeding has been recorded in East Park and several of the cemeteries, such as General Cemetery. Up to two pairs regularly nest in the grounds of Holderness House, on the corner of Holderness Road and Laburnum Avenue. Other scattered pairs undoubtedly go quietly about their business in large gardens and copses in the western villages, such as Hessle and Willerby. The mature trees in the Sutton and Saltshouse Road areas of East Hull perhaps hold a few more.

Passage migrants away from the breeding sites can turn up in any stand of trees or bushes but do not hang around for long. The earliest spring record was on 24th April in 1968 but the species is one of the last to arrive each spring. Most appear between early May and early June. Four in a small copse at the Great Culvert Pumping Station on the Holderness Drain, near Bransholme, at the beginning of June 1998 was the largest gathering of spring migrants reported in the Hull area. Most are alone. Intensive coverage at Saltend in the mid 1980s found the Spotted Flycatcher to be purely an autumn migrant there. Up to four were seen there from mid August to mid September between 1984 and 1986. East Park still had two birds on 12th September 1997 but the latest date for an autumn migrant in the Hull area was on 26th September 1985.

Red-breasted Flycatcher
Ficedula parva

This species is a scarce passage migrant on Yorkshire's east coast and is very rare inland. There have been just a few records in the Hull area, the exact number depending on how much faith you place in one or two of the earlier records, though I include all of them here for completeness.

On 20th May 1907 Mr Haworth-Booth saw a male Red-breasted Flycatcher at Hull Bank House (now called Haworth Hall), on the west bank of the River Hull not far north of Sutton Road Bridge, this being over a mile out into the countryside back then. A very good find and

seemingly straightforward enough, Haworth-Booth reported his sighting in *The Field* later that month and went on to inform an acquaintance, Harold R. Jackson of Hornsea. In August of the same year Jackson reported in the *Naturalist* that he and his sister had seen a pair of Red-breasted Flycatchers on 4th June at Thearne Hall, just a mile and a half north of Hull Bank House. Not only this, Jackson was certain that the birds were nesting nearby. Ralph Chislett, founder of the famous Spurn Bird Observatory and one of Yorkshire Ornithology's most celebrated names, repeated Jackson's record of a pair in his 1952 *Yorkshire Birds*. J. R. Mather repeated this again in his 1986 *The Birds of Yorkshire*, although he noted the strangeness of the date for a passage species. Both authors also gave the location as Beverley. Neither Chislett nor Mather mention Jackson's certainty of a breeding attempt, but looking at Jackson's original account one wonders how such a record had been readily accepted in the first place.

Jackson reported that he first noticed the male bird on account of its low warbling song, which ceased when it was joined by "another evidently of the same species". Jackson took this second bird to be the female. The male, he continued, began flirting with the second bird in the manner of a Robin, elaborately bowing and raising its head. The size of Willow Warblers, Jackson admits that they were seen in bad light and deep shade. The plumage was noted as being uniform light brown on both birds, with the male sporting a bold red patch under the throat that extended partly onto the breast. Although observed for seven minutes, at no point is the most obvious feature of a Red-breasted Flycatcher, the striking white tail-sides, mentioned in Jackson's account.

In my opinion at least one of these birds, probably both, was clearly a Robin and nothing more. Hearing of Haworth-Booth's sighting just two weeks before he visited the area, I imagine Jackson was keeping his eyes peeled for the bird. On hearing a song he did not recognise coming from a red-throated bird that he saw badly, Jackson seems to have put two and two together and made five. The low warbling song was surely just a subdued version of the very variable repertoire of the Robin and the posturing is a classic description of a Robin's threat display to a rival. That Jackson was so certain they were nesting is testimony to the fancifulness of the record - Red-breasted Flycatchers nest no closer than eastern Europe - and I can only assume that Chislett and Mather never actually saw the original account.

A more reliable occurrence was of an autumn passage bird near Hessle on 9th September 1971. The next, and most recent, record was not until 4th October 1989 when I discovered a first-winter bird in a hawthorn hedge along the Foredyke Stream at North Bransholme, just opposite Ladyside Close. I spotted this bird early one morning as a teenager on my way to school. I watched it for five minutes as it came as close as four feet before making typical fly-catching forays into a swarm of gnats, showing the characteristic tail pattern as it did so. It eventually flew off north over my head, giving the typical melancholic alarm note as it went, but it could not be relocated later in the day. Both of these records were accepted by the Yorkshire Naturalists' Union's Reports Committee.

Pied Flycatcher
Ficedula hypoleuca

Breeding no closer than the woodlands of the North Yorkshire Moors and the eastern Pennines, Pied Flycatchers are scarce passage migrants in the Hull area. This is true throughout the East Riding, but they are regular on the Holderness coast.

The first mention of the Pied Flycatcher around Hull concerns a very unexpected breeding record at Hullbank Hall, now Haworth Hall, in 1895 when a nest containing six eggs was found in a yew tree close to a pond. Haworth Hall was a grand country house back then but now sits among the suburbs on the west bank of the River Hull, to the north of Sutton Road Bridge. Passage migrants were noted near Pearson Park at the beginning of the 20th Century, being described as occasional visitors to John Nicholson's nearby town house. At least five were reported in Hull between 10th and 12th September in 1953 but Boylan (1967) could give just one passage record for the years 1960 to 1967, typically offering no further details. Another was seen in Hull on 13th October 1969 and an even later bird was caught at Paull on 13th November 1976. One was seen at Kirk Ella's Kerry Woods on 1st October 1978 and North Bransholme hosted another on 19th September 1983. Two were at Saltend on 22nd August 1984 with another on 8th September. 1985 saw one at King George Dock on 24th September and a lovely male was at Saltend on 9th May 1986, this being the only spring record for the Hull area. There were no more reports in the 1980s, probably reflecting a lack of reporting rather than a lack of birds.

A juvenile Pied Flycatcher was seen to board a Russian cargo ship, carrying timber, at the Spurn lightship on a very hot 2nd August 1995. The bird stayed aboard and caught insects until the ship reached King George Dock. The most recent records for the 1990s, during a rather poor decade for reporting, came from East Park on 9th September and Saltend on 6th October in 1998. Both involved singles.

Any time between late August and early October would therefore seem to offer the best chance of finding a Pied Flycatcher in the Hull area. A small handful of birds probably pass through each year, and they may stop off in any area of trees or shrubs.

Bearded Tit
Panurus biarmicus

Also known as the Bearded Reedling, the Bearded Tit is not a member of the tit family at all but is actually a species of babbler. Babblers are a large group with many species in Africa and Asia. Very rare in Britain during the first half of the 20th Century, Bearded Tits began expanding their range during the 1960s as birds colonised new areas of the country from the huge population in the Dutch polders. It was around this time that Blacktoft Sands at the head of the Humber was colonised, eventually becoming the largest colony in the country. It is irrupting birds from Blacktoft that are seen in the Hull area now and again.

A handful of Bearded Tits are seen among the reeds at Saltend most winters, usually from October to April. Eight were present in January 1978, with a few seen again in January 1984 and at least 24 the following December (when 20 were ringed). Most of the flock remained into 1985 and 17 were counted on 17th January. Birds were still present during February, with the 16 at nearby King George Dock on 24th probably being the Saltend birds. The flock decreased to seven in March with the last one on 1st April.

Numbers were down the following year, with eight at Saltend on 1st January 1986 falling to just two by February. The last one was seen on 22nd March. Two were present again from mid October onwards, staying until 17th March 1987, with one more on 8th April. Later that year eight were back in the Saltend reeds on 7th November. None were seen in 1988, but five were sighted in January and February 1989. Four were counted on 14th October 1990. Breeding occurred at Saltend in 1997, when one pair was seen with a very young juvenile in the reedbeds on 12th August. The adults were present from April to September. Disappointingly, the following year saw only wintering birds again; two were present in February, one in March and another in November.

The reedbeds around Saltend are the only places where Bearded Tits have been seen in the Hull area, albeit irregularly and in varying numbers. Other *Phragmites* beds along the Humber waterfront and elsewhere may well hold a very occasional party in winter.

Long-tailed Tit
Aegithalos caudatus

Continuously on the move in talkative, close-knit family groups, the very cute Long-tailed Tit is a favourite of mine. Although it seems to be thinly distributed as a breeding bird in the Hull area, this species is nevertheless fairly widespread in the region. It is possibly more common now than it has been for many decades.

In 1901 John Nicholson reported that parties of Long-tailed Tits were regular visitors to his Hull garden, near Pearson Park, but only in late summer. Soon afterwards, Nelson (1907) mentioned that it seemed to be decreasing in the East Riding. In 1952, meanwhile, Chislett described it as "nowhere very numerous, but nowhere scarce" in the county. Boylan (1967) considered the Long-tailed Tit to be a rare bird in 1960s Hull, mentioning just five records of occasional winter parties.

The supposed scarcity in the city might seem a little exaggerated now but it appears that the species really was a bit thin on the ground around Hull back then. There were only a few sightings around Kirk Ella in the mid 1970s, for example, mainly in winter, but with 12 in October 1982. Bonavia (1990) also considered Long-tailed Tits to be largely autumn and winter visitors around Cottingham in the first half the 1980s. Regular observation at North Bransholme from 1989 to 1994 revealed parties of up to 15 Long-tailed Tits between midsummer and winter. The presence of odd pairs in spring and family groups in July suggested that breeding was occurring somewhere close by, probably along Old Main Drain. Indeed, the *New Atlas* (Gibbons *et al.*, 1993) indicated breeding throughout the Hull area at the beginning of the 1990s.

Counts at the Bransholme Sewage Works plantation in the early 1990s usually revealed five birds or less, again mainly in autumn, but that decade has witnessed a steady increase in recorded numbers of Long-tailed Tits. There is now also a greater tendency to penetrate further into the city than before. An irregular visitor to Hedon Road Cemetery in the 1970s, by the 1990s Long-tailed Tits were resident all year round and up to 20 could be found in the general area. Small parties were reported along the old railway line in 1996. Several pairs nested around the north end of Priory Road the same year. A site record of 20 were at the Bransholme Sewage Works in September 1998 and 24 were in East Park that November. I saw another party of half a dozen birds in East Park in December 2000. Recent breeding has also been suspected around Pearson Park but, as yet,

there are no records from the city centre.

I only once had Long-tailed Tits in my North Bransholme garden during the 1990s but they are increasingly coming to bird tables all over Britain. Peanuts, sunflower seeds or hanging fat could well attract them to yours if there are flocks close by.

Marsh Tit
Parus palustris

Boylan (1967) regarded the Marsh Tit as a very rare bird in Hull during the 1960s. Just three records were mentioned, all in the extreme north-west of the city where the Orchard Park estate now stands. Bonavia (1990) stated that the Marsh Tit was less common than the very similar Willow Tit (which was itself scarce) around Cottingham in the first half of the 1980s, but it was thought to breed in small numbers. A pair was in the Humber Bridge Country Park in December 1988 but the *New Atlas* (Gibbons *et al.*, 1993) indicated no breeding anywhere near the Hull area at the beginning of the 1990s. There is always the possibility that a lack of reporting meant pairs were missed.

There were no records during the first half of the 1990s and I have never come across one in East Yorkshire, never mind the Hull area, since I started birdwatching in the 1980s. In the last few years of the 1990s, however, lone Marsh Tits started to be seen all over Hull. A single bird was a regular visitor to a peanut feeder in West Hull in the early months of 1997. This or another was seen among a flock of other tits on nearby scrubland in October. It was back at the peanut feeder again throughout 1998.

West Hull is the place where you would have expected to find a Marsh Tit in the area, if they were going to turn up at all, but on 15th January 1998 a single bird was confidently identified in East Park. This was the first record for East Hull. It was followed by another, perhaps the same bird, on the Hornsea Rail Trail near Sutton on 14th December.

Marsh Tits are extremely sedentary, rarely moving more than a mile or two from the woodland in which they were hatched, so the recent sightings around Hull indicate that there may be a small population in the wooded areas to the west of city.

Willow Tit
Parus montanus

An uncommon and, sadly, declining species throughout Britain, Willow Tits have also become much more difficult to find in the Hull area during the last few decades. Now best described as a scarce resident, breeding is very rarely reported and the species is most likely to be found among wandering flocks of tits in autumn and winter.

Chislett (1952) mentioned recent breeding at Wawne and Haltemprice in the late 1940s and the species was regarded as not uncommon on Humberside around that time. Boylan's 1967 *Birds in Hull* makes no mention of the Willow Tit during the first half of the 1960s, although Marsh Tit was included. Despite this, a pair of Willow Tits were seen on Dunswell Road, Cottingham, in July 1967. There were several more sightings around Kirk Ella in the mid 1970s, with pairs seen in Kerry Woods during the breeding season into the early 1980s.

A pair reared eight young at Saltend in 1986 and up to three adults were seen on many dates, all year round, since at least 1984. One or two birds were often seen along the Old Main Drain at North Bransholme between the mid 1980s and mid 1990s, mostly between September and March. A pair was also seen here in June 1993 and breeding was suspected somewhere close by, possibly Woody Carr near Wawne. Two pairs were seen at Priory Road fields in autumn 1995 and they remained to breed in the Raised Bank and Priory Wood areas in 1996. This is the only recent breeding record anywhere in the

Hull area. Sightings in Kirk Ella's Kerry Woods during March in 1995 and 1998 raises hopes that more Willow Tits may be breeding elsewhere. The sight of a single bird along North Bransholme's Old Main Drain on New Year's Day 2001, meanwhile, after several years of absence, showed that the species has not totally disappeared from all of its former haunts around Hull.

Coal Tit
Parus ater

The Coal Tit is a bird of woodlands, particularly those with a strong coniferous element. It is therefore not very surprising that it is uncommon in the Hull area, especially in the relatively treeless east.

The earliest mention of the Coal Tit in Hull comes from Boylan's (1967) account of the birds found in the city between 1960 and 1966, in which he described this species as an irregular breeding bird in the suburbs. Other sources mention occasional winter sightings in Northern Cemetery in the early 1960s, with resident birds in Newland Park. A pair bred in a cranny in Cottingham's St Mary's Church in 1981 and breeding was

noted at the University of Hull's Botanic Gardens in the early to mid 1980s. Birds were also reported to be regular in Cottingham gardens in autumn and winter.

Things are quite different in East Hull. The only record for Hedon Road Cemetery is of a lone bird visiting the bird table for a week in February 1986. Three seen at Saltend the following September was the only record there during intensive coverage in the mid 1980s. An adult was feeding a troupe of recently fledged young down Common Lane, Wawne, in early summer 1995. I suspect that this brood was reared in the nearby Paradise Wood, which has some conifers. A pair were in North Bransholme's Old Main Drain hedgerow in September 2001 and there are also a few sightings from the Ings Road area of East Hull.

Back in West Hull and the western villages, the stronghold of the species in the Hull area, Coal Tits were occasionally seen in the trees down Cottingham Road in the mid 1990s. There were three records from conifers in Hull's Avenues in 1996 and they are often seen in gardens in this part of the city. Breeding is reputed to occur, albeit uncommonly, in old trees in West Hull and they are regular in the Humber Bridge Country Park.

The status of the Coal Tit in the Hull area is probably best summarised by dealing by with both sides of the River Hull individually. In East Hull the species is a scarce breeding bird and occasional wanderer. In West

Hull it nests more commonly, though still rather sparingly, but is a more widespread resident.

Blue Tit
Parus caeruleus

Anyone who has ever put a birdfeeder up in their garden will be familiar with the acrobatic and perky little Blue Tit. They are very common birds in the Hull area and can be found in any area of woodland, scrub, hedgerow, leafy gardens and avenues or even reedbeds. They even nest in the city centre.

Nicholson reported that the Blue Tit was a frequent visitor to his Hull garden in 1901; a flock of eight was present as he wrote his account. Boylan (1967) said that the Blue Tit was a common breeding bird in 1960s Hull and they could often be seen in Queen's Gardens. There were also five pairs in Northern Cemetery alone at this time. Bonavia (1990) considered them to be abundant breeders in gardens and woodland around Cottingham in the first half of the 1980s. I also found them to be common at North Bransholme in the early 1990s, with around 10 pairs along the length of the Old Main

Drain and in the nearby copses. There were a further two pairs at the Bransholme Sewage Works.

Michael Flowers reports that the Blue Tit is very common and nests annually in Hedon Road Cemetery. Crowther's 1996 survey of Hull's Avenues found them to be common there, too, with Milsom coming to the same conclusion at the Priory Road fields the same year. In June 2001 I came across a recently fledged family party of Blue Tits in trees near the Old English Gentleman pub in central Hull. It is, therefore, probably fair to say that the Blue Tit is common everywhere in the Hull area and has always been so.

While most nests are probably located in tree holes, Blue Tits will readily take to a nest box with the right dimensions. Such boxes certainly help them in the suburbs where mature trees are often scarce. Other artificial sites are also used in the absence of anything better, and four pairs were nesting in city gas light standards in 1941.

In 1989 I located five active nests in a half square mile area on the eastern fringe of North Bransholme. One was in a dead sycamore tree, two were in live ash and silver birch trees, with a further two in nest boxes. I decided to keep a close eye on these nests to see how they fared and found that two of them lost a parent bird (one to a Sparrowhawk and the other found dead due to unknown causes). What was notable was the fact that all of the chicks from all of the nests fledged within just a few days of each other, between

6th and 9th June. Blue Tits synchronise their breeding like this to coincide with the hatching of the caterpillars, and they only have one chance to breed each year. With many Blue Tits not living to see a second year it is crucial for them to rear as many young as possible, hence the large broods that offset the heavy predation.

After the chicks leave the nest the family parties can be found roaming the trees and hedgerows from mid June onwards. They often join up with other families of Blue, Great and Long-tailed Tits, Willow Warblers etc. and gatherings of over a dozen Blue Tits may be found in late summer and autumn. Not all of the autumn and winter Blue Tits visiting our gardens and hedgerows are local birds, however. A first winter bird caught at Hull on 27th October 1976 was ringed at Spurn Point, over 20 miles away, just two weeks before. Another ringed at Spurn on 7th October 1977 was found dying at Hull 18 months later, on 7th March 1979. These birds may have come from overseas.

Great Tit
Parus major

The Great Tit is less numerous in the Hull area than the Blue Tit but it is still a common bird and occurs in similar bushy and wooded habitats. As with the Blue Tit, natural tree-hole nesting sites are at a premium in many parts of Hull and a well made, well positioned nestbox will readily be used by local Great Tits. Great Tits are also familiar visitors to most bird tables around Hull, being particularly fond of sunflower seeds, peanuts and 'bird cakes' (seed and nuts set in fat).

John Nicholson had a pair of Great Tits visiting his Hull garden, near Pearson Park, in the autumn of 1901. This contrasted with parties of up to eight Blue Tits. Another early Hull record concerns a little gang of Great Tits going to roost in the glass bowl of gas street light in 1943. A Great Tit caught at Cottingham in April 1952, meanwhile, had been ringed at Sedbergh (95 miles to the northwest) just four weeks earlier.

Boylan (1967) regarded the species as a regular breeder in the parks, cemeteries and gardens of 1960s Hull. Bonavia (1990) listed it as an abundant breeder around Cottingham but, once again, it was noted to be less numerous than the Blue Tit. The peak count at Saltend in 1984 was just four birds, this being compared to 14 for the Blue Tit. I also found Great Tits to be much scarcer than Blue Tits at North Bransholme throughout the 1990s, although two or three pairs bred along Old Main Drain. The largest numbers at North Bransholme were encountered in

June, when the young had just fledged and family parties were roaming the copses and hedgerows. One or two birds visited my garden bird table most days during winter.

Great Tits are reported to be very common down Hedon Road, regularly nesting in telegraph poles between the cemetery and Brigham's factory. A decline was noted in Hull's Avenues in the mid 1990s, however, and they are now infrequent there. Great Tits were still found to be common around Priory Road in 1996, again less so than the Blue Tit, but there were maximum counts of eight birds and breeding was noted in Priory Wood, Wood Lane and the Pickhills.

There are, in fact, few districts of the Hull area that do not resonate to the ringing song of the Great Tit in spring. Breeding birds are fairly common and widespread in all but the most built up and barren areas. Most gardens and stands of trees and bushes will receive a visit from roaming birds in autumn and winter.

Nuthatch
(Wood Nuthatch)
Sitta europaea

Despite being a resident and moderately common breeding bird in much of Britain, including North and West Yorkshire, the Nuthatch is an extremely rare bird in the East Riding. Nuthatches are highly sedentary and very reluctant to move more than a few miles from their territory, especially if this involves crossing open ground. They are therefore unable to easily reach the scattered fragments of woodland in the Hull area. Indeed, the furthest recorded distance ever travelled by a Yorkshire Nuthatch is just under 20 miles, and there are precious few Nuthatches within that sort of distance from Hull and the surrounding villages. Little wonder then that there are just two reported instances of a Nuthatch in the region covered by this book.

On 17th May 1977 Brian Fendley saw a Nuthatch in the Kerry Woods, just west of Kirk Ella. Sixteen years later, in early 1993, Graham Uney saw one climbing down a chestnut tree at Holderness House, on the corner of Laburnum Avenue and Holderness Road in Hull. A fortnight later Uney apparently saw the same bird again at Holderness House, this time at the top of an ash tree right outside the entrance to the grounds. Where these birds came from is a mystery. Were they from an undiscovered population in the Wolds woodlands or were they maverick wanderers from further afield?

Treecreeper
(Eurasian Treecreeper)
Certhia familiaris

The Treecreeper is an unobtrusive bird and this makes its status in the Hull area a little hard to judge. It seems to be rare or scarce in many parts and regular in a few others. The general scarcity of the Treecreeper around Hull is likely to have a lot to do with the patchy distribution of mature trees and woodland, as the species is strongly tied to this kind of habitat.

All of the three Yorkshire avifaunas of the last century (Nelson in 1907, Chislett in 1952 and Mather in 1986) had little to say about the Treecreeper in the East Riding and nothing of it in the Hull area. All of them, however, acknowledged that it could be found in most mature woods throughout Yorkshire. The earliest mention of the species around Hull comes from 1943 when unusually high numbers were seen around Cottingham, Anlaby and Hessle. This was attributed to the felling of extensive woods nearby, forcing the birds out and into new areas.

The Treecreeper was a very rare winter visitor to 1960s Hull, according to Boylan (1967), with just three records. A pair were seen in Cottingham in March 1969 and Brian Fendley found a nest in Kerry Woods, Kirk Ella, in 1976. Birds have been regular there up to the present day. Bonavia (1990) mentioned that Treecreepers were present in woods around Cottingham in the 1980s, occasionally coming to the village gardens. One was seen in a South Street garden in April 1984, April 1991 and November 1993.

Treecreepers were not recorded at Saltend during the intensive coverage of the mid 1980s. A single bird at Hedon Road Cemetery in July 1981 was only the second record there. I saw a pair along North Bransholme's Old Main Drain hedgerow in autumn 1988 and one was calling from woods at Woody Carr, near Wawne, in April 1989, but they were my only records of the species in that area. I suspect that breeding may be occurring at Woody Carr, this being excellent habitat for them, although access restrictions make this difficult to prove. Gibbons *et al.* (1993), meanwhile, recorded breeding in all 10 km squares covering the Hull area between 1988 and 1991.

Helen Crowther's 1996 survey of the wildlife in Hull's Avenues revealed the Treecreeper to be a scarce but long term resident among the more mature trees. A pair was present in the Humber Bridge Country Park the following year, with breeding considered to be regular here. A lone bird was in East Park in the autumn of 1998 and breeding is suspected here, too. Indeed, breeding has been occurring at nearby Holderness House, on the corner of Holderness Road and Laburnum Avenue for many years.

Roaming winter birds offer the best chance of seeing a Treecreeper in East Hull. West Hull and the villages are clearly a better bet for breeding birds, but the species does not appear to be common anywhere.

Golden Oriole
(Eurasian Golden Oriole)
Oriolus oriolus

A scarce passage migrant on the coast of East Yorkshire, the beautiful Golden Oriole was recorded just once in the Hull area throughout the whole of the 20th Century. This was a fine male found near Paull during the first week of May in 1947. The bird was seen by a Major Batchelor and several others during its stay. In the 1860 *Hull Museum Guide* it is reported that "specimens [of the Golden Oriole] have been seen near Hull". Details would have been nice!

Red-backed Shrike
Lanius collurio

The Red-backed Shrike never nested in the Hull area, even when it was a common summer visitor to England in the 19th Century. This is despite Thomas Nelson noting one-off breeding from near Beverley and Easington in his 1907 *Birds of Yorkshire*.

The earliest record for the Hull area also comes from Nelson, who mentions one "observed near Hull" sometime prior to 1845. The next concerns a male that lingered on the city outskirts for ten days in June 1941. It was spotted by G. H. Ainsworth, the then Yorkshire Naturalists' Union bird recorder for the East Riding, as he was cycling in open country on Wawne Road towards Hull, through what is now the Bransholme housing estate. He first noticed a funny bird sat on telephone wires that, as he approached, glided down into some bushes. Ainsworth watched it for some time as it swooped down from bushes and wires to catch insects. During its stay it became very obliging and showed little fear of passers-by. As it hung around for some time

Ainsworth thought that it might be breeding with an unseen female, although he found no nest.

More lingering spring migrants were responsible for the next record, when a pair were seen near Cottingham from 29th May to 4th June 1955. No more were reported for over three decades until an immature bird was observed at Saltend on 23rd September 1989. This was followed by a singing male at the same site on 29th May 1996.

There is a clear trend for spring records over autumn ones in the Hull area, although the number of years taken to acquire the above five records is testament to the rarity of the species in our part of the world. Red-backed Shrikes must have occurred more frequently in the Hull area when the species was a regular breeder in Britain, but it now requires an enormous amount of luck to ever see one here.

Lesser Grey Shrike
Lanius minor

Two of these very rare vagrants from southern and eastern Europe have been claimed in the Hull area. The first concerns a bird seen "in Hull"

on 3rd July 1980. This was rejected by the British Birds Rarities Committee (BBRC), who adjudicate on such matters. The second record, a first-winter bird reported from Saltend by several observers on 16th October 1989, does not appear in any of the BBRC reports.

Great Grey Shrike
Lanius excubitor

The Great Grey Shrike is a very rare autumn migrant and winter visitor in the Hull area, but one may turn up in any scrubby patch during this time. The visits by passage birds are characteristically brief; one found at Saltend on 6th October 1998 was not seen again. Another at Castle Hill, between Bransholme and Swine, on the afternoon of 17th October 2000 left the next morning.

Winter birds, in contrast, tend to hang around much longer if they find a suitable location. One spent several months at West Ella in early 1970, while on 25th March 1996 I found a singing bird near the Foredyke Stream at North Bransholme. I followed the bird as it made its way north along the thick hedgerow on Old Main Drain before it was lost to view near Carlam Hill Farm. The next day it was relocated in the scrubby field that now hosts the Bransholme Fishing Pond. It remained there, attracting dozens of observers, until it was last seen on 7th April. A photograph of this shrike appeared in one of the national birdwatching magazines soon afterwards. Indeed, the bird was very obliging and performed for admirers by gruesomely catching and dismembering a Dunnock among the hawthorns. The only other record concerns one seen behind Hallgate School, Cottingham, on Christmas Day 1982.

Jay
(Eurasian Jay)
Garrulus glandarius

Common over much of Britain, the Jay is a rather rare bird in Hull. It occurs mainly as a passage migrant during autumn dispersal of British birds or immigration of Continental birds. The recent trend has been for single Jays to be seen every few years as they pass through the area. Lone birds have been seen as follows: at Kerry Woods (near Kirk Ella) in 1975; moving west over Paull on 11th October 1986 and again at Kirk Ella on the same day; Kerry Woods again on 20th August 1988; Woody Carr near Wawne on 18th January 1989; North Bransholme on 5th September 1992; Hull Golf Course (Kirk Ella again) on 6th December 1993; Sutton Fields Industrial Estate on 21st September 1997. The spring of 1997 also saw two birds at Kerry Woods on 21st March. This site is seemingly the most productive for the species in the Hull area.

A huge invasion of Continental immigrants in the autumn of 1983 brought thousands of Jays to Britain. The only ones recorded from the Hull area were at Priory Road fields on 27th November and Wawne's Paradise Wood on 29th December. Others likely to have been part of this invasion were at Paradise Wood on 27th February 1984, and again on 12th April, and at Harland Way (between Cottingham and Skidby) on 10th May the following spring.

Jays appear to have visited the region in larger numbers in years gone by, with a flock of four reported from Northern Cemetery in the early 1960s. The largest numbers seen in the area occurred in late April 1948, when two flocks of around 30 birds were seen heading south high over the Humber at Hessle. The flocks were roughly an hour apart, with a few stragglers inbetween and afterwards, and these birds were no doubt homeward-bound visitors from the Continent.

Magpie
(Black-billed Magpie)
Pica pica

Magpies are more common in the Hull area now than at any time in living memory. Nelson (1907) states that they were becoming scarce in the East Riding a century ago due to persecution from gamekeepers and farmers. Around the same time, at the beginning of the 1900s, John Nicholson made no mention of the Magpie when he listed the birds coming to his garden on the outskirts of West Hull. This is despite Nicholson hosting such birds as Hooded Crow, Nightjar and Cuckoo. Game shooting was a major pastime of the social elite in Edwardian Britain and any creature that preyed on gamebirds or their eggs and chicks was ruthlessly slaughtered. Magpies, opportunistic predators and scavengers, were near the top of the game preserver's hit list. They recovered a little during the two World Wars, when many gamekeepers were away fighting, but they were hammered once again as soon as their persecutors returned. Game shooting slowly declined in the latter half of the 20th Century, howev-

er, and by the 1960s there were odd pairs breeding on the outskirts of Hull. Two birds at Kirk Ella in March 1981 were the first recorded in that village. They were uncommon at Saltend in the mid 1980s, although Bonavia (1990) regarded them as fairly common residents around Cottingham between 1981 and 1986. A pair or two were breeding at North Bransholme during the early 1990s, despite being a favourite quarry of the airgunner, and at least one other pair was resident on the Sutton Fields Industrial Estate around the same time. They had also become common along Hedon Road, the western villages and most other parts of the Hull area by then. Magpies were still reportedly increasing around Hull's Avenues in 1996, with four or five seen daily. Increases were also noted from Cottingham in the mid 1990s, with Paul Milsom seeing a pair or two in every hedgerow around Priory Road between 1995 and 1996.

Magpies are usually seen in pairs but they have a tendency to flock in winter and early spring. It is at these times that the largest numbers have been reported in the Hull area. Ten were noted at Priory Road in January 1982, this being a big count back then. An impressive 21 at Priory Road in October 1995 was followed by a whopping 47 in January 1996. A further 17 were on Snuff Mill Lane in January 1993. Seventeen were at the Bransholme Sewage Works in March 1992 and 19 were there again in September. Up to eight were seen the following year and 30 in March 1998. My peak count at North Bransholme was 12 in January 1993, while Michael Flowers recorded 13 in Hedon Road Cemetery in the spring of 1997. It is noticeable that peak counts from most individual sites have increased significantly over the past 20 years.

Jackdaw
(Eurasian Jackdaw)
Corvus monedula

In 1901 John Nicholson, writing in *The Naturalist*, included the Jackdaw among the list of birds that visited the garden of his Hull town house, close to Pearson Park in the outer suburbs. Nicholson described the Jackdaw as a common bird that bred in the vicinity, no doubt in the chimney pots of the smart houses and holes in the mature parkland trees.

By 1967, when Patrick Boylan wrote his *Birds in Hull*, largely based on notes taken since 1960, the Jackdaw could still be found breeding in many Hull suburbs, such as Newland Park. In 1990 Peter Bonavia wrote *The Birds of the Cottingham Area 1980 - 1986* and listed the Jackdaw as an abundant breeding species that was increasing in the area. In the same period, around the mid 1980s, the Jackdaw was described as an uncommon bird at Saltend that was mainly met with in spring and autumn. There was no breeding among the docks. I suspected that thinly scattered pairs were breeding in old trees in the woods and lanes about Wawne at this time. This is probably still the case, although I have never seen a nest.

In 1995/1996 Paul Milsom recorded up to 60 Jackdaws on the Priory Road fields. Breeding was still being noted in the chimneys of old houses in nearby Cottingham. A few pairs may breed in similar circumstances in Sutton and also the outlying villages to the west of Hull, but definite breeding records seem to be very thin on the ground. This is hopefully just a result of a lack of recording and not a genuine lack of nesting birds.

Occasional Jackdaws visit the parks in the inner suburbs of Hull but the species is mainly a bird of the villages, city fringe and outlying farmland. I regularly saw large numbers among the great flights of Rooks east of North Bransholme during the late 1980s and early 1990s. Counts included 50 in December 1989 and 500 with 1,000 Rooks in late November 1993. A great swirling mass of 800 Jackdaws was observed going to roost at Paradise Wood, near Wawne, on 23rd January 1994.

Rook
Corvus frugilegus

The earliest mention of the Rook in Hull comes from the *Zoologist* (1846, p. 1366). This described the unusual nesting and rearing of young by two pairs between chimney pots in George Street, in the town centre, in 1840. John Nicholson reported the Rook as being a common sight over Hull gardens in 1901 and Nelson (1907) regarded it as the most common of the larger land birds in Yorkshire.

By the time Boylan wrote *Birds in Hull* in 1967, however, the only remaining rookeries in the city boundary were in the northeast suburbs, Sutton and Marfleet. Several urban Hull rookeries were abandoned between 1963 and 1966, these being at St. John's in Newland, Trinity burial ground (near the Marina) and at Holderness House on the corner of Holderness Road and Laburnum Avenue. A regular flightline between the rolling fields west of Hull and the rookeries to the northeast was still in evidence, however, ensuring a constant stream of birds over the city. Occasional birds also dropped down to feed in the cemeteries and parks. Three pairs of Rooks tried to nest in an elm tree in the Hedon Road Cemetery in 1972 but the attempt failed and they were never seen again at that site.

The expansion of Hull during the late 1960s and 1970s engulfed more rookeries on land at North Bransholme, but they slowly declined. One at Wawne Lodge, on Pennine Way, became extinct about 1987 and the last Hull rookery, in Ash Plantation on Lothian Way, contained around 30 pairs in the 1980s before being deserted in the early 1990s. Harassment from air-gun-wielding youths had a lot to do with the extinction of the Ash Plantation rookery.

There are still several rookeries in the Hull area, outside of the Hull city boundary, including 60 nests at Wawne village and at least 100 at Long Carr (between Wawne and Skirlaugh) in 2001. There are perhaps more near Swine and in Wawne's Woody Carr but any colonies at this latter site are heavily shot over in spring, as is Long Carr. There have always been large rookeries around Cottingham and Bonavia (1990) reported 199 nests at Harland Way and 133 at Castle Hill in 1984. These figures also seemed about right when I lived near Harland Way in the mid 1990s.

Large, wheeling flocks of Rooks sometimes congregate in the outlying fields around Hull. Up to 250 birds from the Cottingham colonies regularly feed on the Priory Road fields, usually preferring pasture. I counted 300 at North Bransholme in

January 1993 and an impressive 1,100 on 8th November the same year. Over 1,000 were there again in the company of 500 Jackdaws on 28th. Much smaller numbers can often be found in many open spaces in and around Hull, including arable fields, any remaining pastureland, playing fields and also parkland and wide roadside verges. I often see a few Rooks feeding around the North Point shopping centre in the heart of Bransholme and the occasional bird or two may even come to a well-stocked bird table in the outer suburbs.

Carrion Crow
Corvus corone corone

The Carrion Crow is the common, large, black crow that can be seen all over the city and throughout the wider Hull area, from the city centre and Humber shore to the outlying villages and farmland. Their bulky stick nests can be found in the tops of trees almost anywhere, in streets, remote copses, parks and even on busy roundabouts.

The status of the Carrion Crow in the Hull area has changed significantly over the past 100 years. John Nicholson made no mention of the species when he wrote of the birds visiting his garden in the outer suburbs of West Hull at the beginning of the last century, despite including the Hooded Crow and Jackdaw. This suggests that the Carrion Crow was genuinely absent from the neighbourhood at that time. If so, this was surely the result of wholesale trapping and shooting by farmers and gamekeepers. Carrion Crows are still heavily persecuted by gamekeepers to this day on account of their fondness for gamebird eggs and chicks. They are also popular targets for airgunners.

The expansion of Hull over the course of the last century created oases in the parks and cemeteries where Carrion Crows could live in safety from the gun. By 1967 Boylan could say that they were breeding regularly and commonly in most such places in the city. Bonavia (1990) described the Carrion Crow as very common around Cottingham in the 1980s and this status could be applied across the whole Hull area by then. They still seem to be increasing and spreading right across the city and can be seen atop almost any television aerial, lamppost or tree. They are also commonly seen patrolling the farmland fields, playing fields and parklands for worms and other titbits.

Carrion Crows mainly hang around singly or in pairs, but small groups of half a dozen or so are not uncommon and large gatherings can also occur. Fourteen was the highest count at Saltend in 1984, 57 were on the Pickhills fields (off Priory Road) on 14th February 1995 and 30 were in poplars behind Hedon Road Cemetery one winter day in 1999. There is a large winter roost of Carrion Crows in East Park and birds stream in from across the region in late afternoon. Over 270 were counted there on 3rd January 1998, with 375 on Christmas Eve 1998 and 243 on 23rd January the following year.

The Carrion Crow is probably more common now than at any time during the last century and is one of the most familiar birds in the Hull area, but it is admired by few. The Carrion Crow certainly seems to have been lumped in with its larger cousin, the Raven, as a legendary symbol of bad omen in the popular psyche but it is undeniably an intelligent, adaptable and successful bird in both town and country. One wonders how much the jet black plumage, harsh call and apparently stern expression have to do with its unpopularity. Not all Hull Carrion Crows are completely black, however, and many show varying amounts of white in their wings, sometimes forming a distinct white wingbar across the flight feathers.

'Hooded Crow'
Corvus corone cornix

The Hooded Crow is a race of the Carrion Crow and replaces the all-black variety in northwest Scotland, Ireland, Scandinavia and Eastern Europe. Large numbers of foreign Hooded Crows used to winter in eastern England during the first half of the 20th Century and they were scarce visitors to John Nicholson's Hull garden. The proliferation of tips and landfill sites in their homeland since the Second World War meant food was not so hard to find in winter and the annual exodus to Britain became unnecessary. Very few now make the journey.

Boylan noted just two winter records of Hooded Crows in Hull between 1960 and 1966. Two more were at North Bransholme on New Years Eve 1980. One was present down Fountain Road, off Beverley Road, between early February and early March in 1984 and another spent a couple of months on the Priory Road fields that same year. One was at Saltend in November and December 1985 and one flew over North Bransholme around the same time.

An apparent Hooded Crow feeding on a grass verge at the junction of Wawne Road and Honiton Road in the heart of Bransholme in March 1995 was probably a hybrid with a Carrion Crow. A definite hybrid, meanwhile, was in East Park between 2nd and 3rd April 1996.

Starling
(Common Starling)
Sturnus vulgaris

Everyone knows the Starling. For many generations it has been one of the commonest birds in the Hull area, nesting in our roofs, feeding on our lawns and swarming over our skies in its amazing evening gatherings. The last century began with flocks of Starlings being common in the gardens of Hull, such as that of John Nicholson near Pearson Park where it also bred. In 1909 an active nest was found at Sutton on the bizarre date of 29th November. The nest contained five half-grown young, although four were already dead and the fifth looked as if it was about to join them soon enough. The Starling was still a very common breeding bird in Hull in the 1960s, as it was around Cottingham and doubtless everywhere else, and this continued into the 1980s. They were still described as being very common breeders around Cottingham in the mid 1990s, although numbers had been falling nationally for some time and decreases were being noted around Hull. By 1996 the Starling was no longer a daily sight around some parts of Hull's Avenues area, while numbers of nesting birds at Bransholme and across much of the region were falling throughout that decade. Starlings are still quite common breeding birds around Hull, but they are clearly in trouble at the moment and are causing a great deal of concern to conservationists.

Most Starlings synchronise their nesting to begin in April, when the ground is still soft enough to allow them to probe for grubs to feed their chicks on. From March onwards the males gain the bluish base to the bill and sit close to their nest hole, flapping their wings, puffing out their throat and reeling off their incredible song. So easily disregarded as just noisy chatter, the Starling has one of the widest vocal repertoires of any British bird and is our best mimic. The song usually begins with a wolf-whistle, followed by a clicking chatter that can then lead anywhere; one bird that sang outside my window regularly gave perfect renditions of the calls and songs of, among others, Lapwing, Redshank, Curlew, Grey Partridge, Blackbird and Great Tit. The copies were so good that I often looked around for the real thing before realising it was the Starling. They will also weave fragments of man-made sounds into their songs, with favourites being car alarms and telephones. My local bird also produced the revving of a motorbike and the 'clunking' sound of a hammer hitting concrete, the result of him listening to a neighbour during a spot of DIY.

Once the chicks hatch, around mid April, the adults form feeding flocks on areas of insect-rich pasture, playing fields or rough grassland. They can then be seen commuting backwards and forwards from their nests under the eaves of nearby houses, though they will often travel a long way to a good food source. One such feeding flock at Saltend in April 1985 numbered 150 birds and there were often up to 200 conveying grubs from the grassland off Noddle Hill Way to their insatiable broods in the roofs of Bransholme houses.

The young fledge around mid to late May and gather in dense hedgerows or thickets while their parents continue to bring food until their charges are able to follow them. In the late 1980s and early 1990s up to 500 newly fledged Starlings regularly congregated in the hawthorns off Cumbrian Way on North Bransholme at this time. Newly fledged Starlings were often brought to me by local children who thought them to be lost or injured. There was usually nothing wrong with them, except they were now separated from their parents and slowly starving to death, but I invariably found them impossible to hand rear. I have hand-reared many young birds of several species, but there is something in a Starling's nature that will not allow it to submit to hand-feeding, even to the extent that they regurgitate food that is force fed into the crop. It is almost as if they give up and prefer to die when they are isolated from their brethren.

Once the young Starlings are confident on the wing they join the adult feeding flocks to roam their neighbourhood, often seeking out pools of water in which to freshen up their plumage. Between the 15th and 18th May 1989 around 200 of the North Bransholme contingent, most of them juveniles, had gathered to bathe at the shallow pool just opposite Kingswood School on Wawne Road. Many of the juveniles, being fresh out of the nest, lacked the waterproofing element of their plumage and got so waterlogged that they couldn't fly. It was ridiculously easy to pick them up as they sat among the grass waiting to dry. Despite a flock of 60 adults and juveniles feeding on the Pickhills, between Cottingham and Hull, in May 1996 it is getting increasing difficult to find any of these early summer post-breeding flocks that number 100 birds or more. These late May and early June flocks are probably the best indication of the size of the breeding population in the immediate area, and it is depressing to see them dwindling in recent years.

Come June the Starlings begin to form summer roosting flocks in stands of trees, reedbeds along the Humber, dense thickets or any man-made structure with lots of perches. Saltend and the cranes around the docks are often used. Each of the local flocks initially gathers at some suitable pre-roost location. The hawthorns behind Whitehope Close on North Bransholme was the preferred site for my local birds and there is another in Queen's Gardens.

Here they may preen or chatter away for an hour or so until the sun starts to set, then they take their cue and leave for the night roost.

Around 3,000 birds used to gather at a pre-roost site in Northern Cemetery during the 1960s, later moving to their night roost in the Pickhills hawthorns, off Hull Road at Cottingham. The Pickhills roost regularly contained at least 20,000 Starlings throughout late summer and autumn until the mid 1980s when it moved to the reedbeds at Saltend. A total of 21,000 were counted there in early July 1988, although the Pickhills was still used as a pre-roost site. A small summer roost in the trees near Corporation Pier in Hull came to grief in July 1963 when, after a night of heavy rain, over 100 were found water-logged the following morning. Many were already dead, while others drowned as they tried to take off but fell into the Humber. A large number were taken to the RSPCA to be dried off before later being released. During the big freeze of early 1963, meanwhile, Starlings were dying at the rate of 50 per night at one West Ella roost.

Strangely, the summer roosts often break up during the early autumn and by August 1985 the Saltend roost was down to 10,000 birds. The daytime feeding flocks in Hull's outlying fields increase as autumn progresses, however, as huge numbers of Continental Starlings arrive from September onwards. Flocks of 200 or more regularly joined Lapwings and Golden Plovers at Carlam Hill Farm, near North Bransholme, in the early 1990s. Up to 500 were gathering there in December 1989 and a similar number were noted among plovers on Willerby Carrs in September 1995. An East Hull feeding flock contained a pure white bird in November 1942.

As autumn turns to winter, and the number of Continental Starlings reaches a peak, the roosting sites swell with new recruits. The largest roost recorded in the Hull area was at the Pickhills site in February 1968 and represented the largest gathering of any bird ever seen in the Hull area. The figures are truly mind-boggling, with a conservative estimate of at least 200,000 birds. One observer put it closer to a million. Daily variation in numbers due to the nomadic nature of the winter visitors makes this perfectly feasible, and to see and hear a flock of a million Starlings, or any bird come to that, must have been incredible. This was something of a one-off, however, as in January 1969 the roost held only 5,000 birds. As already mentioned, however, it often reached 20,000 or more in subsequent years.

It is unlikely that the number of Starlings in the Hull area will ever again reach the dizzy heights attained during the 1960s, both in terms winter roosts and also summer breeders. Since that time much of the pasture land around the city has been converted to arable or been built on, creating less feeding opportunities for the birds. Fewer now visit us in winter and the British population is declining alarmingly, so there just aren't as many Starlings around these days. I find this a real shame as they are wonderful birds on so many levels, be it the iridescent beauty of their plumage close up, the cheeky wolf-whistle and staggering mimicry, or the pure grace of a flock of thousands twisting and turning in unison like living smoke.

Rose-coloured Starling
(Rosy Starling)
Sturnus roseus

The first record of this rare vagrant from southeast Europe and Asia concerns an adult male shot at Cottingham on 26th August 1865 which went to the Boynton collection. Another mentioned by Nelson (1907) as "Hull, Rolleston Hall, one seen, November 1901" was a little misleading in that Rolleston Hall is actually at Rolston, south of Hornsea. The second, and last, Rose-coloured Starling in the Hull area was an adult at Hessle, seen briefly on 17th September 1994 but not relocated.

House Sparrow
Passer domesticus

The House Sparrow, often less formally referred to as the Sparrow, or even 'Sparrer' in the Hull dialect, is known by virtually everyone. Many people think of the Sparrow as the commonest bird in Britain but this has never been the case and even more so today. Things have been going seriously wrong for this little grey and brown bird for the past couple of decades and there are parts of Hull that no longer support them.

House Sparrows were very common in the Hull area at the beginning of the 20th Century, breeding in the nooks and crannies of buildings almost everywhere. Flocks were frequent in gardens and parks, where they fed on seeds and scraps, and in the outlying fields and farms where they took grain. The use of horses for transport and load carrying during the first half of the century, before the widespread use of the car or van, meant that there was plenty of feed scattered about in the form of spilt oats. This, aswell as other spilt foodstuffs at grain depots and the like, meant that the House Sparrow thrived. In 1967 Boylan could still say that the House Sparrow was a very common breeding bird in Hull, mentioning a large roost at King George Dock and smaller ones at Corporation Pier, Baker Street, Dansom Lane and elsewhere. There was also a late summer and winter roost of around 200 birds in a courtyard at the Highlands School, North Bransholme, in the 1980s.

Around 30 pairs were breeding around Saltend and the Hull docks in the mid 1980s and Bonavia (1990) regarded it as a numerous resident around Cottingham. Birds were nesting in almost every roof on Bransholme around the same time. In late summer large flocks often congregated near abundant food supplies, such as ripening fields of wheat, barley and grasses, or around grain stores and farms. Up to 500 were in fields beside Old Fleet Drain, near Saltend, in August and September 1985. I often saw similar sized flocks in crop fields along Old Main Drain, North Bransholme, in the late 1980s but this had decreased to 200 in 1989, 100 in 1993 and there are probably less than a dozen today. The decline in the number of Sparrows in places where they were once very common has been noted throughout the Hull area. Helen Crowther's 1996 survey of Hull's Avenues found Sparrows to be still common and widespread but gatherings never exceeded a dozen birds. Similarly, Paul Milsom's survey of

the Priory Road fields the same year found them breeding around the farms and houses but they were nowhere numerous and the maximum flock size was just 30. Michael Flowers noted a decrease in House Sparrows at Hedon Road Cemetery since the 1980s but still regarded them as common at the Millennium, while this most typical of garden birds had completely disappeared from Peter Bonavia's Cottingham garden by 1997.

Things are just as bleak in the city centre, where small bands of cheeky Sparrows could be found in Queen's Gardens and in most streets, ready to nip between shopper's feet and steal away with a dropped chip or other titbit. In January 1999, however, Ray Eades found just 20 birds around the *Johnson & Jeff* seed warehouse in Hull's High Street, the last city centre stronghold. A search in spring 2001 revealed no House Sparrows anywhere in the Old Town, although I heard several birds chattering from the shrubberies in the Prospect Centre car park in June. Eades put the decline in the city centre down to the almost complete lack of residential houses and gardens in the Old Town these days He contrasted the dearth of Sparrows there with around 10 pairs in gardens down nearby Wellington Street, on the other side of the Marina, where some people feed the birds.

Several of my local House Sparrows at North Bransholme in the early 1990s often had abnormal white feathers in the wings and tail and such plumage aberrations are not that uncommon. A mostly white bird with a few brown feathers was seen at Newton Garth, between Hedon and Paull, in 1899 but it soon died after being caught and caged as a curio. A totally white bird appeared at the same place the following summer, however, but whether it was also trapped or left in peace is not recorded. Some Bransholme boys brought a newly fledged chick with completely white wings to me in 1998 and I was left with the task of hand rearing him. Only as the bird grew did I find that the white flight feathers were much weaker than the normal kind and unable to support proper flight. I kept the bird during his first summer moult, however, and many of the white feathers were then replaced by the more normal brown, enabling me to release him that autumn.

Regular streams of migrating House Sparrows were noted at the east coast watchpoints in decades gone by. There are many records of birds found dead or dying in the Hull area that were previously caught and ringed elsewhere. One ringed at Gibraltar Point, Lincolnshire, on 20th November 1964 was found dead at Cottingham the following April and a female found dead in East Hull in July 1966 was ringed at Spurn in October 1961. Other Spurn birds, ringed between October and January in the 1960s and 1970s, have been recovered in the Hull area in most months up to five years later and this indicates that there is some movement through the Hull area.

Tree Sparrow
(Eurasian Tree Sparrow)
Passer montanus

Nelson (1907) noted that the Tree Sparrow had undergone a substantial increase in Yorkshire during the latter part of the 19th Century, stating that it was fairly numerous in parts of the East Riding. By 1952 Chislett could say that he seldom visited any part of the East Riding without seeing them, and scattered colonies were breeding around the periphery of Hull at that time. During the 1960s, despite a national decline, nesting was recorded around Little Switzerland (near Hessle), Snuff Mill Lane and northwest Hull, with further breeding suspected on the eastern outskirts of Hull.

Boylan (1967) reported that Tree Sparrows from outside of Hull frequently visited the suburban gardens in winter. They were also seen at Northern Cemetery and flocks were common at the western waterfront. Single Tree Sparrows occasionally visited a garden in Kirk Ella during winter in the late 1970s and 26 were at Snuff Mill Lane in December 1979, but the national decline in numbers was beginning to bite in the Hull area by the 1980s. Bonavia (1990) could only describe the Tree Sparrow as an uncommon breeding bird around Cottingham and northwest Hull for the years 1980 to 1986. A flock of 150 at Snuff Mill Lane in December 1983 indicated that there was still a healthy population in that locality, although these may have been winter immigrants. Evidence of such inward migration comes from birds found dead at Cottingham and Paull in February 1971 and July 1984 respectively. Both were ringed at Spurn the previous autumns.

The regular coverage around Saltend and the docks in the mid 1980s revealed the Tree Sparrow to be a surprisingly scarce bird in that part of the Hull area, with only a handful of autumn records of one or two birds. One bird that spent several months in the company of House Sparrows in Hedon Road Cemetery in the late 1970s was the only one ever recorded there. The Tree Sparrow was found to be faring better around Bransholme, however, and up to a dozen were recorded at North Bransholme in the mid to late 1980s. A flock of 96 was at Bransholme Road (off Noddle Hill Way) on 21st January 1988 and still numbered 70 in early February. In 1991 I discovered a small breeding colony of around five pairs in scattered copses between North Bransholme and the Holderness Drain. The colony persisted into the mid 1990s and breeding was also noted to the north of Wawne in 1994.

Sadly, though, North Bransholme appeared to have been deserted by the mid 1990s.

Since 1995 the only Tree Sparrows known to breeding in the Hull area were all west of the River Hull. Around 15 pairs were found breeding off Priory Road in 1996, mainly around Willerby Carr Farm and Wood Lane Farm to the south of Cottingham. There were unconfirmed reports of Tree Sparrows in Hull's Avenues area during 1996 and small numbers of breeding birds were found at Willerby in 1998 and 1999. A bird chirping around an old oak tree at Dunswell in June 1998 was strongly suspected to be nesting there.

Wintering flocks during the mid to late 1990s included 17 at Willerby Carr Farm in October 1995, 10 at North Bransholme in March 1996, 50 east of Sutton in September and October 1998 and 69 at the Bransholme Sewage Works in April 1999.

Despite a 95% decrease in numbers across Britain during the second half of the 20th Century, it is still possible to find a few pairs of Tree Sparrows nesting in old hedgerow trees, isolated copses and around farms on the outskirts of Hull and in adjoining areas of the East Riding. Protection and monitoring of the breeding colonies is vital if we are not to lose the Tree Sparrow as a breeding bird in the Hull area. Additional help in the form of nestboxes and supplementary feeding, actions which have greatly benefited them elsewhere in Britain, may ensure that our local Tree Sparrows do not go the same was as the Lesser Redpoll.

Zebra Finch
Poephila castonotis

A very common cage and aviary bird, Zebra Finches are native to Australia but exporting the birds has been banned for many decades and the large number of captive-bred birds in Britain are virtually domesticated. Like the Budgerigar, many colour forms have been bred from the original grey and buff variety and escapees are not that uncommon. Around the size of a Blue Tit, Zebra Finches can survive quite well in warm weather and even short spells of hard weather if they can find sufficient food, though most are probably picked off by Sparrowhawks, Tawny Owls or cats before too long. An orange-cheeked, wild-type male was at large on North Bransholme in June 1989 before being caught and returned to captivity, while a white bird was also seen nearby later that summer. Their popularity as inexpensive cagebirds means that escapees can therefore turn up anywhere at any time.

Despite their varying appearance they can usually be identified by their small size and 'beeping' call, similar to that of the Roadrunner in the old television cartoons!

Chaffinch
Fringilla coelebs

Despite being one of the most common and widespread birds in Britain, the Chaffinch is not especially numerous in the Hull area and probably lags behind the Greenfinch in terms of numbers and distribution. That is not to say the Chaffinch is rare or scarce in and around Hull, however. The species is probably best described as being a widespread breeding bird in small to moderate numbers wherever there is a good stand of trees or bushes. The Chaffinch is, perhaps, most common in the Hull area during the autumn when passage migrants and the year's youngsters bolster the local population, though it is often relatively scarce in midwinter.

The Chaffinch was an occasional visitor to the suburban gardens of Hull at the beginning of the 20th Century, with numbers probably being kept in check by the bird catchers who supplied the numerous cagebird shops in Hull at that time. Chaffinches were popular as cagebirds on account of their general abundance, pretty colouring and strident song, with owners often pitting their cock Chaffinches against each other and betting on which bird had the better vocal repertoire. Chaffinches were increasing in the gardens, villages and suburbs of Hull by the 1920s, however, but, even though Chislett (1952) suggested that it may be the most numerous of all Yorkshire birds, Boylan (1967) could only describe it as a regular yet uncommon breeding bird in Hull during the 1960s. Small numbers were breeding in the parks, suburbs and cemeteries at that time, with just one pair in Northern Cemetery giving some idea of their abundance in the city, but Boylan also regarded the Chaffinch as a common passage migrant.

A pair or two were breeding around Saltend in the mid 1980s and up to five migrants were observed heading westwards up the Humber on most days in October 1985. Just two or three pairs breed in the hedgerows between North Bransholme and the Holderness Drain, on the northern outskirts of the city, but small flocks of up to 10 or so birds are frequently met with here between August and November. Bonavia (1990) considered that a lack of woodland was limiting the species' breeding opportunities around Cottingham during the 1980s. Milsom (1997), however, recorded up to four pairs breeding around Priory Road in the mid 1990s, mainly in Priory Wood, Snuff Mill Lane and Wood Lane, with autumn/winter gatherings peaking at seven birds. Following the railway line into Hull, Helen Crowther's 1996 survey of birds in the Avenues found "good numbers" in the embankment hedges. Chaffinches even penetrate right into the heart of the city centre and singing was heard in Queen's Gardens in April 1999, with a female in the Trinity burial ground (at the top of Ferensway). Five males were singing in Hedon Road Cemetery the following spring and Chaffinches have increased here since the 1970s, when they were rare. The cheery 'spink' call and bright song of the Chaffinch can therefore be heard throughout leafy districts of the Hull area, from the Humber Bridge Country Park and western villages to the city centre and urban parks. They will readily visit garden bird tables for seeds or a drink from a bird bath, when the males add a welcome splash of colour during the grey days of early spring.

Brambling
Fringilla montifringilla

The Brambling is a winter visitor to Britain from breeding grounds in Scandinavia and the flocks are largely nomadic in search of their favourite winter food, beech mast. Beech trees are not exactly abundant in the Hull area and there are no extensive stands that produce large crops of mast, so the Brambling tends to be an uncommon and irregular winter visitor in our part of the world. Most Bramblings drop into the Hull area between late October and April, with the earliest autumn arrival being one in East Park on 7th October and the latest spring bird being seen at Saltend on 13th May the same year.

Boylan (1967) regarded the Brambling as a scarce winter visitor in 1960s Hull, but a rubbish tip on the West Hull foreshore attracted large flocks in 1962 and 1963. Up to 300 were feeding on seed heads at the tip in March and April 1962, with a staggering 700 on 20th January 1963 decreasing to 200 a week later before they all left after a fall of snow. Four were in Northern Cemetery around the same time. Since the 1970s single Bramblings or small flocks of up to a dozen birds were noted at many sites around the Hull area, including Kirk Ella (Kerry Woods and nearby gardens), Cottingham (including Newgate Street and South Street), the Saltend area, Hedon Road Cemetery, North Bransholme, Humber Bridge Country Park, East Park and Castle Hill Farm (between Sutton and Swine). A flock of 50 Bramblings was in the company of 20 Chaffinches in Cottingham's South Street on 18th January 1981, this being the largest flock recorded in the Hull area since the 1960s.

Most visiting Bramblings do not hang around for very long and the majority are just passing through. October to November are the best time to catch up with the species as they refuel after their North Sea crossing before pressing on inland in search of their beloved beech mast. April also appears to be a peak month for finding a Brambling in the Hull area, however, as birds pass through again on their way back to Scandinavia. A single bird has visited the Hedon Road Cemetery most springs since 1987, but one fine male nearly didn't make it back to Scandinavia after flying into a window that April. After being picked up dazed it eventually flew off, apparently unharmed, once its photograph had been taken for posterity.

Green Singing Finch
(Yellow-fronted Canary)
Serinus mozambicus

Superficially similar to a Serin or even a Siskin, the Green Singing

Finch breeds in sub-Saharan Africa and many wild-caught birds are imported into Britain each year for the cage bird trade. Some of these birds inevitably escape from their cages or aviaries and in the spring of 1989 a male set up territory in the thick hawthorn hedge near the now Kingswood High School on Wawne Road, Bransholme. The species is quite capable of surviving for some time in the British climate, although predators or a frost probably finish them off eventually, and the Linnet-like song of the Bransholme bird could be heard for several weeks during May.

Canary
(Atlantic Canary)
Serinus canaria

Native to Madeira and the western Canary Islands, the Canary is a very popular cagebird in Britain and Hull is no exception. Kept for over 200 years on account of their song, wild-type Canaries are similar to a Serin in appearance. As with many domesticated cagebirds, however, a variety of colour and even structural forms have been bred from the wild type, and most escapees will have a varying amount of unnatural yellow or white in their plumage. The long history of the Canary in Britain means that birds have been escaping and turning up around Hull for many years. Several writers noted how Hull boys delighted in the novelty of catching Canaries when they appeared in their neighbourhood in the early 20th Century. Although possibly less popular as pets today, the occasional Canary can still be found at large in the Hull area every so often, although they probably don't last long.

Greenfinch
(European Greenfinch)
Carduelis chloris

The Greenfinch is probably the most common and widely distributed finch in the Hull area, breeding in scrub, hedgerows, parks and gardens. They frequently come to bird tables for sunflower seeds, peanuts and grain in winter and spring.
John Nicholson made no mention of the Greenfinch when he listed the birds visiting the garden of his Hull town house in 1901, but in 1967 Boylan wrote that it was a common breeding bird in Hull and small par-

ties could sometimes be found around the docks in winter. Bonavia (1990) classed the Greenfinch as an abundant breeding species around Cottingham and northwest Hull in the 1980s and went on to mention that they bred in Cottingham gardens. Breeding was recorded at Saltend in the mid 1980s and I usually counted four or five pairs breeding on the eastern margin of North Bransholme between the late 1980s and late 1990s. Milsom (1997) noted breeding around Priory Road in 1996, with a possible five pairs, and Michael Flowers considers them to be very common in Hedon Road Cemetery where they breed in *Leylandii* trees. A flock of 28 were at Paull in May 1998, indicating the size of the breeding population in that part of the Hull area, and birds were present all year round at the Hull Ice Arena in 1999 where they were considered to have bred. Breeding is also suspected in Queen's Gardens, so Greenfinches may be found nesting right into the city centre.

Crowther's 1996 wildlife survey in Hull's Avenues area noted a great decline in the local Greenfinch population, with small flocks now being replaced by just occasional visits by one or two birds. I noted a less dramatic decline at North Bransholme towards the end of the 1990s and this is broadly in line with national trends, where many once abundant farmland birds are becoming scarcer due to intensive farming methods and loss of habitat. Greenfinches still breed rather commonly throughout the Hull area, however, especially in the more leafy suburbs and outlying villages as well as in the parks, cemeteries and wilder parts of the surrounding farmland.

Late summer and autumn sees the largest gatherings of Greenfinches around the Hull area as the local population, already swollen with the year's youngsters, is further bolstered by incoming migrants. Up to 180 Greenfinches were counted at Saltend in October 1984, with 120 in December. A flock of 60 were among over 100 House Sparrows in a ripening field of rape at High Bransholme Farm, northeast Hull, in June and July 1993, with 40 again in October. A flock of 15 were at Thwaite Hall Lake, Cottingham, in December 1984 and 26 were feeding on ash keys just south of the village in November 1995. A flock of 25 were feeding on rosehips near the Makro store at St. Andrew's Quay in early October 1999 and a "large flock" was roosting in bushes near the Birds Eye factory on Hessle Road in early 1997, with lesser numbers again in 1998.

That a large number of the Hull area's Greenfinches are not permanent residents is proven by the recovery of many dead birds in and around the city that were ringed as migrants at Spurn Point earlier in their lives. The majority were caught and ringed as immature or first-winter birds in autumn and many were found in the Hull area the following spring, although one bird was found in Cottingham just eight days after having being handled at Spurn.

Goldfinch
(European Goldfinch)
Carduelis carduelis

The Goldfinch has had its ups and downs in the Hull area. Probably quite common in the mid 1800s, by 1907 all Nelson could say of it in our area was that it had "nested sparingly near Hedon". Nelson attributed the scarcity of Goldfinches to a decrease in the cultivation of flax and linseed and, in no small part, to the professional bird catchers that operated in the area back then. Nelson tells us that the Goldfinch was once exceedingly numerous in these parts but as soon as it made an appearance it was eagerly sought out by the bird-catchers. In early autumn the men would target the family parties that gathered on weedy commons and waysides, easily capturing the youngsters, known as Grey Kates or Grey Pates, early on while the warier adult birds, the so-called King Harry Redcaps, would usually fall victim later. In just a few days a noted bird-catcher named Greenhough caught over 400 Goldfinches at Beverley and, as there were many of his ilk scouring the whole region at that time, there is little wonder that these delightful birds quickly disappeared.

The trapped Goldfinches eventually ended up as cagebirds in Victorian sitting rooms. There were at least 11 bird-dealer shops in Hull in 1892, some trading solely in British birds, that acted as outlets for the bird-catchers' harvest. In 1901 John Nicholson's Hull garden was attracting such birds as the Linnet, Yellowhammer and Chaffinch, but he made no mention of the Goldfinch as even a rare visitor. Between the old farmers and the bird-catchers, they must have virtually wiped them out.

The pressure on Goldfinches for the cagebird trade slowly subsided throughout the first half of the 20th Century and by the 1940s the species was noted to be increasing steadily as a breeding bird around Hull. By the 1960s the Goldfinch was an irregular breeder within the old Hull boundary, most frequently in West Hull, and small parties occasionally visited Northern Cemetery. Numbers continued to rise throughout the 1970s but by the 1980s they were falling again around Cottingham and northwest Hull, with breeding described as uncommon and irregular. This decline was a national one, thought to be linked to a decrease in food supply and increase in trapping and shooting pressure in France and Spain where many of our British birds spend the winter. Wild-caught Goldfinches are still extremely popular cagebirds around the Mediterranean.

In 1984 breeding was reported at Saltend, with an influx being apparent between late August and late October. This autumn flock averaged around 30 birds but 67 were counted on 15th September. On 28th September 1986 a 100-strong flock was twittering around nearby Alexandra Dock. In the late 1980s and early 1990s a pair or two bred most years at North Bransholme; flocks of 50 birds or more could occasionally be found on the ripening rape fields or teasel heads around High Bransholme Farm and Foredyke Stream between August and October. At least 55 were counted here in September 1993 and 33 were nearby in November 1998, indicating that good numbers can still be found in those parts during autumn.

By the mid 1990s numbers had picked up again around Cottingham and northwest Hull, with up to 20 on thistles and autumn hawkbit near Willerby Carr Farm, north of Wold Road/Carr Lane, in the autumns of 1995 and 1996. Breeding probably occurred in this area in 1996 at least, with a handful of birds present throughout the summer from May and family parties seen from August onwards. This period, from August to November, is the best time to look out for flocking Goldfinches anywhere around Hull and the villages wherever thistles, teasel or other weed seeds are available. The birds gather at such good feeding sites to fatten up before most of them move out to winter on the Continent by mid November. They are often uncommon again until the spring, when returning birds arrive back at the nesting sites.

Goldfinches have been increasing in suburban, and even urban, areas throughout the past decade. Despite a decline in Hull's Avenues area up to 1996, there was a general increase noted in the western suburbs, such as where the freight line crosses Chanterlands Avenue near Huntley Drive, and right into the city centre. In East Hull, meanwhile, a pair nested in clematis in Hedon Road Cemetery in 1999 and 2000. In December 2000 I saw a trio of Goldfinches flitting overhead near George Street and such a sight is not that uncommon these days. Goldfinches are now increasingly being reported from gardens throughout the Hull area, coming either for seed on bird tables (they love poppy and teasel seeds) or water in bird baths, and they have visited gardens in North Bransholme, Chamberlain Road and Kirk Ella to name but a few.

Siskin
(Eurasian Siskin)
Carduelis spinus

Siskins are rather uncommon winter visitors to the Hull area, with small flocks or odd birds usually being seen anytime from September to late April. Numbers are unpredictable, some years seeing a good sprinkling of birds while others are more or less barren. Siskins have a great affinity for alder and birch trees and anywhere where a few of these trees grow in close proximity to each other, providing enough cones to feed a few birds for a couple of days, will attract Siskins sooner or later. Lesser Redpolls may also associate with them but, in light of the current status of that species in the Hull area, it would be a fairly good day to find a mixed flock of Siskins and Lesser Redpolls in these parts.

As with the Goldfinch and the Redpolls, the East Riding birdcatchers of the 19th and early 20th Centuries were very keen on the Siskin, calling it the Aberdevine in the olden days, and many must have passed through the hands of the dozen or so bird dealers operating in Hull in the 1890s.

There were just three reported sightings of Siskins in Hull during the 1960s, all in autumn, and a late spring bird was in a Kirk Ella garden on 14th April 1975. Another was in the nearby Kerry Woods on 23rd April 1980, with a singing bird at Kerry Drive, Kirk Ella, on 3rd May 1986 begging the question as to whether nesting ever occurred here. Breeding is very rare in the East Riding, however, and has never been recorded around Hull.

Siskins were not infrequently recorded at Saltend in the mid 1980s, with 63 on 22nd September 1985 probably being passage birds. A further 24 flew northwest on 1st January 1986 and 22 went north on 22nd. A single was at Saltend on 25th April the same year, with another late bird on 3rd May and then none until the first of the autumn, a flock of six, on 13th September. The plantation at the eastern edge of the Bransholme Sewage Works, on the east bank of the River Hull just south of the new Kingswood development, was once a good site for Siskins. The Thomas Clarkson Way, which leads from Ennerdale to Kingswood, was actually built over the eastern half of this plantation in 1993. The lost section was much more scrubby and diverse than the remaining portion, with lots of alder trees that the Siskins loved. Flocks were annual here but their visitations went virtually unrecorded. I remember seeing them there myself on several occasions between 1991 and 1993 but the only count I made was 15 on 15th March 1992. This figure was probably about right on most other occasions.

During the mid 1990s Siskins were occasionally seen in the gardens and scrub of the Avenues area of Hull and they were said to have occurred "consistently over the years", so it's fair to assume that they still do. The draw of alders was again demonstrated in 1997 when a small flock was feeding in the trees in Hessle Square in January. Seven were among a tit flock on the Priory Sidings, off Clive

Sullivan Way in West Hull, on 15th September that year, while three were back in Hessle Square in January 1998. Another three were in East Park in February and four were at King George Dock on 6th October, with another at Saltend. A female that spent the day feeding on peanuts in the Hedon Road Cemetery on 20th April 2001 was another typical late spring sighting in the Hull area, but it was the first Siskin record for that well-watched site.

Linnet
(Common Linnet)
Carduelis cannabina

The Linnet has always been a rather frequent breeding bird in the scrubby corners tucked away in Hull's outer suburbs, tending to avoid the heavily built-up areas but becoming even more common in the hedgerows of the outlying lanes and farmland. Numbers have fallen nationally since the 1970s, as with most farmland birds, and this accelerated as the century drew to a close. Some thinning out of the population around Hull has become quite evident in recent years. The Linnet is still a fairly common breeding species in the Hull area, however, being more numerous as a passage migrant with occasional flocks staying to winter if conditions are favourable.

The earliest record of the Linnet in Hull comes from John Nicholson's description of the birds in his townhouse garden in 1901, being on the outskirts of Hull near present day Pearson Park, when he tells us that small flocks often came to feed on sunflower heads and dahlia seeds. Sadly, the Linnet was another favourite with the local bird-catchers of the time who snared them for the cagebird trade, there being at least 11 bird-dealers in Hull in 1892, although they don't seem to have suffered as much as the Goldfinch which became very rare.

By the 1960s the Linnet was a regular but thinly distributed breeder on weedy and bushy ground around the docks, allotments, cemeteries and outlying fields of Hull, never far from the outskirts. At least one pair bred in Northern Cemetery around this time and it was also a winter visitor there in small numbers. Breeding birds were said to be considerably reduced in 1963, however, after the severe 1962/3 winter. Cold weather displacement brought 150 to the West Hull foreshore at the end of December 1962, this being an unusually large midwinter flock.

Breeding numbers soon recovered though, and in the early 1970s Linnets were very common in Hedon Road Cemetery where at least two pairs bred. In the 1980s Linnets were also breeding commonly around Cottingham and northwest Hull, but 35 at Snuff Mill Lane on 1st May 1984 was considered a large flock in those parts and they were scarce in winter. Several pairs were breeding at Saltend around this time, too, but by now Hedon Road Cemetery hadn't seen any Linnets for several years. Between 1989 and 1994 between five and 10 pairs bred between North Bransholme and the Holderness Drain (mainly along Old Main Drain hedgerow), up Bransholme Road and along the Holderness Drain itself, and 60 were counted on 4th June 1993. In 1996 several pairs were nesting in the hedges bordering the Priory Road fields, between Cottingham, Hull and Willerby, being present from April to September but never numbering more than 10. In June 1999 a few Linnets were still found to be breeding off Hedon Road near King George Dock. A pair was also seen on and off throughout the summer near the entrance to the Courtney Street Industrial Estate at Mount Pleasant, where they probably bred. Linnets still breed along the road that runs from Wawne up towards Routh, as they have always done.

Autumn flocks of Linnets are a common feature of many weedy areas and stubble fields around Hull from August to November. A flock of 140 was at Saltend on 27th August 1984, with up to 100 again the following autumn. At North Bransholme I counted 100 on 8th October 1989, 150 throughout September 1993 and between 100 and 120 from October

to December that year. A flock of 60 were at the Holderness Drain nearby on 5th September 1998 and autumn flocks were regularly seen at Victoria Dock and the Makro store near St. Andrew's Quay throughout the late 1990s. It is often said that most British Linnets leave the country for France and Spain by December but, while it is true that the species is often much scarcer at this time of year, good-sized local flocks have often been recorded throughout the season. Aside from the aforementioned 150 at the West Hull foreshore at the end of 1962, I counted 160 on stubbles at Carlam Hill Farm, east of North Bransholme, in January 1994 and 180 in February. A further 60 were at Victoria Dock on 7th February 1999, 80 were on Priory Sidings in February 2000 and a nice little flock of 30 alighted a few yards from my feet on a clump of thistles at the Bransholme Sewage Works on 27th December 2000. I have often noted a modest build up of, presumably, spring passage birds at North Bransholme in March and April. Flocks typically number 50 or less but there are occasionally big influxes. A gathering of 100 was present there on 4th April 1993 while the large wintering flock of late 1993 and early 1994 at Carlam Hill Farm, mentioned above, swelled to 240 by 1st April and 250 on 18th.

While Linnets seem to be faring tolerably well around Hull, in the spite of the national decline, it is worrying that the large flocks of just a few years ago are no longer being reported. The bushes and scrub along the railway lines as well as along the major drains, along the River Hull and around the docks, outer suburbs and foreshores are still visited by unobtrusive pairs of Linnets during the breeding season, giving themselves away only the twittering song of the male. This only goes to show the value of so-called 'waste ground'.

Twite
Carduelis flavirostris

Twite are rather rare passage migrants and winter visitors in the Hull area, but it is likely that their status is a little clouded by their similarity to the much commoner Linnet and their love of rather windswept and barren places. The first record is of two birds at the eastern docks from 2nd to 3rd February 1962. The next were not until 1985, when the Saltend stalwarts found that Twite were not that infrequent during October passage. The first were four on 5th October, followed by eight on 8th, two on 20th and finally one on 24th. These birds were either around Saltend Channel or on the gravel at the chemical works. The next were not reported until 1997, when 12 were feeding on weed

seeds on the Priory Sidings, off Clive Sullivan Way near Gipsyville, in West Hull. The same 12 were still there on 8th January 1998, while the most recent record was of two flying east at King George Dock on 29th September that year.

It appears that Twite can turn up in the Hull area anytime from late September through to late winter, with areas close to the Humber seemingly the most attractive to them. I would also not be surprised if scrutiny of autumn or winter finch flocks elsewhere revealed Twite to be more regular than the documented records suggest.

Lesser Redpoll
Carduelis cabaret

The Lesser Redpoll was only assigned full species status in 2000, after previously being considered as a sub-species (*Carduelis flammea cabaret*) of the nominate Mealy Redpoll (*Carduelis flammea flammea*). Lesser Redpolls have always been the only type of Redpoll breeding in Britain, but their fortunes in the Hull area have been mixed over the past century. They went from being very scarce to locally common and, now, at the beginning of the 21st Century, they are all but extinct as a breeding species in these parts.

In *The Birds of Yorkshire* (1907), Nelson described the Lesser Redpoll as "rare" in the East Riding and Nicholson made no mention of them visiting his West Hull garden a few years before, despite having Linnets and Yellowhammers occasionally. Lesser Redpolls are not at all shy of visiting leafy suburban gardens, even for nesting, so their omission is a strong indication that they weren't to be found in the neighbourhood. A significant factor in this absence was probably the depredations of the professional bird-catchers of the day, who systematically trapped finches for the cagebird trade. These chaps virtually wiped out the Goldfinch population in the southern Hull valley, so it is fair to assume that they were taking large numbers of locally breeding Lesser Redpolls too. By the 1950s, however, Chislett (1952) implied that Lesser Redpolls were by no means rare in the East Riding, though the only Hull record around that time was of six in Pickering Park on 13th April 1948. Lesser Redpolls are usually back on their breeding grounds in April, so these birds may have been nesting nearby. Numbers had definitely grown by the 1960s, with nesting recorded in Newland Park, Cottingham Road and Chanterlands Avenue. Up to six pairs were nesting in the silver birch trees in Northern Cemetery by 1965, although they were considered to be localised, irregular and generally uncommon within the old Hull boundary. Lesser Redpolls were more common outside of the city at this time, with a total of 20 being counted at Little Switzerland, Hessle, in late May 1966, this being the height of the nesting season.

Things seemed to improve into the 1970s and the Lesser Redpoll was a very common breeding bird in the birch scrub that had grown up along the Hedon Road stretch of the abandoned Hull to Withernsea railway line. When these birches were cleared around 1985, however, the Lesser Redpolls left and did not return. Despite this setback birds were probably breeding in northwest Hull and around Cottingham in the early to mid 1980s. The fluttering display flight was noted over Cottingham gardens and the grounds of Hull University, but the only confirmed breeding in this area was at Wood Lane, in the Priory Road fields near Cottingham. A remnant of the Hedon Road colony was found clinging on in the Saltend area in 1985, when two pairs bred and a post-breeding flock of up to 30 was present in August and September. Passage along the Humber was also recorded at Saltend that autumn, with 10 to 20 birds passing westwards overhead on most days in late September and 79 were grounded on 28th. Around 10 per day could still be found passing over throughout October, with up to 50 grounded on occasion. Passage petered out into November and birds were then scarce until the breeders returned the following April.

The passage birds were probably immigrants from the Continent and such as these are likely to be responsible for the occasional winter records in the Hull area. These winter birds may turn up on any weedy or bushy ground, but records are usually few and far between away from the summer haunts. One was at the Bransholme Sewage Works on 6th January 1988, another visited a Kirk Ella garden on 3rd January 1990, three were at High Bransholme Farm on 1st February 1992 with another there on 20th November 1993, one was at the Holderness Drain at North Bransholme on 14th January 1999 and two were there on 28th, with seven over West Hull on 6th October. It is interesting to note that most of the scant winter records are in the depths of winter rather than spring or autumn, when one would expect birds to be passing through, suggesting that they are the result of hard weather movements.

The number of Lesser Redpolls breeding and wintering in Britain has plummeted since the 1980s, and the situation around Hull mirrored the national trend. By the mid 1990s Lesser Redpolls were very difficult to find and breeding was rarely proven. The Saltend colony died out, with just one bird present on 30th April 1998, and the displaying birds around Cottingham and northwest Hull did not return. The odd bird was very occasionally recorded in garden bushes in the Avenues area, however, and may have bred. The last breeding site in Hull was at the Priory Sidings, off Clive Sullivan Way near Gipsyville. Family parties were present there in 1997 in an area where breeding had previously occurred and in 1998 one pair reared young. This is the last breeding record I have received from anywhere in the Hull area. In 1999 single Lesser Redpolls were seen once during the breeding season at the Bransholme Sewage Works (4th May) and Hedon Road Cemetery, with another at the latter site, again just once, in summer 2000. Sad to say, it is very likely that the Lesser Redpoll is now locally extinct as a breeding bird.

Mealy Redpoll/Common Redpoll
Carduelis flammea

The Mealy Redpoll was previously considered to be the northern race of Redpoll that visits Britain in winter, breeding as they do in the forests of northern Scandinavia eastwards. Recently, however, the 'Lesser Redpoll', the form that breeds in Britain, was split from the nominate Mealy Redpoll by the British Ornithologists' Union, the guardians of the official British List, giving us two species as opposed to one.

Nelson (1907) said that the Mealy Redpoll was a very scarce winter visitant to the East Riding, giving no records nearer to Hull than Beverley. Chislett (1952) said that they had occurred at too many places to mention and Mather (1986) summed it up by saying that only a few Mealy Redpolls are seen in Yorkshire in most years while invasions occur in others, giving 1980 as a year when an invasion hit the East Riding. None of these county avifaunas give any specific records for the Hull area. The earliest local record I have is of three birds in the Kerry Woods at Kirk Ella in March 1976, seen by B. Fendley, with another "probable" there on 9th April 1983.

The dedicated observation at Saltend and the eastern docks in the mid 1980s gave the best indication yet of the likely status of the Mealy Redpoll around Hull. The first of 1984 were three at Saltend Marsh on 19th November, one again from 1st to 18th December, up to five throughout January 1985 and up to eight in February, with six on 26th March and the last on 8th April. The first of autumn 1985 was back at Saltend on 24th September, with four on 25th November, six on 14th December and two on and off throughout those months. A flock of 10 were in the Old Main Drain hedgerow at North Bransholme on 6th January 1986, a good record there, while singles were at Saltend again on single dates in January and February and a flock of 11 was at St. Andrew's Dock on 22nd February. 1987 produced just one record, with a single bird at Bransholme Sewage Works on 10th March, but the next was not until 1997 when another single was at Paull on 29th September. Later that year, on Boxing Day, the weedy ground surrounding the newly built ASDA store at Kingswood attracted Hull's biggest ever flock of Mealy Redpolls, an impressive 15.

Judging by the above records, the first Mealies of the autumn are likely to turn up around the last week of September and after that they may be encountered at anytime until mid April. The biggest numbers and most frequent occurrences are in midwinter between December and February. Any scrubby or weedy ground may attract them, with a few dozen in some years and none in others.

Arctic Redpoll
Carduelis hornemanni

Nesting in the forests bordering the Arctic tundra, the Arctic Redpoll is a rare winter visitor to Britain and one, identified as an adult male of the race *C. h. exilipes*, at Saltend Marsh on 25th November 1985 was part of a small national influx that year. The finder was S. L. James and the record was subsequently accepted by the British Birds Rarities Committee.

Crossbill
(Common Crossbill)
Loxia curvirostra

The scarcity of Scots pine and other conifers around Hull means that Crossbills are very rare and irregular visitors to the area. Nelson (1907) reports that Crossbills had occurred in various places near Hull in the late 19th Century, sometimes quite close to the town, although he gives no specific dates or locations. Boylan (1967) gives just three records for the period 1960 to 1966, stating that these were after continental post-breeding irruptions but giving no details as to numbers or dates. Crossbills often breed quite early in the year, as early as February, but their breeding season can be protracted so Boylan's "post-breeding" comment probably implies late summer or autumn. There were three more records during the mid 1980s, all flyovers by single birds on the eastern waterfront during a time of intensive coverage in that area. The first was a female or immature heading east over West Wharfe, near Alexandra Dock, on 27th December 1985, with another unsexed bird passing south there on 20th February 1986 and another west past Saltend on 26th July. The curious spread of dates for these records shows how unpredictable, not to mention fleeting, a visit by a Crossbill can be in the Hull area. The only other record to have reached me concerns a party of six flying west over East Park on 6th November 1997. It is notable that Crossbills do not appear to have actually alighted in Hull for over 35 years!

Bullfinch
(Common Bullfinch)
Pyrrhula pyrrhula

The Bullfinch is a scarce yet regular breeding bird in the Hull area, being more widespread in autumn and winter.
Boylan (1967) regarded the Bullfinch as a scarce bird generally in 1960s Hull but breeding was suspected at East Park, where 10 birds were seen in January 1967, and another unspecified location.

Nesting was proven at Little Switzerland, near Hessle, in 1967 and other birds were present around Kirk Ella in the mid 1970s. One pair reared four young at Saltend in 1984 and others bred nearby at the Holderness Drain and Old Fleet Drain the following year. Two to five birds was the usual count in that area. One or two birds, occasionally up to five, can still be found around Saltend in most months. Breeding also occurs along the old Hull to Withernsea railway line, near Hedon Road Cemetery. Another pair was present in allotments close to the Maternity Hospital throughout the summer of 1998, though Hedon Road Cemetery has seen a decline in numbers since the 1970s.

Breeding was noted in a conifer plantation at Risby, northwest of Cottingham, in 1985 and other Bullfinches have regularly been sighted around Cottingham and northwest Hull since the 1980s at least. Small numbers of Bullfinches were often seen in the walled orchard of the convent on the corner of Beverley Road and Cottingham Road in the 1980s, though they seem to have become much more infrequent there. Hull's Avenues area has also witnessed a decline in recent years.

Up to five birds were occasionally seen along the Old Main Drain hedgerow, North Bransholme, during the 1990s, usually in autumn, but they are not thought to nest there. Wandering pairs or small groups sometimes visit the Bransholme Sewage Works, too, but,

again, breeding is unlikely. Other wandering birds can be seen almost anywhere on the fringes of Hull and around the surrounding villages, although they are clearly not averse to following bushy corridors further into the city suburbs. The most reliable location in the Hull area for Bullfinches seems to be the Humber Bridge Country Park, however, where nesting was recorded in most years throughout the 1990s.

Hawfinch
Coccothraustes coccothraustes

The earliest record of this sturdy finch, with its formidable-looking beak, in the Hull area is of successful breeding at Hull Bank Hall in 1893 and 1895. Hull Bank Hall, now known as Haworth Hall, sits on the west bank of the River Hull just upstream of Sutton Road Bridge and is now virtually derelict and surrounded by housing estates but, back then, Haworth Hall was a country estate several miles out of Hull. The master of the house, Colonel Benjamin Blaydes Haworth-Booth, remarked how the 1893 birds were very shy but both the adults and young remained until December of that year. In 1907 Nelson wrote that Hawfinches had also been observed near Hedon in the nesting season, probably before 1900, and that it was fairly common in certain parts of the East Riding as close as the Beverley area.

The next specific record was not until 1953 when breeding occurred at West Ella. Chislett (1952) tells us that Hawfinches were "not very infrequently" met with in the Hull area. At least one was at West Ella again in March 1969, others were at nearby Kirk Ella in late May 1970 and "Hull" in June, with one or more at Hessle in October 1971. This southwest corner of the Hull area, particularly the Humber Bridge Country Park and surrounding districts, is now the only place where the species occurs near Hull and it is worth giving the records in full. In 1985 a pair was seen at Hessle on 29th May and singles were seen again throughout June but there was no proof of breeding. One was in the Humber Bridge Country Park on 19th March 1987, three were there on 1st April 1990, eight were seen on 3rd March 1991 with others throughout the year, at least one pair reared nine young in the Park between 1992 and 1994 and a single was seen again in April 1997. Hawfinches are very shy and unobtrusive, however, so it is likely that they have regularly bred around the Park for decades but were often overlooked. Beyond the Hull area the Hawfinch is more numerous out towards North Ferriby and those birds in the Humber Bridge Country Park seem to represent the easternmost extremity of this population.

The only record of a Hawfinch east of the River Hull since the 19th Century is a very curious one indeed. On 12th April 1998 Michael Flowers heard a loud bang on the kitchen window of West Lodge in Hedon Road Cemetery. Thinking little more of it, he was very surprised when, half an hour later, he found the head of a Hawfinch, complete with the characteristic beak but almost devoid of feathers, below the same window. Just how it got there is a complete mystery, as Flowers has seen Hawfinches there neither before nor since. The only likely explanation I can think of is that a wandering Hawfinch, attracted to the Cemetery's whitebeams, was caught by a Sparrowhawk and taken to a tree near West Lodge to be plucked and eaten. It is possible that while plucking the head, which would be cumbersome and unappetising with the huge beak, the Sparrowhawk maybe pulled it off and tossed it aside as they so often do with their victims feathers, feet and other bony extremities. This could explain the bang on the window, as the falling head struck it, and also why it had no feathers.

White-throated Sparrow
Zonotrichia albicollis
There is one very curious Hull record of this rare vagrant from North America and I give the details here so that readers may make up their own mind. At the beginning of 1893 G. W. Jalland spotted an odd

looking Sparrow as he fed the birds on the lawn of Holderness House, a Georgian mansion on the corner of Holderness Road and Laburnum Avenue in East Hull. In those days Holderness House was on the outskirts of Hull and was mainly surrounded by fields and parkland. Jalland, an accomplished naturalist, immediately recognised that the bird was unusual and may have been "from some distant corner of the world". How right he was. The bird was still present on 13th February when, as was usual at the time, it was shot in order to get a better look at it. John Cordeaux, the highly regarded Humber-side naturalist, identified it as an adult male White-throated Sparrow on 25th February, when he examined it in person, and the esteemed Professor Alfred Newton (author of the landmark 1893–96 *Dictionary of Birds*) confirmed this.

The origins of the bird were called into question from the start, however, with Thomas Nelson deciding in his *The Birds of Yorkshire* (1907) that it had probably escaped from a cage while being transported to Britain by ship. This theory was generally accepted by other ornithologists at the time and, as a result, this particular bird does not feature in the 'official' list of genuinely wild birds recorded in Britain. The reasoning for this attitude to the record probably stems from the belief, which was prevalent well into the 20th Century, that North American land birds simply did not occur on our east coast in a natural state. That the bird was found a short distance from a major port was also a large factor to consider. We now know, however, that wild North American land birds have reached Britain's east coast on numerous occasions. Indeed, White-throated Sparrows in Lincolnshire and Suffolk in 1992 were readily accepted as genuinely wild birds and an American White-crowned Sparrow was recorded at Hornsea in 1977. This Hull White-throated Sparrow was, potentially, the first European record of the species and while the 'assisted passage' argument is a distinct possibility in the origins of this bird so, in my opinion, is genuine vagrancy. Unfortunately, we will never know which it was.

Lapland Bunting
(Lapland Longspur)
Calcarius lapponicus

A regular winter visitor to the Yorkshire coast, albeit in varying numbers, the Lapland Bunting is an uncommon straggler inland. The Humber waterfront of the Hull area has never really proved as attractive to 'Lap Bunts' as the regular, truly coastal, sites of Barmston, Spurn or Filey and there are just three records from the Saltend and Paull area which, on the face of it, would appear to be the most likely place for them around Hull. The first were two birds at Paull on 13th October 1985, a typical date for passage migrants, and another was there on 5th January 1986. What was conceivably the same bird had flown south over Saltend Marsh just four days earlier. In December 1987 B. Richards discovered a small flock on fields east of North Bransholme, with at least five on 9th, two on 10th and then again on 22nd. Surprisingly, another three were back there on 11th March 1988 with two the next day and a male again on 10th April, last being seen on 12th. I am rather envious of Richards for these sightings, for I watched these same fields for the next 10 years and never saw a single Lapland Bunting in all that time!

Snow Bunting
Plectrophenax nivalis
Snow Buntings are very pretty little birds that breed among the boulders of alpine slopes and the tundra of the far north of Europe, with a small population in Scotland. It is in winter when flocks arrive in East Yorkshire to flutter over the coastal fields like flurries of snow. Only small numbers visit the Hull area, however, and not in every year.

The first record also concerns the largest flock seen in the area, when 40 were near Hedon on 16th November 1963. Boylan (1967) mentions a small party flying west at the East Hull waterfront some time between 1960 and 1966 but gives no further details, while four flew west on the West Hull foreshore on 14th January 1968. There were no records from the 1970s, although 15 flew northwest over the Holderness Drain at North Bransholme on 15th December 1980. There were six sightings from the area around Saltend and the eastern docks between 1984 and 1986, all singles, with the earliest on 28th October, three in November and one in December and February with the latest on 28th March. All were fly-overs heading north or west, except for the March bird, in 1986, which was a full adult male feeding in the Earles Road car park, off Hedon Road. Another was on the ground at Alexandra Dock on 21st February 1989. A party of six Snow Buntings were feeding on weedy ground near the Makro shopping centre at Hessle on 22nd February 1991, with a single bird at Saltend on 19th February 1998.

The best time for finding Snow Buntings in the Hull area would appear to be between late October and late March, with the peak months being November and February. The windswept Humber shoreline, particularly the Saltend area, offers the best chance of seeing a flyover bird or two, while feeding birds may turn up further inland on stubbles or weedy expanses.

Yellowhammer
Emberiza citrinella

An irregular visitor to large suburban gardens in Hull at the beginning of the 20th Century, the Yellowhammer was a very common bird of open country and agricultural land throughout the East Riding. Boylan (1967) wrote that the Yellowhammer was a regular but uncommon breeding bird in 1960s Hull, being confined to the city outskirts but commonly frequenting grain depots at King George Dock during winter. Breeding was reported from Little Switzerland, near Hessle, in 1967 at least and nesting was also occurring at Saltend during the mid 1980s, with a favoured site being the hay meadow next to the railway line at Corner Farm. Bonavia (1990) considered the Yellowhammer to be a common breeding and wintering bird in farmland and open country around Cottingham during the 1980s and I regularly counted up to five singing males between North Bransholme and the Holderness Drain during the late 1980s and early 1990s. Up to four pairs were breeding on Swine Bank, Willerby Carrs, in 1996 but by 2001 I could only locate three pairs on territory at North Bransholme, this being in line with the national downturn in fortunes for British Yellowhammers. North Bransholme may be the only breeding site for Yellowhammers left in Hull, as no other nesting birds have been reported within the city boundary for many years. Scattered pairs still breed in adjoining parts of the East Riding, particularly around Paull, Wawne and Skidby, but in nothing like the numbers of just a few short decades ago.

The Yellowhammer has always been more numerous and widespread in the Hull area during autumn passage and winter. Up to 20 frequented the Saltend area during the latter part of the year during the 1980s, with a site record of 60 in January 1985, while the usual autumn count of 15 at North Bransholme was inflated to 33 in mid December 1992. The 1996 peak count in the Priory Road area was 10 at Wood Farm in late January, while Paull held an encouraging flock of 60 in February 1999. On this basis it is still possible to locate a small flock of Yellowhammers in likely winter habitats, such as stubble fields or wasteland, but as a breeding bird they are still declining with alarming persistence.

Reed Bunting
Emberiza schoeniclus

The first specific mention of the Reed Bunting in the Hull area concerns a late nest containing five eggs at Hedon on 25th August 1900. Boylan (1967) referred to the Reed Bunting as a regular but uncommon breeding bird in 1960s Hull, being confined to the drains and dykes during the breeding season. They were noted to be occasional winter visitors around Kirk Ella in the mid 1970s and were found to breed at Snuff Mill Lane and Willerby Carrs, between Cottingham and Hull, during the 1980s. Bonavia (1990), however, considered them to be rather uncommon around Cottingham and northwest Hull.

A healthy population bred at Saltend Marsh, between King George Dock and the Saltend chemical plant, dur-

ing the mid 1980s, with 17 pairs there in 1984 and a further four at Victoria Dock. Most of the suitable habitat at both of these places is now gone. Between five and eight pairs were breeding on the marshy fields and drain banks between North Bransholme and the Holderness Drain in the late 1980s and early 1990s, with a similar number still doing so. Up to four pairs nested along Swine Bank ditch, on Willerby Carrs, in 1996. Other recent breeding records have come from the rough land on southwest Hull's Priory Sidings (five territorial males in 1998 and one in 1999), the Queen Elizabeth Dock area (breeding in 1998 and three territorial males in 1999), Anlaby Common (one pair in 1999) and also the Bransholme Sewage Works and surrounding area. Scattered pairs of Reed Buntings are still likely to breeding in several other outlying parts of the Hull area, along reedy dykes and hollows, bushy and overgrown drain banks and along the northern stretches of the River Hull. They are nowhere very common, however, and are tied to the ever-decreasing wet and boggy habitats. Geoff Dobbs, the respected local birdwatcher and co-founder of the Hull Valley Wildlife Group, considers the Reed Bunting to be threatened within the city of Hull due to loss of habitat and this is undoubtedly true.

The number and distribution of Reed Buntings in the Hull area increases during late summer and autumn as local birds roam and passage migrants pass through. Up to 25 were occasionally found to the east of North Bransholme during the early 1990s, with a site record of 40 on 9th October 1993, while 20 were at Saltend in October 1984. Reed Buntings often become harder to find during the winter months as most local birds move out, but individuals or small flocks can occasionally be found on the breeding grounds or weedy areas and stubble fields. Winter weather may well bring Reed Buntings to you, however, as odd ones and twos are increasingly turning up on suburban bird tables to take seed and grain. One visited my North Bransholme garden during a period of snow cover one winter in the early 1990s and another recently turned up again in the early months of 2001. Gardens in Lapwing Close (East Hull), meanwhile, were visited by a couple of birds in February 1998.

Red-headed Bunting
Emberiza bruniceps

On 16th September 1989 R. Eades saw a male Red-headed Bunting land on a ship in the Humber and remain aboard until the ship docked at Hull. The bird then flew off, never to be seen again. Red-headed Buntings breed across central Asia and winter in India but, while they have been recorded in East Yorkshire on several occasions, the large trade in wild-caught birds of this species means that all occurrences, and particularly those of the colourful adult males, are treated with suspicion. It is, however, almost certain that some of the birds seen in Britain are true vagrants and the credentials for this individual are quite good. Firstly, the bird first appeared on the east coast, as many rare migrants do, and the time of year is just about right for an eastern vagrant. In addition, a second Red-headed Bunting came ashore at Filey on the very same day. The Filey bird, also a male, could theoretically have arrived from Asia on the same airstream as the Hull bird. Sadly, and some would argue more likely, the possibility of both birds escaping from the large bird markets in Holland cannot be ruled out.

Corn Bunting
Miliaria calandra

Reports in *The Naturalist* in 1922 stated that the Corn Bunting was absent west of Hull and was decreasing in the areas where it persisted, the implication being that Corn Buntings were present in the Hull area at that time. Boylan (1967) knew of only one breeding locality in Hull during the 1960s, this being patronised only irregularly. A respectable 20 were at the Bransholme Sewage Works in January 1978 and Bonavia (1990) considered it to be a common and widespread breeding bird in the open country around Cottingham and northwest Hull during the 1980s. James (1985) reported that the Corn Bunting was rare around Saltend during the mid 1980s, with just two records of wandering birds in 1985, despite being a common breeder on farmland around Paull and Hedon.

A flock of 28 at High Bransholme Farm, east of Bransholme, in late April 1989 gave a rough idea of the breeding population in that area back then, but the number of singing males gradually dwindled throughout the early 1990s to just two by 1994. The main breeding sites in this area were in fields between Castle Hill Farm, north of Sutton, and Fairholme Farm, northeast of North Bransholme, including several birds within the Hull city boundary. Corn Buntings were rarely heard there after that, but a flock of seven in mid March 1997 was more encouraging. Breeding seems to be more common around Wawne, however, particularly in the fields along the road up to Meaux and Routh, and I have often heard

males singing around Wawne Grange and Wawne Common Farms. The Corn Bunting was once a common and characteristic bird of the waving crop fields and scrawny hedgerows that fringe many parts of Hull but if any still nest within the city boundary then they are surely among the last. They are still thinly distributed in adjoining areas of the East Riding but are declining fast, as the British Corn Bunting population has plummeted over the last few decades and this was mirrored in our area. As ever, changing farming practices are thought to be at the heart of it, with autumn sowing, improved crop spraying and 'tidying up' robbing farmland birds of the summer insects and winter stubbles and weed seeds that they depend upon.

BIBLIOGRAPHY

Bonavia, P. (1990) *The Birds of the Cottingham Area 1981-1986*. Cottingham Bird Club, Cottingham.

Boylan, P. J. (1967) *Birds in Hull; Hull Museums Publication no. 217*. Hull Museums, Hull.

British Birds (1907 – present). Monthly journal. *www.britishbirds.co.uk/*

Broughton, R. K. (1998). *Eutrophication of a Shallow Lake in Northeast England: the impact of feral geese*. Unpublished dissertation, available to view at Map Room, Geography Dept., University of Hull, HU6 7RX.
See *www.hvwg.co.uk/framearticle.html* for abbreviated report.

Chislett, R. (1952) *Yorkshire Birds*. A. Brown & Sons, London.

Crowther, H. (1997) *Birds of the Avenues Area, Hull*. In: Middleton (1997) Hull Natural History Society Newsletter No. 9. C.M Kirk, Hull.

Dobbs, G. E. (2000). *Kingston-upon-Hull Local Biodiversity Action Plan: response from the Hull Valley Wildlife Group*. Report prepared for Hull LBAP committee.

Gibbons, D. W., Ried, J. B. & Chapman, R. A. (1993) *The New Atlas of Breeding Birds in Britain and Ireland 1988-91. Poyer, London.*

Hull Natural History Society Newsletter. Twice-yearly newsletter of the Hull Natural History Society, edited by R. Middleton.

Hull Valley Report, later the *East Yorkshire Report*. Annual report since 1997, edited by F. Moffatt & I. Forsyth for the Hull Valley Wildlife Group. *www.hvwg.co.uk/*

James, S. L. (1986). *Saltend and Hull Docks Bird Report 1985*. produced by the author, Hull.

James, S. L. (1990). *Saltend and Hull Docks Bird Report 1986*. produced by the author, Hull.

Mather, J. R. (1986) *The Birds of Yorkshire*. Croom Helm, London.

Milsom, H. P. (1997) *The Ecology of a Hedgerow and Grassland Habitat in Relation to Its Use By Birds: a report on a study of Priory Road Fields and the Snuff Mill Lane area, 1995-96.* Unpublished project report for the Certificate in Ornithology, University of Hull.

Nelson, T. H. (1907) *The Birds of Yorkshire.* A. Brown & Sons, London.

Yorkshire Naturalists' Union *Ornithological Report,* later the *Bird Report* (1965 – present). Annual report.

Yorkshire Naturalists' Union *The Naturalist* (1887 – present). *www.tka.co.uk/ynu/*

INDEX

Curlew		98
Diver,		
	Black-throated	1
	Great Northern	2
	Red-throated	1
	White-billed	2
Dove,		
	Collared	132
	Rock	128
	Stock	130
	Turtle	134
Dowitcher,		
	Long-billed	94
Duck,		
	Ferruginous	39
	Long-tailed	43
	Mandarin	30
	Muscovy	29
	Ruddy	48
	Tufted	40
	Wood	30
Dunlin		90
Dunnock		170
Eagle,		
	White-tailed	52
Egret,		
	Little	13
Eider		42
Falcon,		
	Gyr	62
	Peregrine	62
	Red-footed	59
Fieldfare		181
Finch,		
	Green Singing	230
	Zebra	228
Firecrest		200
Flycatcher,		
	Pied	203
	Red-breasted	202
	Spotted	200
Fulmar		6
Gadwall		32